My
Mother
the
PSYCHOPATH

My
Mother
the
PSYCHOPATH

Growing up in the
shadow of a monster

OLIVIA RAYNE
& S.M. NELSON

EBURY
PRESS

1 3 5 7 9 10 8 6 4 2

Ebury Press, an imprint of Ebury Publishing
20 Vauxhall Bridge Road
London SW1V 2SA

Ebury Press is part of the Penguin Random House group of companies whose
addresses can be found at global.penguinrandomhouse.com

Penguin
Random House
UK

First published by Ebury Press in 2019

www.penguin.co.uk

A CIP catalogue record for this book is available from the British Library

ISBN 9781785038990

Typeset in 10/15 pt Bulmer MT Std
by Integra Software Services Pvt. Ltd, Pondicherry

Printed and bound in Great Britain by Clays Ltd, Elcograf S.p.A.

Penguin Random House is committed to a
sustainable future for our business, our readers
and our planet. This book is made from Forest
Stewardship Council® certified paper.

To my grandmother, who helped me gain my freedom,
To my best friend, who gave me the strength to cut ties,
And to my boyfriend, who has loved me unconditionally ever since.

'If you say it, it can't hurt you'
Olivia Rayne

This book is a work of non-fiction based on the life, experiences and recollections of Olivia Rayne. In some cases names of people, places, dates and sequences of the detail of events have been changed to protect the privacy of others.

CONTENTS

PREFACE

I always thought that if I met a psychopath, I would definitely know. For years fascinated by criminal psychology, I devoured every book on the subject I could find, watched every documentary, every film. I could recite the hallmarks of psychopathy as easily as my ABCs. I knew the most important weapon in a psychopath's arsenal is charm, because it's that which lures you in – but that charm, I knew, wouldn't work on me. There'd be *something* there that would tip me off – a hardness to the smile perhaps, maybe an iciness in the eyes. Something would set the alarm bells ringing – after all, I'd read the books.

The reality was very different.

I met Olivia in 2013 when we worked for the same company. Olivia is bright, funny, playful and vivacious. I thought she had an infectious laugh, a warm smile and a quick wit. I was also struck by what a lovely mother she had. When I first met Josephine I observed her zeal, the way she seemed genuinely interested in everything and everyone around her. I noticed her smile, her earnest eye contact, the heartfelt way she talked. On each occasion we met, I thought, what a magnetic woman. Later, I noticed the gifts she sent Olivia that came to the office: designer shirts, dainty gold necklaces, sets of expensive make-up. 'You're so lucky!' I would say to my friend. 'Your mum's so generous.' Olivia would smile thinly and say nothing.

As time went on and we became closer, Olivia began to open up about her mother: all the awful things that had happened in the past, all the terrible things that were happening now. I listened, incredulous.

Her story seemed so outlandish that initially I wasn't sure how much I believed – she must be exaggerating, surely? How could a young woman in her early twenties be caught up in such an intricately toxic situation? Moving from one destructive relationship to another, being passed back and forth between her abusers as if they were playing catch. It was an unlikely story, wasn't it? And besides, her mother didn't just seem 'nice', she was positively lovely.

But then I started to see it for myself. Olivia showed me the hateful emails that flooded her inbox. I heard the furious messages her mother left on her phone. I witnessed Josephine's attempts to control her daughter, I watched as she tried to sabotage her life. Intimidation, manipulation, blackmail, threats, exploitation, gaslighting, lies and deceit; Josephine utilised all forms of psychological abuse against her daughter, but physical abuse wasn't beneath her either. I saw the visceral effect this persecution had on Olivia: the flushing, the shaking, the way she picked at her skin like it itched.

Never would I have thought that the enchanting woman I'd chatted with would be capable of such overt cruelty; I could never have imagined my cheerful friend with the wicked sense of humour could hide such a brutal secret. I was by Olivia's side during her mother's final campaign of harassment, and later, I would be on the receiving end of it myself.

Olivia's story is so outrageous and so dangerous that I simply had to tell it. With her blessing I wrote an article, which later led to this book. Reliving memories that she tried for years to suppress was extraordinarily painful for her, and hearing truths from family members that were concealed for decades was both distressing and humiliating.

At times I wondered if it was too much, recalling 22 years of torment at the hands of the one person you're meant to trust the most, but Olivia never wavered in her conviction: she wanted her story told. If her experience could help one person escape a situation similar to her own then it would all be worth it.

No more shame, no more pain, no more fear, no more grief: by untangling herself from the bind we're taught from birth to trust, Olivia took back control, and now her story is an open book.

I want to thank Olivia for having the courage to share her ordeal. No one has impressed me more with their strength, humour, generosity and resilience – and above all, such unwavering determination to move forward and heal.

This is Olivia's story.

– S.M. Nelson

1

DREAM

In my dreams, my mother watches me drown. She stands above me, her head tilted to the side, and as I stare at her from beneath the surface, I see her looking down at me. She looks cloudy, as though I'm peering through mist. Her eyes meet mine.

She watches me with a distant interest, like she's studying a painting she isn't sure she likes. She watches the bubbles drift up like pearls as my breath comes in panicked torrents; she watches the ripples swell to the surface as I churn through the water. She watches as I'm dragged beneath the depths, blind eyes blinking as I float face down. She does nothing but wave me on, her palm circling in the chilly air as I wash down the river. *Goodbye, Olivia*, each wave says. *Goodbye. Don't forget your mother*.

I don't wake up until the end, until I'm suffocating in stagnant blackness and I know that it's over. I try to feel relief – it was just a dream – but as I settle down and try to sleep, the fear creeps in and waits silently by my bed. It feels sharp, like a paper cut, and it smarts like a burn, but it's also an ache, like the dull throb of stomach cramps, or the fading hurt of a yellow bruise. Whenever I feel I am rising up past it, it presses down on me until I'm limp and shaking and it squeezes me to pieces.

Whatever is happening to me is my fault. I must have done something wrong, something so huge I can't even see it, something that's drowning me. In the pit of my stomach I can feel my own cold contempt – guilt and

5

horror, shame and disgrace. But I don't know where these feelings have come from; I'm not quite sure what I've done.

What did I do?

What have I done?

PSYCHOPATHY SYMPTOM #1

Glib, superficial charm

Psychopaths are unusually charismatic. They are entertaining, articulate and quick-witted, and their easy charm is very alluring. Frequently described as magnetic and seductive, their flattery and perceived empathy disarms people, helping lure their targets in. They are excellent conversationalists, able to tell the most implausible stories in a powerful and authentic way.

2
CHARM

'Psychopaths are unusually charismatic,
magnetic and alluring.'

The thing about my mother is that if you met her, you'd like her. Everyone did – at least at the start. It took a while to see through her pretty mask of charm. She wore it like armour, and it was so powerful, so effective, that the idea it wasn't genuine was absurd. To other people, looking in, she was respectable, successful and generous. She taught art to children, either in schools or privately, in our home. Sometimes, when her pupils came to our house, I listened outside the room, pressing my ear as close to the door as I dared. The kind, patient way she spoke to other children was alien to me.

In the evenings she marked her pupils' homework, glancing over their drawings and paintings and sighing from her brown leather chair. Sometimes I could see she was impressed: she never said anything, but I could tell by the slight raise of her brows that she was looking at good work. When she didn't like something, she told us. 'Look at this!' she would say, holding up a painting of a fruit bowl. 'What a load of shit! How did I get here, marking this drivel? God help me!'

When the pupil arrived for their next lesson she would squeeze their shoulders as they came through the hall and say, 'Well done on your painting!' and it was as if she really meant it. I peeped at them through the banisters, wondering if they could somehow tell she didn't mean it, that she'd been mocking their drawing the night before. They never seemed to. When their parents arrived to collect them an hour later, I wondered if maybe they would sense it. But they never did. They said, 'Josephine, thank you *so* much for what you've done for Annabelle, she looks forward to coming here every week,' and Mother would glance down at the floor as though embarrassed and she'd say, in a soft, demure voice, 'Oh please, the pleasure is all mine.'

She had this way of looking you right in the eye and making you feel as though she understood you completely: she just *got* you. But it was more than that, because when you looked into those wide, earnest eyes you got her too.

She had the most beautiful eyes. It wasn't the colour that was startling, a steely grey, but how expressive they were. She could make you feel whatever she wanted, just with a look. She'd turn her eyes to you, reproachful or ecstatic, solemn or wry, and you'd feel it, all of it, like a hammer to your gut. But that was only sometimes, when she wanted you to feel that. Other times I looked into her eyes and there was nothing there, only a dark vacuum staring back at me.

Mother could walk into a room and befriend anyone – but not only befriend them, captivate them. Throughout my childhood she had a pattern of making very close, very intense friendships. They never lasted much longer than a year or two; either she did something so disturbing the other person never spoke to her again, or else she cut ties herself, casting them off and discarding them like they'd never existed. But still, she had a gift of connecting with people almost instantly. It was like she knew your deepest worries and would do anything to help. She stroked arms as she listened, rubbed backs, wrinkled her brow in concern. She knew exactly what to say, what strings to pull, what compliments people ached to hear, and she delivered the goods each time. She did it to me, too, showering me with praise and gifts and making me feel special, then ripping it all away the next minute. She could sniff out vulnerability in seconds. Show her your belly, show her any weakness, and she'd rip you apart.

Her voice was sweet, but her words sharp as a blade. She had a thing for pet names. I was alternately her darling, her love, her sweet angel face – or a fucking bitch, a stupid whore, a sad disaster of her past. I was her sweetheart, her flower, the love of her life, but also a slut, a pervert, a cockroach ripe for zapping. One week she was my best friend, teaching me to paint, reading me my favourite stories, spending hundreds on baking kits so we could make cakes together; the next, she wouldn't even speak to me. I followed her around the house like a dog, begging her to tell me what I'd done wrong. 'If you don't know,' she said with that wry smile, 'I'm not going to tell you.'

Yet from the outside she had this way with her, this lightness. She'd breeze around the room, her perfume trailing behind her, throwing her head back and laughing. Mother had a beautiful laugh and she knew it. She laughed a lot whenever she was around other adults, particularly men. She always did this thing when she laughed: she tilted her head right back, exposing her long, elegant neck, then she put her hand to her throat and traced her fingers all the way down until they tugged on the neckline of her shirt. She glanced down then, tucking her hair behind her ear as though self-conscious; then she'd look up through her lashes and smile at the man goggling back, maybe sigh breathily through parted red lips. It seemed like a spell to me, when I was young. How silly men were, that with a laugh and a look and a stroke of her neck, they'd become prey. How funny that they thought they were special. How simple they must be, not to realise Mother's game.

Mother had beautiful hair too, back then. It was thick and golden and curly, and she wore it in a braid when she was working, or else loose down her back, where it hung in glistening coils. I always envied that hair. I used to stroke her plait lovingly, tracing my fingers over the smooth shafts. 'It's my pet snake,' I'd exclaim, smoothing the length of it as if it were alive. She'd turn around, pick up the end of her braid and jab it at my neck. 'Watch out it doesn't bite you, then!' she'd say, and I'd shriek with nervous laughter.

Every evening she brushed her hair until it crackled. She was so alive, so pulsing with energy, that to me she seemed to crackle too, to buzz and fizz with electricity she could never quite expend. Next to her I felt grey and flat; two-dimensional and squashed, pressed into myself like a dried flower.

Mother loved flowers – one of her only traits I've inherited that I'm glad about – and our house was always full of them. 'If you were a flower, you'd be a foxglove,' I once told her when I was 12. She was arranging flowers in a vase, about to start painting a still life. She glanced up, surprised but apparently pleased.

'Why a foxglove?'

'Because they're beautiful and exciting and exotic,' I replied. I knew how much she prided herself on being exciting and exotic. She's French, after all, totally different to us stiff, boring Brits, and she was spontaneous and fun and free-spirited.

'They're also deadly,' she said. Then she laughed. 'That's a good comparison, sweetheart.'

'What flower would I be?' I asked, glad she liked my game. She thought for a moment, her head on one side. Then she smiled.

'You'd be a dandelion. But when they're seeded, not when they're yellow.'

'Why a seeded dandelion?' It certainly wasn't the flower I wanted to be: I liked peonies – bright and beautiful and maybe a little blowsy, but soft and delicate inside.

'Well, they're boring, not very pretty, and totally insubstantial. You can blow them away with a single puff!' She turned those big amused eyes to me. 'Oh Olivia, I'm jooooking! Don't be so sensitive, I'm just playing.'

I looked into her grey eyes, wishing I knew what she was thinking. It was like gazing at the surface of a dark and murky lake; I wanted to see what was underneath, but was afraid to stir around and disturb the depths below.

* * *

Mother grew up in France but when she was 17, she moved to England – or, as she always said, was 'thrown out of the house' by her parents, though I later learned that wasn't true. It was the first of countless moves for her; she was impulsive and restless, and chased stimulation like it was crack. When I was a child, she moved us around the world on a whim – from England to Martinique, Germany to Monaco. Before I was 16 I'd lived in four countries, been to eight schools and lived in nine different homes. She was always getting itchy feet and uprooting us somewhere new. 'I'm bored,' she'd say. 'It's time to go. I need a fresh start. Somewhere new, somewhere different.'

But in this instance, back when she was 17, she moved countries for love, so she says. She'd fallen in love with a married man and followed him back to England. It didn't take him long to extract himself from her, although not for want of trying: she used to tell me, in a strangely blasé manner, that she'd stalked him for a while. She'd stand outside his house and cry and shout as he drew the curtains and refused to come out. He was terrified, she chuckled, truly terrified. Even as a child I always thought it was odd how she found that funny.

But then, several years later, she met my father at a party. Josephine gravitated towards the tall, dark stranger with the gentle smile. They say opposites attract, and in my parents' case this was true. My father has always been an introvert. Since he was a child he was content with his own company, happy to sit by himself in the sandpit while his three brothers played around him. He was so reserved that his brothers used to take turns teasing him, just to see how long it took him to react. Eventually, his face would turn pink and his tiny fingers would curl into angry red fists, but that was as far as little Clive's rage ever dared to flare. This type of meekness seemed sweet in a boy. It's not quite so endearing in a man.

The night they met Mother was 'the life and soul of the party'. My father is chatty enough if he knows you, but he's always been shy. He was mesmerised by how Mother worked the room. She didn't know many people there, but somehow managed to place herself at the centre of everything, where she belonged, burning like fire, luring pale moths to her glow. She was louder than anyone, livelier, funnier. Mother invited herself over to his flat the next night to cook for him – 'Nobody is as good a cook as I am,' she'd said – and that was it. Clive was ensnared.

But Clive wasn't the only one beguiled. When he first brought Mother home to meet his family, his brothers nudged him and said, 'Talk about punching above your weight! Clive, how did you bag *her*?' His friends began inviting him to more events and social occasions – 'You'll bring Josephine, won't you?' they asked – and my father was proud at how alluring his partner was, delighted that his loved ones wanted to be around her. When I was born five years later, it was the same, and when people met her, they thought what a lovely mother she was, this attractive, chatty woman with the lilting, beautiful laugh.

At times she was kinder than I predicted. Often she was crueller than I could imagine. There was no consistency to her behaviour, no pattern I could follow. I was perpetually on edge. When she was nice it left me feeling guilty, certain the problem must be me. Was I paranoid to doubt her? Was I mean to suspect? Could I not see that she loved me?

Sometimes when I turned around I'd catch her looking at me, and her face unnerved me. She didn't look away when our eyes met but kept staring at me, her eyes glinting, her mouth a thin line. Other times, I'd catch her looking at me with an expression I can only describe as hate; the type of hate that twists your face and curls your lip. When she saw me look at her she'd walk over to me, place her hands on either side of my face, kiss my forehead and say, 'My darling girl, I love you so much.'

Had she wanted me? Did she love me? Sometimes I thought she did.

We used to have this mixtape in our car, and whenever we had a long journey, we played it. I know that tape so well, even now – every song, the order they played, how long the hiss of the tape fizzed between each track. Whenever Eurythmics' 'There Must Be An Angel (Playing With My Heart)' came on, Mother turned it up full volume and sang at the top of her lungs, and when the chorus kicked in, she twisted around in her seat, faced me with a smile, put her hand on my knee and sang to me. She sang like she meant it, like she'd written every word for me, and whenever she sang 'angel' she gave my leg a squeeze. I loved those moments but I always wondered, how long will this last? How long will I be her angel before I'm that bitch again? How long will she love me before she hates me? I wanted to believe she meant what she was singing but I also knew who she was. This was how it always was: reel me in, make me relax, make me feel loved, then take it all away. It was a game to her; she was playing with me.

When I was with her there was always, always, this underlying sense of dread. It was almost worse when she was loving and kind, because it came with this twisted knot in my stomach, this feeling that I was continually holding my breath and waiting for the switch. In the car I tried to act like I was relaxed but I could see her looking at me in the rear-view mirror, her eyes boring into me. I would flinch and wonder, *Do I not seem grateful? Am I not being happy enough? Should I thank her, for singing these words to me?*

Even now, when 'There Must Be An Angel' comes on, a feeling of apprehension sweeps over me. It's a song people can't help singing along to, and sometimes when I'm with friends they belt out the words while I smile and twist my fingers together. I close my eyes and lean back, like I'm enjoying the song, but behind my closed lids I'm back in that car again, dread rising up from my belly. The lyrics whirl around in my mind as Mother's face floats in front of me, my heart pounds, my stomach shrinks.

I hear her singing about bliss, that no one else could feel like this, that I must be her angel. Then I see her eyes look at me from the rear-view mirror, and then I know the truth: she's playing with my heart.

* * *

My mother is a psychopath. By definition she lacks conscience, remorse and empathy towards others. Underneath her carefully constructed veneer of charm she is deceitful, manipulative, narcissistic and callous. She was one person in public and another behind closed doors. She wore different masks depending on her mood and what was useful in that moment, and she flitted effortlessly between her roles like a seasoned actor. Who would she be today? The loving mother? The cancer victim? The trusted teacher? The antagonist destroying my life?

Most people who knew her had no idea that Josephine Lacroix – charming, quirky Josephine Lacroix – could do what she did. Even those she was close to, even my grandparents, never saw the full extent of it. And of course, her worst moments were juxtaposed by her best, and when Mother was at her best she was brilliant: spontaneous, funny, flirtatious, exciting.

For a long time I tried to rationalise her behaviour, to make excuses for her. It was because she was ill … because she was stressed … because I was naughty. It was because I gave up on her, that awful time when I was eight. Regret chased me, relentless. It was like running down a long and winding dark tunnel; every time I saw the glimmer of light at the end, it swallowed me back into its windowless depths.

It's astonishing, when I look back now, to realise what a good job on me she did. What an excellent job it was. Everything I knew – or thought I knew – about love was warped. For years I thought control and manipulation were normal in relationships. She used and discarded me at her leisure, she reeled me in only to cast me off. I was entirely at her disposal, but I willingly went back for more – I had no idea it could be different. How would I know? It couldn't be bad, what she was doing, because my father was there and he saw, he knew, and he did nothing.

She knew exactly how to play me, and she did it expertly for more than 22 years. For 22 years I couldn't see the truth, and even when it was upon me, I barely recognised it. For 22 years, cold self-loathing flowed through me like blood, and the damage she inflicted distorted me, warping my mind, scarring my body.

I need to go back and tell my own story – the way it was, not the way she told me it was. Time may comfort but it doesn't cure. I'm better now, it's true, but the damage done can never be undone. It's still there, itching quietly beneath the surface, like a sharp metal wire cutting into me for too long. Even though I've snipped through the barbs and finally discarded it, the angry red imprint is etched forever into my skin.

PSYCHOPATHY SYMPTOM #2

Lack of empathy

Psychopaths are unconcerned with the feelings of others and have a near universal lack of empathy. People are seen as mere objects to be used for their own fulfilment, and they are unable to put themselves into the shoes of others. They care nothing for the suffering of those around them, and are scornful of the weak and vulnerable. To the psychopath, strangers are disposable; family members are possessions.

3
CONTEMPT

'Psychopaths have a near universal
lack of empathy.'

There's a photo, hanging on the wall of my mother's house. Or at least, there used to be; she's probably burnt it now, along with all the other pictures that went on the bonfire that day. I used to look at that photo and use it as proof of Mother's love. Because look how happy we were, the two of us, cuddled up together on the sofa. Look at her arms wrapped around my shoulders, her proud, wide smile, the way her head rests gently on mine. How could she not have loved me? Look at me, at my wide, bright eyes, the innocent glee. Of course I was loved, of course my mother loved me.

It's strange, thinking about this photo today. How misleading photos can be – but at the same time, how alluring. I was so desperate to believe Mother loved me that I would pore over old pictures of us, urging myself to remember that moment when the camera went off, right then, that exact moment in time, because *then* Mother loved me. *Then* it was real. It was almost like I was taunting myself, staring into these snapshots of another life. It felt voyeuristic, like I was looking at something I wasn't meant to, something off-limits. I would hold these photos close to my face as if somehow, if only I were close enough, some of the love and contentment in the photos would escape its paper constraints and be real. It seems silly now, but for a long time it wasn't.

Mother – or 'Maman', as I called her then – loved having her picture taken. Usually, when I begged to have a photo with my father, she'd refuse. 'Let's have one of us together,' she'd say. 'Don't you want to have a picture with Maman?' And of course I'd agree that I did, and she'd pull me towards her, snake her arm around my shoulders, twist her body towards me and smile that toothy grin.

Our happy photos were proof of happy families. Tangible, undeniable proof, and she wielded them like a shield, but also a weapon. After we'd had arguments, before she 'forgave' me, she loved getting the photos out. She'd wave one in front of my face and say, 'Remember this? Remember this day? Look how happy we were, look what a good girl you were. What happened to that sweet girl? What did you do to her?'

And I would look at the photo and try to remember. Because the photos really were happy ones: we looked happy. We were happy. *We were, we were.*

'Remember this day? Remember how special it was and how happy we were? Remember how we went swimming in the lagoon and made sandcastles? Remember how you felt sick and I wrapped you in my arms and looked after you? Remember? Remember?'

I wanted so badly to remember. I would strain my brain, I would close my eyes and clench my fists as Mother's words drummed away. Remember, remember?

I want to, I want to.

And then suddenly, I would remember, and the memory hit me with a swooping gust of familiarity that made my belly ache: I'm a small child on a beach; I'm squinting in the sun, grains of sand scraping between fingers smeared sticky with sun cream, lips cracked and dusted white with salt, baby-soft hair crusted coarse; Mother scrubbing me dry, the feel of the towel against my face, the way her arms wind tight around me; how the wind is sharp, how she holds me close, how I screw up my eyes, how orange orbs of sunlight whirl behind my lashes. It's so clear, how could I not have remembered?

'Yes, I remember. I remember it.'

And then came the line she'd always say after a big fight, her favourite line of all: 'I'm the best fucking mother in the world, aren't I? Aren't I just the best?'

She would wait next to me for the answer. Her words hung between us. Silence shuddered through the room; it hovered, heavy with the unsaid, those words I could feel rising in my throat but didn't have the energy to utter.

'Aren't I just the best?'

Very quiet this time.

'Yes. You're the best mother in the world.'

* * *

I didn't really remember that moment on the beach, of course. I'm sure the reality was worlds away from my desperate imaginings. But I wanted to conjure up a happy childhood and those photos became my fuel. I looked at my younger self and wished more than anything that I could go back to that point, back before I ruined everything by being devious and scheming and demanding. Why did I have to spoil it? What was wrong with me? I'd had a wonderful childhood. Look at all the places we went, the fun things we did, the gifts I received – what more did I want?

I believed her, when she said it was my fault; when she said I ruined the special memories, all those happy years we'd shared. I believed they really were happy. I know the photographs played a part in that, and to this day I think it's why Mother was so keen on taking pictures. Because they were 'proof': 'Look how happy we were, Olivia. Look what you've ruined. Look what you've done …'

I collected fragments of memories like treasures, piecing them together like mosaics; I reconstructed events and believed they were real. For so long I was in denial. Until I accepted that these photographs were just illusions, how could I accept there was something wrong? How could I understand that it wasn't me, it was her? It was easier to think that there was something wrong with me than to think it was her. I never wanted to think that – that hurt too much.

Eventually I had to abandon the idea that things used to be good, that I'd had this happy childhood and somehow, along the way, I'd ruined everything. Because Mother had always been like this, hadn't she? She was just good at hiding it. But I didn't know any of this for a long, long time. Even after I broke away, I didn't realise the whole truth until I spoke to my grandmother, until I begged her to reveal everything that had been kept hidden for years. Poor Granny, she only wanted to keep me safe. She'd bitten her tongue, terrified Mother would take me away again, terrified of what she might do. My grandparents – my father's parents – were the only people in my life who saw through Mother, who never fell for her facade, and when Granny told me about my early years, those things I'd forgotten or tried to erase, everything I'd held dear for so long came tumbling down around me.

'Do you remember Christmas '95?' she asked me. 'You probably don't, you were only three. You came to stay with us that year in the cottage, all of you – your parents and cousins and uncle. It was that Christmas that changed everything. I never looked at your mother in the same way after. But once you'd all gone home, your grandfather and I never talked about what happened. It was too hard.' She spoke slowly; partly to gather her thoughts, but also to coax the words out. It wasn't an easy story for her to tell; I wasn't the only one repressed.

'We just couldn't confront the reality of what was happening. We thought they were just episodes, you see … isolated incidents. Your father said they were – "Josephine sometimes has episodes, that's all," he'd say – and, you know, we didn't see that side of her often. At that time anyway.' Granny paused, looked at me, sighed. 'She was capable of being so lovely – to you, as well as to us. Your Grandad never liked her, from

21

the beginning, and she knew it, but I did. I thought she was odd, and sometimes she reacted so strangely, but fundamentally … fundamentally, I thought she was a good person.

'A few times I tried to talk to her. I suggested maybe she was being too hard on you. That you were a sensitive child, you weren't tough like her. You needed more from her: more empathy, more affection. But every time I did, she brushed it off – she smiled and laughed and chatted lightly about other things. Other times she looked at me with hurt in her eyes – those big wounded grey eyes – and she'd say, "Jean, how can you think this of me? You only see one side of Olivia. She's a difficult child, an angry, aggressive child. She needs to be disciplined now, while she's young, or where will we be in a few years?" But after that Christmas …' Granny trailed off, tears in her eyes. 'It was so awful to see, it was awful.'

There was a sinking in my stomach, because I did remember that Christmas. In my mind it was a happy Christmas. I remembered the photo from that day, that for years was pinned to our fridge. It was right in the centre so every time you went to fetch a drink or snack it floated in front of your eyes. The bottom corner was folded up, and whenever I looked at it, I tried to flatten it down, to protect and preserve it, this precious pictorial proof: proof we'd been happy, evidence I'd been loved.

In the photo are my cousins, my grandparents, Mother and me. We're gathered in the living room and Mother's kneeling by the sofa, holding me from behind. Her chin is on my head, her curly hair on my shoulder. She's beaming up at the camera, at my father standing behind it. My hands are clasped together, my eyes wet, my cheeks pink, my round toddler's tummy straining against my velvet dress. There's torn wrapping paper in front of us, jigsaw puzzles and games and new books on the carpet. On the coffee table are glasses of half-drunk wine, chocolate stars wrapped in foil, plates of mince pies with thick smears of cream. We looked full and happy and hearty.

When I looked at that photo I thought I remembered it. I thought I remembered charging around the living room, hot and breathless with excitement; eating mince pies until my little belly stuck out; that my cousins took turns poking it and squealing with laughter. I remembered that – I did, I *did*.

Or did I? Was it just the photo that made me think I remembered? I knew that I remembered one thing from that day: Mother, gently stroking my forehead. But what else?

'Do you really not remember what happened that day?' Granny asked, and I shook my head, squeezing my eyes tight. The memory of Mother stroking my face hovered in my mind but I pushed it aside. What was behind that? At first there was only grainy darkness, but as I dug there were flashes of something else: a floor, a cold floor; pain, heat. I thought there was another memory there – a door, a silhouette? – but it was bleary and it made me feel nervous. What else?

I couldn't see. I didn't know.

'Tell me what happened.'

So Granny told me, and as she spoke the gaping holes in my mind refilled, and my meticulously constructed memories shrivelled away as though they were burning.

It's dark, it's night-time. I'm locked in the bathroom, lying on cold tiles, sobbing and crying for Maman to let me out. I'm rattling the bathroom door in desperation, pleading and weeping so hard I can't breathe. *Please let me out, Maman, please open the door. I feel sick, I'm scared. I'm scared, Maman. Maman!* She's standing outside the door – I can see her silhouette through the glass – but she doesn't say anything, she doesn't respond.

I'm hot, I'm tired, my head hurts. I press my cheek to the cold floor to cool myself. I'm lying face down, arms spread wide, feet turned out. Sobs hiccup through my chest but still she doesn't come to me. I call for her, again and again, and I know she's listening because I see her silhouette turn towards me. Still she says nothing.

This is what Granny told me about the Christmas I thought I remembered.

It was Christmas morning. Granny came into the living room where I'd slept with Mother and Father. She was carrying a tray: mugs of coffee for the grown-ups, hot milk for me. My parents were still lazing on the pull-out sofa, and as Granny came in, Mother sat up with a smile.

'Morning, Jean!' she said brightly. 'Merry Christmas!'

'Merry Christmas, Josephine!' Granny replied. 'Merry Christmas, Clive!' She glanced around the room, looking for me. 'Where's Olivia?'

'Oh,' Mother said, and there was a pause. 'She's in the bathroom,' she added, picking up her coffee and sipping it slowly. Granny glanced at the bathroom door adjoining the living room. Her bookcase, that old, heavy mahogany bookcase, was dragged across the door like a barricade. Granny's head flicked back to my parents. My father was making a great show of blowing on his coffee, staring straight ahead at the wall. Mother was watching Granny steadily, unflustered, smooth as silk.

'Why is she in the bathroom?' Granny asked. She remembered that her voice quivered, but she didn't know why. Mother sighed, shook her head like she was in pain.

'She kept her father and me awake until the early hours. She wouldn't stop crying, howling for attention like a little madam, so in the end we had to lock her in the bathroom for the night.'

Granny stared from Mother to Father and back again. 'But she's three, Josephine. She's only three.'

'I'm aware how old my daughter is, thanks,' Mother returned crisply, standing up and smoothing back her hair.

'But she's only a little girl.'

When Mother didn't reply, Granny stepped towards to the bathroom, but then Mother spoke loudly.

'I'll let her out,' she said. 'She's *my* daughter.'

Mother strode towards the bathroom and opened the door. Granny stared at her son, my father. He was still staring at the wall, gulping down his coffee even though it was too hot to drink.

'Are you ready to come out now?' Mother said into the bathroom. 'Are you ready to behave?'

First, Granny heard my snuffles from inside the bathroom, then she saw me wobble out, red-faced, tear-stained, sticky.

'Sorry, Maman,' I said, and then I burst into tears. Mother knelt down and drew me into a hug, and I sobbed into her chest. Granny stood there, staring, disbelieving.

'She was in there all night?' she eventually asked.

'Not *all night*,' Mother replied. 'What do you think I am?'

Something contracted in Granny's stomach but she forced a smile on her face and said, 'Merry Christmas, Olivia! Let's get you washed and cleaned up for breakfast, shall we?' She took my hand and led me into her own bathroom, where she washed my hot face and brushed my matted hair. After breakfast my uncle and cousins arrived, and Granny watched me play with them, running around the living room like a caged animal released. But then, after a while, my flushed face and bright eyes caught her attention. I kept bumping into things, and when she called my name I didn't seem to hear. She placed her cool hands delicately on my forehead, frowned, stroked my face again.

'You're burning up,' she said to me. 'Poor love, and there I thought you were just looking rosy. Josephine ...' she called to Mother, who was sitting with my cousin Jack, reading from his new storybook. 'Olivia's got a temperature, it feels very high. Come here, have a feel.'

Mother sighed, rolling her eyes upwards as if Granny was being annoying. She passed Jack's book back to him, gave him a sympathetic smile and a pat on the head and walked over to us. She leaned over me, planting her fingers on my forehead, trailing them gently down my cheek, stroking me like she loved me.

25

'She doesn't seem hot to me,' she said. 'She's probably just overexcited, what with all the presents and mince pies.'

But Granny knew there was something wrong. She led me back into her bathroom, away from the fun and games in the living room, and undressed me quickly but carefully. Then she wiped my feverish face and burning body with a wet towel, swept my sweaty fringe away from my eyes.

She didn't know it then, but I'd never felt a woman's hands touch me like this before, in this affectionate, benevolent, distinctly maternal way. Mother hugged and kissed me when I was good, especially when we were with friends or family, but there was always an impatience to her embrace: an edginess, an eagerness for me to unwind my arms from around her neck and let her go; and also there was a heaviness to it, like holding me was a burden, something tiresome and gratuitous, but something she must endure all the same.

My temperature didn't go down, and as the hours passed I became more and more distressed. I lay on the floor, squirming and groaning, and only then did Mother concede something must be wrong. 'Call the emergency doctor!' she ordered grandly as she stooped over me. When the doctor arrived, I was lying on the sofa with another cold flannel on my forehead. He examined me, quickly and sympathetically.

'She has a severe ear infection,' he told Mother, standing up and smiling down at me. 'That's why her temperature's flared. She's in significant pain and sleeping will be difficult tonight, but it should have eased up by tomorrow. I'll write you an antibiotic prescription in case it hasn't, but see how she goes.'

Granny remembers this next bit like it was yesterday. Mother leaned over me, smoothed my face gently, tenderly, and said, 'Oh no! Oh Olivia, my darling! Oh, my little Olive!' Her voice shook, tremulous, as if she were about to cry, but as Granny craned her neck to look at Mother she saw that her face was smooth and blank. Mother looked at me, blinked

26

slowly: once, twice. 'You poor little thing!' she said. 'You've been so brave, my darling, darling girl!' Her voice wavered and trembled again – she sounded like she was on the brink of tears – but as she looked at me, her face was still that strange blank mask.

Something shivered through Granny, but as she tried to process what she'd seen she was suddenly flooded by anger. 'Well, I suppose we know why she couldn't sleep last night,' she said. 'Why she was crying. The poor girl needed love and attention, not—'

'None of us are mind readers, Jean,' Mother said lightly. 'If Olivia doesn't tell us what's wrong, how are we supposed to know?' She placed a hand on the doctor's arm and guided him out of the room. 'Thank you *so* much for coming, Doctor,' she said, flashing him one of her lovely smiles. 'We really appreciate it, especially at Christmas.'

After the doctor left, my ear began leaking and I screamed and wept, inconsolable with pain. Granny gave me baby paracetamol but it didn't seem to work, and I lay on the sofa, shuddering with sobs. As Granny rocked me gently in her arms, my grandfather sang 'Twinkle, Twinkle Little Star' in his comforting baritone and my father fluttered in and out of the room, bringing me water and patting my head. After a while Mother came back in, and as she walked over to me my whole body began convulsing.

'No!' I cried '*No, no!*' and I buried my face in Granny's lap, clutching at her arms. Mother rolled her eyes and wrapped a scarf around her neck.

'I'm going out for some fresh air,' she said. 'It's Christmas, *I* deserve a break too.'

After she left, my father sat down gently beside me and pulled me from Granny's arms. What he said next broke her heart.

'It's okay, little Livvy,' he murmured to me as he rubbed my back. 'It's okay, my little Olive. Maman is gone. You're safe now, Maman is gone.'

* * *

How could I not have remembered this? How could I have forgotten her locking me in the bathroom, but remembered her stroking my face? Because that was also true: she did do that. Both those things were true.

I felt a strange sense of betrayal from that photo I'd loved, the photo on the fridge I'd so carefully tried to unfurl. But it was only then that I realised what the photo showed didn't matter, it was what it *didn't* show that was important.

The photo didn't show the night I spent barricaded in a cold bathroom, trying to cool my flaming face on the tiles. It didn't show a mother who locked her feverish three-year-old away, forcing her to sleep on the hard, shiny floor. And nobody would have guessed, from looking at Mother's smile and the way she held me close, that she'd spent the day denying me the most basic motherly compassion.

If I close my eyes I can see her now, standing behind that door, listening to my cries with that strange blank look upon her face: unfeeling, unknowable; unreadable, impenetrable.

PSYCHOPATHY SYMPTOM #3

Need for stimulation

Psychopaths have an extreme need for stimulation. They continually search for new thrills, and enjoy living on the edge and taking risks. This persistent yearning for excitement can lead them to move from place to place as they seek exhilaration; equally, psychopaths are easily bored and have no time for mundane, monotonous or strenuous experiences.

4
THRILL

'Psychopaths have an extreme need
for stimulation.'

For all Mother's faults, being boring wasn't one of them. If there was fun or excitement to be had, she'd make sure she was having it. She was fearless in her pursuit of adventure and proud of it too. That was always one of the jibes she'd throw at me when I showed any degree of hesitance or anxiety: 'You're scared,' she'd say. 'You're a silly, scared little girl.'

She didn't fear anything, whether it was the unknown or people's reactions or the consequences of her actions. Whatever the situation, she was audacious and bold; whatever the outcome, she could handle it. Both invigorating and terrifying, it was the best and worst thing about her. It was so easy to get carried away in her vigour and zest for life that when she said we were moving to Martinique when I was six years old it was hard not to get caught up in her exhilaration. For most people, moving across an ocean to a tropical island you've never even visited before wouldn't be a spur-of-the-moment decision. For Mother, it was like deciding she wanted another cup of tea.

We were having breakfast one morning, sitting around the table. There'd been no warning, no prior conversations – just an announcement from her that we were moving to Martinique. I can still hear the clink of metal on china as my father set his knife down and stared at her.

'What? Why? Why Martinique?' He was utterly bemused.

I looked between the two of them, holding my breath, trying to think where in the world Martinique was.

'Why not?' Mother shrugged. 'It's hot, it's sunny, they speak French. Why not?'

'But *we* don't speak French,' my father said, gesturing towards himself and me as if she had forgotten something vital.

She shrugged with one shoulder, elegantly, dismissively.

'But *I* do.'

Then she looked at me. 'And Olivia speaks it well enough, don't you? You'll soon get better.' She leaned forward. 'Don't you want an adventure, my flower? Don't you want to live in the Caribbean? The Caribbean, Olivia! The *Caribbean*! You'll love it, I know you will.'

'I think we should discuss this later,' my father said, laying his cutlery down with an attempted air of finality.

Mother smiled. 'Oh Clive! I've already made the arrangements. We *are* going, all you need to do is get excited. Live a little! What are you scared of? Life's short, and I want to enjoy it. I want our daughter to see the world, instead of being cooped up in a little house in grey old England. Don't you want more for her?'

I remember my father's blustering then, trying to find the right words to argue with her. He never could. She looked at him, almost sympathetically, then winked at me. I felt the warm glow of being her conspirator. When he left for work a short while later she put her face in her hands, propped up on her elbows, and looked over at me.

'You want to go to Martinique, don't you, sweetheart?'

I nodded that I did. 'It's too cold here,' I said. 'I want to be somewhere hot.'

It was a lie. I have my father's fair skin: I'm pale as a lily, I burn rather than tan, and when it gets really hot, I feel heavy and useless. Mother always went golden in the sun, all burnished and glowing, and she laughed at how we struggled in the heat. 'Oh, your poor English skin!'

she'd say, tossing us the sunscreen. 'Maybe you should go inside, or at least put a towel over your head.' And then she'd laugh like she'd said something really funny. In spite of her mocking, she was careful I didn't burn. On a hot day, she never let me out without rubbing sunscreen in herself, and she did it carefully, as if the idea of me burning hurt her.

She smiled at me. 'It's not just about the weather, you know. It's just …' She sighed, glanced around as if looking for something to help her explain. 'I'm bored,' she said. 'I'm so *booooorrrrrred*.' She drew out the word, nudging me as she did so. 'It's boring here, it's time for something new. You'll love Martinique, I know you'll love it.'

* * *

So, we moved to Martinique. As I stepped off the plane, holding tight onto my father's hand, I walked into a wall of heat like I'd never experienced before. We sat quietly in the car on the way to our new rented home, which none of us had seen. Mother had only looked at photos from the estate agent's brochure, but she promised us we'd love it. 'Wait until you see the garden,' she'd said to me with a grin.

I sat by myself in the back of the car, surrounded by suitcases and boxes and coats we'd shed as soon as we landed. I remember looking at the backs of my parents' heads as we drove along the winding roads of this new country. Everything seemed lighter, brighter than back home: the sky was bluer, the trees greener, and as I looked at the horizon stretching out between my parents' heads, I remember feeling that this was the beginning of something: something was about to begin here.

When we pulled up to our new home – big, white, square, isolated – I didn't wait to be shown around, I didn't even want to see my room. I rushed right into the garden and just stood there, looking at this new place where I now lived.

The garden was long and narrow and faced north. In the distance I could see mountain peaks, dark green ribbons of rainforest, sandy beaches, the capital Fort-de-France, and all around was the glistening turquoise sea. There was no wall to separate our home from the land that sloped towards the coast, and where the clipped grass of our garden finished, ferns as tall as trees shot up, in a thousand different shades of green. I'd never seen so many beautiful flowers, and I saw myself picking bouquets for Mother to paint and place around our home. Just beyond the flowers were mango and papaya trees, and I imagined myself picking and collecting them in baskets and bringing them in to Mother ... how happy she'd be. I could adventure here, dig around in my very own secret garden, like some intrepid explorer. Maybe I would even discover a new species of bird or lizard or insect there.

At the end of the garden where the ferns shot up was a steep rocky path. I stood at the top and looked down. It led down the hill to the coast, where a shallow lagoon shimmered. It was more than anything I could have dreamt up. It didn't feel real. Father walked up behind me and followed my gaze.

'We can go swimming there later,' he said, nodding towards the lagoon. 'It looks like a great place to get some practice in.' I was so overwhelmed, I couldn't speak. I threw my arms around him and hugged him tight, feeling like I was going to explode. I could see myself splashing in the lagoon with all the new friends I would make, laughing and screaming and running along the beach, then heading back up our path to pick fruit, eating fat, juicy mangos and drinking from fresh coconuts. There was a sense of possibility here, of things bursting free and shooting upwards; time curved ahead of me, full of sunshine and opportunity and freedom and joy.

* * *

Mother found work almost instantly. She'd arranged a meeting with an artists' showroom before we left the UK, and within a week had been contracted to create several paintings. It was harder for Father – he taught

33

geography but none of the international schools were hiring. Unable to speak French, he was impotent and isolated, and spent much of those first few months sitting around while I was at school, or playing with me when I was home.

'Are you happy here?' he'd often ask. 'Do you want to stay?'

I told him I was happy; that I did want to stay. I hadn't made many friends at the international school yet, though the other children were nice, but I loved the outdoors lifestyle: running through the ferns in our garden, digging in the sand on the beach, shimmying up the mango trees as far as I could. But most of all I loved the extra time I spent with my father.

He took me swimming in the lagoon almost every day, and I improved so much I joined the swimming team at school. I had my very own white swimming cap that said OLIVIA on it in red letters; Father helped me get it over my hair, tugging and twisting and pulling at the elastic, and he looked so proud of me once it was on, even though I looked like a boiled egg in it. He came to all my swimming practices, and after each one we'd enjoy some special time together. In the evenings he'd take me for dinner and a milkshake, and daytimes we'd go for walks, or to an adventure park, or we'd take the car and drive to a beach and have a picnic.

Once we went right into the rainforest – a word I found magical beyond belief. It poured down almost as soon as we arrived, but I didn't care. Pale green light filtered through mist-wrapped trees, and it was like being in a cathedral, but one that was outside, one that was alive. I remember running my fingers over the knotted bark and feeling so happy I was there. As I looked across at my father, he smiled at me and I knew he felt it too, that sense that we were somewhere otherworldly, somewhere enchanted.

We'd never spent so much time together and I loved every moment. It shaped my memories of Martinique, and when I think of that time now, even after the bad things that happened, the first thing that comes to mind is my father and me, smiling at each other in the depths of that forest.

The second thing that comes to mind is loneliness. Martinique was the first time I remember feeling lonely – perhaps it was the first time I was old enough to recognise the emotion – and at times, it was consuming. Father finally managed to find a job, and he often didn't come home until it was nearly my bedtime. Mother was going through another phase where she was ignoring me, and I felt alone, emotionally and physically. I spent hours in my room and the garden playing by myself: talking to my teddies, doing different voices and having long, animated conversations. I filled diaries and notebooks with my wobbly script, writing stories and painstakingly recording what I did that day, what I ate, what I said, what I felt. I had always been good at entertaining myself, but it was harder here.

My new white room was so big that the yawning corners never seemed full, even though I had plenty of furniture and books and we'd bought posters and frames for the walls. I began collecting things to place about my room: an old pair of my father's gloves he had no use for in Martinique, a bright knitted shawl Mother made years ago, maroon-stained corks from my father's wine bottles that I lined up neatly on the window ledge. But my room still felt empty, so I began to collect things from the garden. I brought in armfuls of colourful flowers, but that didn't do it so I began gathering boughs and branches from the lawn – only ones that had naturally fallen, never picked from trees – and propped them up against my walls. I loved how they made my room look, like a cosy woodland grotto, but Mother said, 'For God's sake, Olivia, will you stop with all the damn twigs!' So I did.

Sometimes at night I couldn't sleep. I looked up at the glow-in-the-dark stars on the ceiling that my father stuck on, and felt alone. 'I'm by myself,' I whispered, like it was a comforting mantra. 'I'm alone, I'm by myself.'

* * *

Mother had never seemed to mind that I so obviously preferred my father to her, but in Martinique, she began to resent our closer bond. She tried to take me for special days out, buying me whatever I wanted, treating me to anything I asked for. One time she took me to the toy shop in Fort-de-France and announced I could have everything in there. She handed me a basket and we filled it up with toys and books and colouring books and stickers and pencils. It was a lovely day, but when we got home and I started unpacking my toys, she started looking at me in that way again.

By that time, when she'd decided she'd been nice to me for long enough and could start the punishment phase, I could sense the change in her as clear as day. To an outsider the shift would have been imperceptible, but I saw it in her face, her stance, the fix of her shoulders. I drew out each toy from the bag as carefully as I could, wincing at the rustle of plastic, and placed them gently on the kitchen table, holding my breath and avoiding her gaze. Then I felt her hand on my shoulder: light, gentle. Her voice was even gentler.

'You aren't grateful,' she said. 'You aren't grateful for all the gifts I've bought, for all the money I've spent.' She swept the toys up into a black plastic bag, smiling at me as she knotted it. Then she marched into the front garden and threw the bag into the bin. 'If you *dare* try to get them …' she said, knowing I wouldn't.

I realised then that there was nothing I could say that could make things better. If I thanked her and told her that I was truly grateful for what she'd bought me, she'd say I was lying; if I cried and apologised, she'd brand me weak or stupid or scared. Whatever I did was futile: it always ended with her screaming and me weeping at the table. So it was in Martinique that I developed a new mechanism for dealing with those bouts of rage.

When she stood in front of me screaming, I simply sat there, my face impassive, my back straight, staring at either my hands clasped in front of me or a spot on the wall. Anywhere except my mother's wild, red face. In my head I said all the things that I wanted to say to her – that she was wicked, that I hated her, that I would run away – all the while remaining impassive and emotionless. It rarely had the intended effect. If there's one thing Mother hates it's not being acknowledged. When she didn't get the reaction she wanted by screaming, she had to step it up a notch.

That was when she began hitting me – rarely across the face, usually on my bottom or arms, but hard and repeatedly. It got to the point where whenever she started screaming, I began backing up against the wall. One day, mid-screaming fit, she noticed: she stopped so suddenly that her right arm was still raised, bent at the elbow as though she was waving.

'Are you afraid of me?' she asked. I nodded that I was. She looked hurt, though her hand stayed raised, ready in case she changed her mind. 'I won't hit you again, I promise.' She didn't keep her promise, but it was as close to an apology as she ever got.

* * *

There were also good times. One odd thing Mother did in Martinique was to buy a motorbike. A second-hand Honda Nighthawk, it was red with black seats. I remember the cracked leather on the back seat, the way the sides used to hum with heat, the acrid smell of the gasoline as she revved. Father hated the bike, hated her using it, but she dismissed his worries with a wave of her hand: 'It's the ultimate freedom, Clive. Something *you* would never understand!'

What my father didn't know was that sometimes, when he was out and Mother was in a good mood, she took me out on the bike. She walked into my room and smiled mysteriously before saying, 'Put your jeans on, two pairs.' I dashed to the wardrobe and wriggled into my jeans as quickly as I could. I suppose this was Mother's way of protecting me, seeing as she didn't have a child's set of leathers for me to wear – not that two pairs of jeans would have done much if we'd crashed.

By the time I shuffled downstairs she was waiting by the bike, helmet at the ready. The helmet was enormous and heavy; so heavy that if I tilted my neck back just an inch I became terrified my head would fall off. I could see it happening: the giant helmet – with my head still in it – bouncing down the road, Mother whizzing along on the bike, trying to scoop it up. She fixed the helmet on me and then lifted me onto the bike.

What she was thinking, having me ride along behind her, I don't know; I was seven years old. I was scared of the bike itself – how noisy it was, how it rumbled beneath me and shook between my legs – but I was truly terrified of riding. When we were speeding along I barely had the courage to open my eyes, and I pressed my helmet into Mother's back, wound my arms tight around her stomach, and pushed myself against her as close as I could. Sometimes, as the bike screeched around corners or Mother sped up along a straight, I felt a scream rising in my throat. I would clamp my mouth shut, and swallow and swallow and swallow until the scream was quashed and I could breathe again. Mother never knew how scared of riding I was – something I took pride in. After she leapt from the bike and ripped off her helmet, she'd remove mine and look at me, her face pink with pleasure.

'Well?' she'd say expectantly, proudly. 'Did you have fun?' And I would stagger off the bike, throw my arms around her, squeeze her tight and say, 'Yes, Maman. *So* much fun!'

It was a strange type of fear, though: it made me feel reckless, indomitable. Power seemed to run through me, clear and unwavering, and it ignited something inside me. It was the opposite of weak, it was the opposite of scared, which Mother always said I was. But in those moments, I wasn't weak or scared, I was resilient and brave.

* * *

One day we took a trip to a deserted cove on the other side of the island. It was a beautiful beach, with a band of palm trees at one end and a cluster of brown rocks at the other. The rocks were warm against my back when I lay against them, and I was happy to sit there, watching the boats go slowly by on the horizon and listening to my father tell me about how he used to sail as a boy. But Mother had heard there were secret caves and she was itching to explore. She swam out to see whether she could spot them from the water, and I watched her strong arms chop through the waves until she became just a speck in the sea. Ten minutes later, she came back to shore, squeezing the water from her hair and smiling excitedly.

'There are definitely caves,' she announced. 'But it's too far out for you to swim.' There was a small speedboat on the shore, and Mother looked at it. 'We could take this boat out,' she said, glancing over her shoulder at Father and me. 'What do you think? I can start it up, no problem. It's small enough that we'll be able to get into the caves as well!' Her whole face had lit up; she looked like a child, giddy with excitement.

'It's someone else's boat,' my father said. 'You can't just take it out.'

'Why not? There's no one here, no one's using it. What's the problem?'

My father stared at her. 'Josephine, it's *stealing*.'

'It's not stealing,' she scoffed. 'It's borrowing. I'm not going to take it home, am I? We're just going to go out on it for a bit. It'll be fun!'

'Absolutely not.' My father was resolute. 'It belongs to a fisherman, he'll probably be along soon. What'll he think when he finds it gone?'

Mother rolled her eyes. '*Fisherman*! It's a speedboat, Clive. No one's going to come for it while we're here. And if they do, we'll see them and can bring it back. What's the big deal?'

'Think what you're teaching to Olivia!' I'd rarely seen my father so animated. 'You're teaching her that stealing is acceptable!'

'*Borrowing*.'

'You're being ridiculous.' Father reached out a hand to pull her away from the boat, but she slapped it back.

'Ridiculous? For wanting to have some fun once in a while?'

'This isn't fun, this is a crime.'

She laughed in his face, then turned to me: 'You want to come for an adventure, don't you, Livvy?'

I nodded. I did want to – the idea of finding secret sea caves made my heart thrill. Also, I wanted Mother to see that I was fun and exciting like she was, not drab and boring like my English father.

'You're not taking Olivia,' Father said, putting his hands on my shoulders and pulling me close. 'I won't have it.'

'Oh stop it, you sad, boring man!' Mother jeered. 'You should be glad she's inherited my sense of adventure.' She took my hand and lifted me into the boat. I glanced at Father to see if he would protest or try to stop her, but he didn't; he just stood there, a few metres away, looking at us while Mother untied the boat and started the engine.

'Ready for our maiden voyage?' she shouted over the buzz of the engine as we began to zoom across the water. I nodded, and she leaned towards the shore and cupped her hands around her mouth, her wedding ring glittering in the sun. 'You pussy! Where's your sense of adventure?' Father didn't react, just stared at us as we moved away from him. 'You do realise you'll be the one in trouble if the owner comes back and finds his boat is gone?' she yelled. He could hear her – we were only metres away – but still he said nothing, just stood stock-still on the beach. Mother looked at me and smiled: 'Let's amp things up a little, shall we? It's time to go full throttle!'

It was a sunny but windy day, and the boat careered over the waves. Every time we rode over a crest and hit the water it hurt, and seawater showered over us. The thud winded me and reverberated through my ribs, but I didn't care, I really didn't care, because it was fun and I was happy, and Mother was happy too. Every time we passed Father she screamed insults at him while laughing like a madwoman.

'You don't have the balls, Clive! You don't have the guts!'

I can still see that moment now, just as it was then: her mouth open with laughter, her teeth glinting, wet hair streaming behind her like seaweed. The salt spray in my mouth, my hair whipping my eyes, the distant, lonely figure of Father on the shore. At times like this, I loved my mother. When I remember them, even now, I still love her. How invigorating she was, how free-spirited.

'Wave to your father, Olivia!' Mother shrieked. I laughed back, and we rotated our wrists and waved to the lonely man stuck on the shore – the man who didn't have the guts to join us in the sun.

PSYCHOPATHY SYMPTOM #4

Criminal tendencies

Psychopaths view themselves as far more important than anyone else, so they do not believe the rules of society apply to them. They think nothing of breaking the law; laws are for ordinary citizens, not extraordinary people like them. Some psychopaths are considered 'successful psychopaths'; these people usually express their antisocial impulsives in more subtle ways – for example, white collar crime, or committing acts that, while not illegal, are immoral. To these pscyhopaths, escaping detection is part of the thrill.

5

IMMORALITY

'Psychopaths do not believe the rules of society apply to them.'

I turned eight in Martinique, and my parents threw me the best birthday party of my life. It was weeks in the planning. I'd been invited to a classmate's birthday a few months back, and she'd had a big blue inflatable swimming pool in the garden, and Mother decided we had to have one too. The weekend before my birthday we drove to Fort-de-France to rent the pool, and Mother insisted we had to get the biggest size. It was five metres long – far too big, my father argued, for our tiny car.

'We need it to be that size,' Mother said. 'Those small pools are ugly! I want the biggest one for Olivia. It's her birthday, it must be special. It must be bigger than that other girl's.'

'But why?' My father didn't get it. 'Why does it need to be bigger? What's wrong with the smaller pool? It's still big enough for Livvy and her friends to splash around in.'

Mother shook her head. 'No, I want the biggest one. What's the matter with you? Don't you want Olivia's birthday to be special? Why are you always so tight with money? Big pockets, short arms!' she scoffed.

And so, inevitably, we ended up with the biggest inflatable pool. When we got home we carried it into the garden, and Father and I spent what seemed like forever filling it with the garden hose. I remember standing on a stool, hose in hand, looking into the inch of water at the bottom and thinking I'd be there all week because the pool was so big.

When the Saturday of my birthday arrived, my parents went all out. I didn't have many good friends at school, but I'd invited the whole class, and I was delighted to see so many of them turn up. Mother had written on the invitations that parents were welcome too, and she'd set up little areas where the grown-ups chatted in groups and sipped fizzy wines and nibbled snacks like smoked salmon and dips.

We had a clown and a magician and a little ice-cream stall with so many flavours – strawberry and chocolate and vanilla and cheesecake. I felt very grown-up that day. Mother had given me my first proper piece of jewellery – an intricate silver necklace with an amethyst pendant. This was the stage where I loved anything purple, and the necklace was the most beautiful thing I'd ever seen. If you pinched the chain in your fingers, the amethyst swung from side to side; gently at first, then more purposefully, like it had a life of its own. The clasp was too fiddly for my fingers, so Mother put it on for me, and I stared at myself in the mirror, terrified to be wearing something so delicate. I was a tomboy – did I even want jewellery for my birthday? Had I asked for a necklace? I think I'd asked for a bike – but then, when I saw the necklace shimmering inside the box, I knew I was glad.

Mother made decorations for the garden – banners and paper chains and posters saying 'Olivia is eight today!' – and Father set up a face painting stall. In the photo from that day I'm a pink and purple butterfly, my nose the delicate black body, my cheeks the colourful wings. Mother joined in the fun too, and a few gold stars glinted by her eyes. In the photo she's laughing, squeezing me to her with one hand, the other holding a champagne flute, curly strands of hair escaping the bun on top of her head. I'm smiling too, but I look flustered. I'm wearing purple patterned trousers, baggy at the knee, and a lilac T-shirt with a floral motif. I still remember how it felt, the flowers raised from the cotton T-shirt, firmer and stiffer and a little bit itchy on my chest. Between my collarbones my pendant glitters.

Mother was the perfect hostess that day. She carried around trays of pretty sandwiches – cucumber and cream cheese, egg and cress, ham and tomato – and plastic tumblers of pink lemonade with curly straws; for the grown-ups she offered sparkling wine and fancy canapés, and she chatted and laughed and said, 'It's a pleasure! Oh really, don't mention it.' She put together party bags for my friends to take home, packed with sweets and balloons and birthday cake and glitter pencils. Sophie from my class rummaged in her bag, squealed with excitement, then said, 'Your mum is the best. I wish she was my mum!'

But as the day drew on, I sensed Mother's growing coolness. It was the first sign that something was going to happen, that I'd done something wrong. The old familiar stress began to churn in my belly. She began ignoring me when I spoke to her, and fussed even more over my friends, laughing and hugging them and saying how beautiful they looked with their bright painted faces. I tried to think what I could have done. I'd been on my best behaviour all afternoon, thanking my friends and their parents for their gifts, tidying up the wrapping paper from the lawn, sitting patiently while my father painted faces.

As the first evening shadows appeared, I went into the house to use the bathroom. When I came through the kitchen, Mother was waiting for me by the sink. She pulled me aside. 'What's wrong with you?' she said, digging her fingers into my shoulders.

'Nothing's wrong,' I replied. 'I needed a wee.'

'You could try to show some appreciation,' she hissed. 'I've been planning this for weeks, and you're just swanning around like it's any other day. What the matter with you?'

I stared at her. 'Maman, this is the best day of my life,' I protested. 'It's the best birthday ever, thank you.' I reached for her hand but she pulled it away, shaking her head.

'You're a spoilt brat! This is the last time I throw you a birthday party. Why do I even bother? You don't appreciate anything I do. Just you wait!' She marched back into the garden, and after a few moments, I followed her. For the rest of the party I could feel her eyes on me, and I didn't know whether I should act happy or sad. If I seemed upset, she might get angrier because I wasn't enjoying all the effort she'd gone to. But then, if I acted happy, I knew she'd hate that she hadn't made me sad. I tried to straddle the two, being polite and attentive and gracious but not having too much fun. Every time I laughed spontaneously, I cringed that she'd seen.

As people started to peel away and leave, panic began to rise inside me. Once everyone was gone, Mother would unleash, and I couldn't bear the thought of what she might do. I tried to get my friends to stay longer, bringing board games into the garden and suggesting we play. Or what about a film, maybe we could watch a film on the projector? Mother realised what I was doing at once.

'Olivia, your friends need to leave now, come on,' she said loudly. 'They've been here all afternoon. Your birthday can't last forever, you know.' The other parents overheard, as they were meant to, and she raised her eyebrows in that 'Ah, kids!' way, and they all laughed. I ducked my head, ashamed.

As the guests trickled away my scalp began to prickle. This wonderful day was ruined already, and Mother hadn't even done anything yet. After she had cheerily waved goodbye to the last guest, I ran over to Father, throwing my arms around his waist and mumbling my thanks for such a special day. I could feel her, rather than hear her, walking up behind me.

She grabbed me by the top of my arm and without saying a word dragged me away. I twisted around, entreating my father with my eyes to help, but he was looking at his feet. As I dug my heels into the grass my smooth-soled sandals had no grip. She yanked me up the stairs while I cried my apologies. *Sorry I wasn't grateful enough. Sorry I didn't smile enough. Sorry I didn't say thank you enough. Sorry, sorry, sorry, Maman.*

When we got to the top of the stairs she pushed me into my bedroom and then stood there in the doorway, one elbow propped against the wall, fingers trailing on her chin. 'Now you can sit here and think about what you've done. Don't even try calling us to let you out. You're a disgrace, and I'm ashamed of you. I'm ashamed to be your mother!' She watched my face for a reaction. I tried my hardest not to give her one. She turned to step out of the room, hovered for a second, then looked back at me, hesitating. My eyes were foggy with tears but I held my breath. Maybe she'd thought better of it. Maybe she wasn't going to lock me in. Maybe she was sorry, maybe she didn't mean to do this.

I blinked, and tears pooled over my eyes and spilled down my cheeks. She reached out a hand, and for a wild second I thought she was going to wipe my tears away. Instead she grabbed my necklace, twisted and pulled, and my neck jerked forward as the silver chain broke. She stood there in front of me, my birthday pendant hidden in her balled fist, the delicate chain trailing from her fingers. She smiled that smile of hers I hated, and I couldn't stop the howl of misery escaping as she shut the door and turned the key.

I wept bitterly for a long time. When my nose was blocked and my face felt hot and puffy, I dragged a hand in front of my eyes and wiped away the tears. If I was stuck here, fine. If she took away my necklace, fine. I never asked for it anyway, I never wanted it. What *did* I want for my birthday? What did I really want?

I wanted a bike, so that my father and I could go cycling along the winding coastal paths. My old bike was in England, and I dreamed of cycling so fast the wheels were a blur, zooming along with the sun on my back, the wind in my face and Father grinning behind me.

I wanted some seeds, so I could plant flowers and grow my own garden. I was captivated by *The Secret Garden*, this magical book about the healing of lonely, damaged children. I wanted to be like Mary, planting roses and snowdrops and 'daffydowndillys' and shrugging off my solitude as I watched flowers bloom.

I wanted a real friend, a best friend. Someone who didn't think Mother was the best mother in the world, someone I could tell the truth to. Someone who would squeeze my hand whenever she was cruel and tell me that it wasn't my fault; someone who wouldn't look away, or down at their feet when I begged them to help.

I wanted a mother who loved me. A mother who was proud of me and proud to *be* my mother. A mother who didn't give me something only to take it away, a mother who didn't say with a smile on her face that I was stupid and silly and scared.

It was still my birthday, but I didn't make a wish – I was too old to think it might come true. I fingered the hollow of my collarbone where my pendant had sat and waited for morning to come.

* * *

A couple of hours later, when it was dark but still not very late, I heard our doorbell go. I was lying on my bed, looking up at the glow-in-the-dark stars, wondering if I should go to sleep or see how long I could stay up. I was hungry, but I knew there was no point thinking about that until morning. There was a little bathroom attached to my room, so with access to water and a toilet, Mother would be in no rush to let me out.

I heard the rumble of voices downstairs – men's voices. This was unusual: we never had many visitors. I got up, crept to the door and lay on the floor, pressing my ear to the thin gap between the carpet and the door. Mother was angry with the men, whoever they were. She was speaking in French, and straining my ears, I could hear her voice, staccato with fury. I could speak French by this point, and words and phrases floated up to me from the hall. *'Menteurs ... ce ne sont que des mensonges ... ils sont ridicules ... no, no ... des mensonges ridicules!'*

49

I held my breath. What were lies? Who was ridiculous? Who were these men? And then I heard footsteps coming up the stairs – not the light, quick tread of Mother but my father's slow, heavy pace. I flew back to my bed, lay down and pulled the duvet up to my chin and turned to face the wall. I tried to take slow, deep breaths, but underneath the covers my chest was rising and falling, my heart hammering.

'Olivia!' Father whispered from the door. 'Olivia, wake up! You need to come downstairs.'

'Why?' I said, rubbing my eyes sleepily as if he'd woken me.

'The police are here.'

I sat up. The police? 'Why?' I whispered back.

'It's nothing important, just a misunderstanding.' His voice shook. 'They're speaking French, it's hard for me to follow. But you should come down. Just … show your face. I just … I don't think you should be shut in your room now.'

I followed him downstairs, remembering how he'd looked away from me earlier. My head spun. Why were the police here? Would they take Mother away? Would she go to prison? If she did, would I be sad? I tried to think whether I'd be sad; I tried to imagine missing her. Without a mother I'd be lonely, surely?

The police were scary – tall and frowny, though they smiled at me when I came into the living room. They were dressed differently from British police, in short-sleeved white shirts and dark trousers and shiny black shoes. They wore blue baseball caps, which I remember thinking was strange for a policeman, and around the waist they had thick leather belts with all kinds of things attached: a walkie talkie, keys, a torch, a gun.

'We hear it's your birthday,' one of them said to me, in French. He had a friendly smile but I was still scared of him, of the way his big forearms were so close to his belt; how quick it would be for him to grab his gun and shoot me if he wanted. I nodded slowly, afraid to speak. 'Happy birthday,' he said, and I nodded again. I felt small, inconsequential, like a foolish nodding dog. 'Did you have a nice day?'

'Don't speak to them,' Mother ordered before I could find my voice. 'They're accusing me of stealing ... Me, as if I would steal! It's outrageous! I have plenty of money, this is ridiculous, I've never been so insulted in my life ...' She rattled away in French, her head flicking between me and the police. The police sighed a lot. They said I didn't have to be there, that I could go upstairs, but Mother said anything they wanted to say to her, they could say in front of her daughter, thank you very much. So I picked up a book from the coffee table and settled into the big green chair in the corner of the room. I pretended to read, and while I did so, I learned what Mother had done wrong.

She worked at the artist's showroom, creating paintings and sculptures. I'd visited a few times and I loved the couple who owned it, Elodie and Nicolas. They let me browse the aisles for as long as I wanted and I got to pick up the smaller sculptures even though they had signs on them saying 'Do not touch'.

Elodie and Nicolas had accused Mother of stealing expensive art supplies from their showroom. They said she had been doing it for months but they hadn't been able to prove it until now. Once she'd got the art supplies – large canvases and bags of clay and brand-new sets of acrylic paints – she'd taken them home and made new paintings and sculptures and sold them illegally across the island. Mother denied everything, even though it sounded like they had lots of proof: they said they had photos from the security cameras of her entering the property at night and leaving with art supplies under her arm; there were several people on the island who'd bought these creations from Mother, and she'd passed herself off as an independent artist, unattached to any showroom or artists' organisation.

'Please,' one of the officers said after Mother finally stopped talking. 'Let's not make this any harder than it has to be. We want you to come to the station to answer some questions there. It shouldn't take too long.'

'And if I refuse?' she said, hands on hips, that disdainful look that I knew so well on her face.

The officers looked at each other, paused, then looked back at Mother.

'Mrs Lacroix, this is not a request.'

My stomach flipped: Mother was in trouble, and it was serious. Would they arrest her when she went to the station? Would they keep her there? I flicked through the pages of the book I was pretending to read, but I couldn't stop the thrill coursing through me.

'Fine,' she said, somehow managing to sound haughty. 'Let me get my bag.'

She flounced down the hall towards the kitchen. I tried catching my father's eye but he was sitting away from me and looking at his knees. I didn't dare look at the policemen again, even though at this point I felt quite warm towards them: they were taking Mother away. Even if she was allowed to come back, they were taking her away and maybe she would learn a lesson. I was cross with her, for stealing from Elodie and Nicolas when they'd been so kind to us. Despite her denial, there was never a moment where I questioned whether or not she had stolen the art supplies. I knew she had. Why did she do such things? Why did she steal from people who trusted her?

And so we waited for Mother to come back. It was taking her a very long time to get her bag. I held the book higher in front of my face and turned a few pages loudly and quickly, as though trying to find a specific page. Just as I darted another look at my father, one of the officers stood up and headed down the hall to the kitchen where Mother had gone. The other officer walked towards the window, looking out into the garden. He leaned forward so the brim of his baseball cap gently touched the glass. I stared at the back of his neck and wondered what he thought of Mother, of our family. Then the policeman stiffened, craned his neck to the right and shouted. The other officer raced into the room. Both glanced out the window, spun around and ran out the front door. I heard it slam and I rushed to the window myself. Father was still sitting on the sofa, looking at his knees. For a moment, I thought how silly he was.

It was dark outside, the only light coming from the hanging lanterns on the porch and the slice of translucent moon overhead. Dimly, far across the water, I could see the lights of town flickering. I peered through the glass, fingertips pressed against the pane. In the dark I could see the hulking shadow of the inflatable pool in the garden. How I hated it. I wished it wasn't there. Then I saw Mother coming up the path.

She was on the far right of the garden, the path that led to the road. She was walking quickly, pushing the motorbike silently, but as she approached the road she revved the engine. Then she swung a leg over the saddle and with a roar and a rumble the bike awoke. Without glancing back at the house, she leaned forward and zoomed away. Father leapt up as the engine revved but he was too late to see her; as he pressed up against the window the red brake lights disappeared behind the house. He let out a strange groan, like he was in pain. I couldn't see the police car from the back of the house, but I heard the frantic wail of the siren start up and pressed my hands against my ears. I hated the sound of the siren – its shrill screaming, the ceaseless keening, like some terrible, vicious baby.

'Oh Jesus!' Father staggered backwards and dropped back into his chair, hands over his face. 'Oh Jesus!'

I sank to my knees in front of him. 'She's gone,' I announced, as if he didn't know. But he said nothing. 'What will they do when they catch her?' I asked, holding my breath. He shook his head a few times, sighed, then put his face back in his hands.

'I don't know,' he murmured through fingers. 'I don't know.'

I knew I should feel scared, but instead I was excited. I wondered if he could tell how excited I was.

'Where has she gone?'

'I don't know, I don't know,' he groaned. '*Why* did she go?' He looked at me desperately, as if I somehow had the answers. I looked back at him, shook my head and shrugged.

'I don't know.'

'I mean, it's an *island*; we're on an *island*. Where does she think she's going to go?'

'I don't know.' I paused. 'Maybe she won't come back.'

He jerked his head and swatted his hand as if a fly was bothering him. 'Of course she'll come back. But why … why …?' He was pacing around the living room now, fingers pressed against his lips, thumbs cupped under his chin, as if trying to keep his face together, or stop his mouth from swinging open. 'It's dark outside … she's trying to run on a bloody motorbike … Oh God … My God, what if she crashes, what then, then what happens …?'

He was talking to himself now, barely aware that I was still in the room. I tried to imagine my mother crashing; how quick it would be, a flash of fear, of jolt of surprise. A sliding tyre on gravel, the grinding of metal. I thought of Mother's body, delicate as the chain on my necklace, spinning through the air as if she were cartwheeling. I saw her hitting a tree and I saw her shattering like glass into a million dark red pieces. I thought of her lying still, arms splayed, legs twisted, her hair tumbling from its bun as it had that afternoon.

How would I feel if that happened?

I didn't know.

I thought of Mary from *The Secret Garden*. Her mother died – her father too – and in the end she was alright. She moved to the countryside and she made friends with Ben Weatherstaff and the robin and Colin and Dickon, and she had her own garden where no one would bother her or be cruel to her. I could start my own garden here – there were already so many flowers growing, I just had to plant my own and make it mine.

'Olivia. Olivia, I need to go out for a while.' My father's voice was soft, scared. 'Not for long,' he added, seeing my face. 'I just need to sort out a few things … see that your mother's okay … You know … You'll be alright here, won't you, by yourself?'

I nodded.

'Just go back to bed. I'll lock up, and then when you wake up everything will be back to normal. Okay? Okay?'

'Okay.'

He reached out a hand, patted my head. 'You're a good girl. Little Olive.' And then he was gone, running out the front door like he was going to join the pursuit, chasing after Mother and leaving me behind. I walked to the front of the house and watched him as he rushed to the car, as he opened the door and got in and pulled his seatbelt across him. He started the engine. The headlights blinked at me, and I saw him glance in the rear-view mirror as he pulled away, careful and methodical as always, even now, when his heart was racing and there were fingernail marks on his face.

I stood there alone in the window, and as I watched him drive away from me it was as if he were driving away forever. I thought I could still hear the awful howl of the siren, echoing in the distance. There was a flash of light as the headlights skimmed my face, the crunch of wheels on the gravel path, then the empty silence of night.

PSYCHOPATHY SYMPTOM #5

Impulsivity

Psychopaths are extremely impulsive and impetuous, and their behaviour often shows a striking lack of reflection. Guided by a desire to achieve immediate pleasure, gratification, or reprieve, they are rash, reckless and erratic. Pyschopaths rarely consider consequences, and resisting temptation is extremely difficult. Whatever a psychopath feels like doing, most times they will do it. Homes are left, relationships are ended, jobs are dropped – all on a whim.

6
SCORN

'Psychopaths are impulsive and impetuous.'

When I woke up, I knew Mother was home. I could hear her, shouting like she was in one of her rages, from downstairs. Disappointment surged inside me. So, she was back. I didn't know what that meant. Was she back for good, or just for a bit, before they took her to prison? I tried my door handle even though I knew it would be locked, and then sat beside the window and waited to be let out. I couldn't bear being locked in my room. But it wasn't being stuck in my bedroom I didn't like – it was being confined to the house, the feeling of being stuck inside when I should be outside. I wanted to be sitting in the mango tree with a gentle breeze on my neck, looking out at the sea. Climbing the tree always left angry red scratches on my arms but that view was worth it. Despite its modernity our house felt stale to me. It was light and airy, but sometimes the bare white walls pressed too close, and even from my room I swore I could hear the hum of the fridge, the rush of the fan, the purr of the water heater. It was too much, inside. Outside was better, with the sweet fragrant smell of frangipani and that wonderful, rustling silence.

There was a storm brewing – not one of those grey, depressing storms you see in England, but a tropical storm. I loved the storms in Martinique, with the warm rain that poured down in sheets, lightning splintering across the sky, and the way the garden smelt afterwards: all damp and citrusy and clean. I leaned my forehead against the window.

58

My stomach was growling; I'd drunk so much water to try to feel full, I could feel it sloshing around in my belly.

It was late afternoon before Mother unlocked my door and came into my room. She looked jaunty, like she was proud of her escapades from the night before, as if she was desperate for me to ask what happened so she could spill the beans. Somehow she also seemed tense, wired; her face looked taut, as though her skin had shrunk and was stretched too thinly over her skull. She ran her eyes over me for a few seconds and then: 'Dinner's ready.' It was like yesterday had never happened: not my party, not her locking me away, not the police coming, not her spontaneous motorbike escape.

In silence I followed her downstairs. I could smell cooked food and suddenly felt sick with hunger. By our front door there were cardboard boxes stacked neatly, and Mother's green suitcase propped against the wall. She watched me look at them, glance back at her, then look at the boxes again. I knew she was waiting for me to ask.

'Why are there boxes?'

'There are boxes because we're leaving tomorrow,' she said nonchalantly. 'After dinner you need to go and pack up your own suitcase. We can send for the rest of the stuff later.'

I sat down at the table and thought about what to say. My father was already sitting down, looking everywhere but at me.

'Where are we going?' I asked slowly.

Mother looked at me like I was stupid. 'Where? Home, of course. England.' She smiled. 'Don't you want to go back home?'

'I don't know,' I answered, truthfully.

'Of course you do,' she said, laying plates down in front of us and dishing out food with a flourish. I remember thinking that her brisk, carefree attitude was strange, and though I knew I shouldn't, I had to ask the question.

'What happened with the police?'

She laughed, a high-pitched trill. 'Oh, it was nothing! A mix-up, nothing to worry about.'

'Then why do we have to go?'

'Because I'm bored of this stupid fucking island!' She had started swearing, and I knew then that her breezy exterior was a lie, and underneath she was seething. 'I'm bored of it, I want to go back. There's no culture here, nothing but beaches and sun and stupid fucking liars! It's time for a new adventure.'

I couldn't think what to say to that so I was silent, pretending to be fixated on the contents of my plate while Father muttered to Mother from the corner of his mouth. He didn't want us to leave Martinique. He said he couldn't go – not just now, anyway, because of his job, because he had commitments. Let's just wait a couple of months, he argued, then we'll all go home. It'll be a new start, just in time for summer! He couldn't leave in the middle of the term, what would they think of him at the school?

'That's fine,' Mother said, smiling behind closed lips. 'Olivia and I will go by ourselves.' I felt my back stiffen as I glanced up from my plate. 'I'm sure we'll be just fine.'

'Don't be silly,' Father said. 'You can't go off by yourselves. There's no need to abandon everything because you got in trouble, the police––'

'*You're* abandoning *us*!' Mother screamed, so loudly her voice cracked, all attempt at calm now gone. 'How dare you talk about abandonment! You don't love me, you don't love Olivia! The first chance you get, you run off by yourself!'

'Josephine, I'm not running off.' Father's hands were flitting up and down. 'I'll come home, of course I will – you know I will – but I can't just up and leave in the middle of the term. If I want to get a job when we're back home I need to stay, just until term's finished. I have commitments––'

'*I* am your commitment!' Mother shrieked, hands balled up by her sides. She was standing now, leaning over the table as I studiously cut my sausages into tiny pieces. 'You stupid fucking bastard, you should be committed to ME! Be loyal to ME!'

'I *am* loyal,' my father started, in a would-be-calm voice, but it was too late. Mother looked like a madwoman, her face dark red, a vein ticking on her forehead.

'I am done with you!' She began pulling on her wedding ring, furiously trying to rip it off. 'I'm going tomorrow, and Olivia's coming with me. Just try and stop us! Who do you think you are? You're not a husband, you're not a man ... you're a weak and pathetic little dog! Well you know, I'm *bored* of having a dog!'

She threw her wedding ring across the room; it bounced off the cupboard where the plates were, then rolled back and clattered into the corner beside her with a hollow clang. She screamed in frustration. I looked at my sausages, at these torn slices of putrid pink flesh, and I felt sick.

'Olivia!'

I looked up at her. She pointed to the ring, her eyes wide and staring. 'Pick up my ring, pick it up!' she insisted when I didn't move. I stood up, chair legs grating against the tiled floor. She gestured to the back garden. 'Take it and throw it off the cliff.'

'Oh, for God's sake!' Father was very agitated now. 'Olivia, just go upstairs please. Your mother doesn't mean what she's saying—'

'Oh, don't I?' Mother snatched the ring from the floor herself and stalked around the table. She pressed it into my hand, folding my fingers over the top as if it were some priceless package. 'Go down to the rocky path,' she said, eyes glaring into mine. 'Throw it off the cliff. I don't want it anymore. I'm done with it, I'm done with *him*!' As she licked her lips, unblinking, her eyes never left mine. 'Do it!'

I looked between her and Father. He looked back at me, his mouth slightly open. Mother moved to the side so she was blocking him from view: 'Olivia, do it. Throw it!'

I hesitated a moment longer but I knew what I was going to do. I was suddenly furious with my father, for his inaction, for his listlessness. For once, I agreed with Mother. He wasn't a man. What type of man is so passive, so weak? I couldn't imagine any of the fathers from school being shouted at in this way. How could he let her scream at him like that? How could he let her extinguish his spirit, his sense of humour, the fun-loving person I knew he really was, and allow her to turn him into a husk of a man? To me, at that moment, he seemed like an empty shell. As I looked into Mother's eyes, I could feel her words, unspoken, in my head: *Throw it.*

I turned on my heel and ran outside into the pouring rain, breathing in the pungent smell of wet leaves, glad to be outside again. I ran through our darkening garden, my feet squelching in the sodden grass, and only stopped when I reached the rocky path leading down to the sea. It was a steep path, but walkable – if I followed it, I'd be on the beach in minutes – but on either side of the path it was wild, and where the ground tilted treacherously, gnarled branches and knotted stems and arrowlike ferns rose from the dirt. If I threw the ring, it would either bounce down the path, ricocheting off the rocks and sinking into the sand, or it would be hidden in the dense undergrowth. Whichever way, it would be lost forever.

I remember this moment so well, like it happened yesterday and not nearly 20 years ago. I looked at the ring, turning it over in my hands, feeling the worn engraving on the inside where my father's name and their wedding date were written. For some reason, as I stood there in the rain with Mother's ring in the palm of my hand, fear began to rise inside me. The wind rushed over the trees; they rippled, like they were moving by themselves, like they were alive.

I clenched my fist. I knew, deep down, that Mother didn't really want me to throw her ring. That when she'd calmed down and forgiven Father she would want it back. But I didn't want her to have it back.

I threw the ring as hard and as far as I could down towards the sea. It was too dark to see where it went, but in my mind's eye I saw it clearly, arching up into the stormy dark sky, silhouetted for a moment in front of plum-coloured clouds, then plummeting down to earth, careening down the path and bouncing from rock to stone until it rolled into the inky ocean.

There was a sense of relief, like burying something that needed to be hidden, or drawing a line underneath something that had gone too far. But I wasn't sure what I needed to bury, I didn't know what had gone too far. Still, I was glad that I'd thrown it, even though I knew Mother would punish me terribly.

It wasn't until the next day, as we sat in the back of a taxi on the way to the airport, that she asked me where her ring was. I told her I had thrown it off the cliff. As soon as the words were out of my mouth I flinched, ready for her rage. But instead, to my surprise, she merely raised her eyebrows and shrugged. 'Well, I did tell you to throw it,' she said, glancing at me in the rear-view mirror. 'You were just doing what you were told.'

That was the thing with my mother. Just when I thought I'd figured her out, she changed yet again.

* * *

And then just like that, we were back in England. As soon as we landed, back into the drizzle and the grey, Martinique seemed like a dream. Did we really go? Did I really walk through mist-cloaked rainforests with my father, running our hands over gnarly ancient trees and grinning at each other? Did I really swim in a warm turquoise lagoon and shin up mango trees and play among ferns that were taller than I was? It seemed unbelievable already, but I knew that I had done those things.

I'd wondered whether Mother was bluffing, the day before. She wouldn't really leave without Father, surely? But she had. She didn't kiss him goodbye, or allow him to help carry the bags or drive us to the airport. She batted his offers of assistance away like they irked her, smiled tightly through his insistence that he'd be on the first plane home as soon as term ended.

'There's no need to try to convince anyone, Clive. I daresay you've made your position quite plain.'

That day I wrote in my diary about how strange grown-ups were, the way they spoke so formally when cross, as if nothing could express furious restraint better than crisp, old-fashioned phrases.

My father cried when he hugged me goodbye. Not sobs, just silent tears that streamed from his eyes and glistened on his cheeks like snail trails. I hugged him back, but I didn't know what to feel. When he told me he loved me, I didn't say it back. I was cross with him, though I didn't know why, and everything felt panicked, rushed. I didn't even know why we were leaving. Was it because Mother had been in trouble and was ashamed, or was she was still in trouble with the police and making a run for it? She never answered me, those few times when I asked her what really happened with the police in Martinique, even years later. She just smiled an odd, twisted smile and said, 'Wouldn't you like to know?'

None of it felt real, even when we were on the plane. It wasn't until we were sitting in the back of a taxi from the airport that I realised I didn't even know where we were going. 'We're going home,' Mother had said – but where was home now? It wasn't in our old house in Salisbury, where strangers now lived. It wasn't across the ocean in Martinique, where my father lived alone.

'Where is home, Maman?' I asked. She looked at me and for the first time that I can remember I felt she was really seeing me: the anxiety swirling in my gut, the anguish at leaving my father, the doubt that stretched ahead of me endlessly. The fear, too: of the unknown, of being jerked away from a life where if I wasn't happy, I was at least settled; and the fear of her, of being alone with her. It was just me and Mother, now. She reached across from the backseat and took my hand.

'Home is with me, my sweet angel face. Home is with Maman.'

* * *

It's funny, when I look back now, how old I felt when I came home – a big grown-up girl of eight. I got on that first plane aged six, sandwiched between two parents, my head swimming with possibility. I returned home two years older, minus one parent, feeling like a different person.

Mother was nicer to me in England – for the first month at least. We stayed in a hotel in London for the first week, and it was a fancy place, with fat cushions on the bed and fluffy white bathrobes with matching slippers. She took me to afternoon tea and we ate scones and cream with strawberry jam, and dainty sandwiches with wafer-thin cucumber, and sipped dinky cups of tea. All the while she bitched about my father, as if now he wasn't there she needed me to be her ally instead. For every scathing remark she made about him, she complimented me or showed affection in a way she never had before. It was unsettling, her being kind, but I can't say that I didn't enjoy it.

We moved to a less-fancy hotel the second week, and daytimes I followed her around the city as she made phone calls and flicked through newspaper adverts and tried to find somewhere for us to live. 'I'm recently separated,' she said on the phone when she spoke to estate agents. 'I need to find a new place for my daughter and me.' *Recently separated*, I thought. *Maybe she was serious, after all.*

I was separated from my father, too. I missed him enormously. I'd just learned about phantom limbs in a children's science book – the sensation that an amputated or missing limb is still there – and I was fascinated by it. I remember sitting back in my chair after reading about it and thinking, *this is how I feel*. It's like my father was a part of me, an actual part of my body, and now he was gone, but I could still feel him, like the ghost of a severed limb. I could feel the space where he used to be attached; by my shoulder, above my stomach, across my heart.

I thought about him all the time; I thought about him in our house and wondered what he was doing. I hoped he wasn't lonely, but in my heart I knew he was. I imagined him sitting in his favourite chair by the window, and I wondered if he had his legs propped on the purple pouffe as he sometimes did, or whether his right foot rested on his left thigh. Was he flicking through a newspaper or trying to lose himself in a film, or was he content, polishing his glasses on the bottom of his shirt and humming away to himself? It bothered me that I didn't know, and sometimes I would get a pain in my chest, I missed him so much. I wanted to rush over to him, to fling my arms around his neck and have him lift me up and swing me around, to breathe in his familiar smell of clean cotton and faint cologne and that distant earthiness, like fresh soil or damp leaves.

In those first few weeks back in England Mother was more consistent than she'd ever been in Martinique, where I'd been living permanently on the edge. Here, I relaxed – just a little, never all the way. But time passed in a blur. Unlike the rest of my childhood I had no diary entries to jog my memory. I'd always hidden my diary among my things – between the pages of my fattest book, in the side-pocket of an old tattered backpack, places I knew Mother would never look – but we'd left with so few belongings there was nowhere safe to hide it. The idea of Mother finding my diary was too horrendous to entertain, and this period of my life remains the hardest to recall.

But I remember some things very clearly. I remember leaning my head against the window in the hotel and gazing out at London as it spread out before me, this stern, foreboding city I didn't know. I remember watching the crowded pavements streaming like rivers towards me, the cars humming and whizzing like brightly coloured beetles. I remember staring at trees that didn't have their leaves and imagining the terrible fire that must have torn through this city, for the trees to be so barren. I remember that Mother bought a car, a little blue Ford that smelled funny no matter how often she cleaned it, and we left London and drove to Sussex. I remember sitting in the backseat as she drove down the motorway and thinking, *Granny and Grandad live in Sussex. Does Mother remember that Granny and Grandad live in Sussex? Are we going to see them?* I felt like I had almost forgotten their faces, but I knew that I missed them. I missed the way Grandad would pick me up and whirl me around until I was dizzy and giggling, and Granny would hug me so tight that I would tell her to *stop, stop, stop or I'll pop!* But I knew I shouldn't mention them to Mother, not yet.

* * *

Of all the places we could have lived in England, we ended up just outside Lewes, a pretty town by the South Downs. I never asked why Mother decided to move us there, but now I would guess it came down to two reasons: that the town is known for its artistic community, and the fact it's only a 20-minute drive to my grandparents' house, though I didn't know that at the time.

We moved into the attic apartment of an old building that had been converted into flats. It was tiny, with a sloping roof and old-fashioned latticed windows smeared with other people's fingerprints. Once we'd unpacked, I stood by the window and I remember, quite clearly, tilting my head to one side and seeing fingerprints appear on the glass, delicate as cobwebs. Whose prints were they, I wondered. Who had lived here before us? I placed my own fingers onto the prints for a moment, wondering if I could somehow sense who'd been here before, but Mother knocked my hand away.

'Don't do that,' she snapped. 'It's filthy!'

The next day I saw that she'd cleaned the windows and wiped the prints away, and I felt sad, like the fingerprints were the last trace of someone who lived here before us, someone who'd once been loved, but would now be forgotten.

The flat had three rooms: the 'big room', as I called it (basically a living room, kitchen and Mother's bedroom all in one), a poky bathroom with a low roof that I bumped my head on whenever I climbed out of the tiny bath, and a box room – my room – with just enough space for a little bed and chair. Now that it was only Mother and me, I was more aware than ever of the importance of staying in her good books. I did exactly what she said, when she said it. I made my bed, I dried the dishes, I thanked her every time she passed me a plate or ran me a bath. I told her I loved her every night. I think that I meant it.

'You need to go to school,' she said to me one day when we'd been back for a few weeks. I looked up from where I was drawing at the desk in the big room.

'I don't want to go to school,' I said.

Mother closed her eyes and sniffed. I remember she had a cold and her face was puffy and pink. She lay on the overstuffed brown sofa, a cold flannel over her eyes, a ripped tissue trailing from her fingers.

'It doesn't matter what you want,' she sighed. 'It's the law.'

I thought it was rich that she now cared about the law, given the circumstances of our return, but I stayed silent.

'Your father's even more selfish than I thought,' she muttered. 'He left me to be a single mother, and now look at me! I'm sick, I'm tired, I'm by myself, how am I meant to find work *and* look after you too?'

'Can't I just go to Lewes school?' I asked. The town had a primary school, a squat, red brick building we'd walked by several times.

'School finishes at three,' Mother said, rolling her eyes. 'Who's going to look after you when you come home? I need to work – this money won't last forever.'

The week before she'd called her parents and asked them for money. She was rarely in contact with them and she didn't let me speak to them.

'Let them earn that right,' she told me mysteriously. I didn't know how much money they gave her, but it must have been a lot – enough to buy a car, and pay for our hotels, and go on shopping sprees, where she bought me expensive toys and herself new clothes.

'Maybe … maybe Granny and Grandad could help?' As soon as I said the words I held my breath, but Mother didn't react. I was afraid she'd get angry, but I hadn't seen them for more than two years, since before Martinique, and now that my father wasn't around, I ached for their familiarity. 'Maybe they could pick me up after school and cook me dinner. Aren't we … aren't we close to Granny and Grandad?'

'We are.'

I paused. 'Are we going to see them?'

'We'll see.'

I glanced back down at my drawing, not daring to let her see the smile that was beginning to play around my mouth. I couldn't blow it. If I carried on being good and not making Mother cross, she might let me see my grandparents.

It was a sign of how much Mother hated the banality of looking after me that a few days later, she announced we were paying my grandparents a visit. I tried to keep the excitement from showing on my face – it was important she didn't know how much I wanted to see them again. As we drove to their cottage, Mother was silent. She seemed nervous and it scared me, because she was never nervous.

'I'm going to tell you a story, Olivia,' she said suddenly. 'A true story, from when you were a baby.' She was looking at me in the rear-view mirror in that way she did, and my palms began to tingle. She always liked telling stories about when I was a baby. I was the best baby in the world, she said, that was why it was so strange that I was such a naughty child. I was a sweet, chubby, rosy little thing; I hardly ever cried. Mother just had to come in the room and I'd coo with joy. 'You were the perfect baby,' she'd say. 'My perfect baby, you were so sweet. You were so pure.

We used to call you "little Clive" because you looked just like him, with your mop of hair and your big green eyes.'

But somehow along the way I became rotten. And no matter her best efforts, no matter how hard she tried and how patient she was, the rot wouldn't out. As I grew older, it crept over me like vines, festering and poisoning me until I was black and spoiled inside. I heard these stories so often I could have mouthed the words along with her.

'Do I know this story?' I asked, and she smiled.

'No. I've never told you this before – out of loyalty to your father, I suppose.' She snorted. 'But I'm done with being loyal now. You need your grandparents right now, but you should also know what they're really like. This is the story of what happened when you were a few months old and I took you to see your Granny and Grandad for the first time.'

'Okay,' I said, and her eyes smiled at me in the mirror.

'You were just a little baby, so small you could sit in the crook of my arm. Your father wanted you to meet his parents. You'd already met your *Grand-mère* and *Grand-père* – even though they were all the way in France and your grandparents were in England!' She laughed at this, and I smiled back tentatively. 'Anyway, we drove for hours to their little cottage. We knocked on the door. I had you all ready in my arms for them, so they could take you and hold you and kiss you, their new baby granddaughter. But do you know what they did, Olivia?'

'No, Maman.'

'Nothing, absolutely nothing! They were all over your father – "Clive, how wonderful to see you, Oh Clive,"' she mocked. 'But all I got was a cold smile and one of their stiff British hellos. They barely looked at you. My beautiful baby girl, they didn't want to hold you. "I thought all babies were supposed to be cute" – that's what your grandmother said. I was so hurt. I thought maybe, if they held you, they'd realise what a special baby you were, but when I gently placed you in your grandfather's lap, he pushed you off. "She's too heavy," he said. "I don't want that thing in my lap." They didn't like you, they didn't want you, and it broke my heart. They didn't even look at you. Wasn't that terrible of them?'

'Yes, Maman.'

'Why would they do that? Why do you think they would be so cruel?' she asked me sadly.

'I don't know,' I answered truthfully.

'Your Granny and Grandad have always resented me, you know. I tried so hard with them, from day one. I tried to be friendly and polite and I never complained, even though they always made these stupid inside jokes to exclude me. I always smiled and laughed. But they never made me feel like one of the family. I was never one of them – they're so British, with their silly habits and closed feelings and stiff upper lips. They hated the fact that your father married a Frenchwoman, they still do. They hate that I'm passionate and wild and they can't control me, however much they try,' She paused, looked at me again in the mirror. 'And you know they want to control you too, Olivia?'

I shook my head; I didn't know what to think. Granny and Grandad had always been kind to me. I didn't think I believed her, but her face looked sad, and I couldn't understand why she would say these things if they weren't true.

'They do. They want to change the way you think, the way you speak, the way you act. They want to make you as cold and unfeeling as they are. They want to turn you against me, your own mother. But they won't, will they, my angel face?'

'No, Maman.' We turned a corner and finally, finally, Granny and Grandad's cottage appeared. Mother pulled the car over and looked at me.

'Come and sit in the front seat for a moment,' she said. I did so, and once I shut the car door, she reached for my hand. 'The thing you must understand, Olivia, is that you are *mine*. You are *my daughter*,' she said, and the fervour in her voice startled me. 'And your Granny and Grandad know that. They want you to be weak, colourless. Bland, like their son. But they know you're like me, and that's what they don't like, and that's why they want to control you and turn you against me.' She brushed my hair away from my face. 'I need to hear you promise that they'll never succeed, my darling.'

'I promise,' I said. My hands were twisted together in my lap, and I looked down at them because I didn't want to look at her.

'Good,' she said. She leaned forward and gripped my upper arms, twisting me so that I faced towards her. 'I need to speak to you about something else before we go in.' She glanced towards the cottage. 'Now, your grandparents might ask you why we left Martinique. Why your father didn't come back with us.' She was staring at me so intensely that I felt her eyes were branding me. 'What are you going to tell them?'

'That …' I swallowed. 'That we left because we were homesick?' I said hopefully. Mother's hands tightened around my arms and I winced.

'No,' she said. 'Today, I'll tell them the real reason we came home, and if you ever, *ever* tell them otherwise …' She left that sentence unfinished and I looked up at her slowly. Her eyes shone with fury, and I realised I was just as afraid of her as I'd always been. I knew I would never speak about what happened with the police. 'Do you understand?'

'Yes, Maman.'

'Good,' she said, her voice light again. 'Come on then! Let's go inside.' She held my hand as we walked along the garden path, leading me towards the door as I trailed after her.

Seeing Granny and Grandad was wonderful, but I wished Mother wasn't there too. I couldn't relax. I remembered faintly, as though in a dream, that bad things had happened in this cottage with Mother, and I wanted her to get in the car and drive away, back to the little attic flat and leave me here. But she didn't.

I didn't say a lot during that first meeting. Mother didn't give anyone else much of a chance. She described the past weeks as though they'd been hell, telling my grandparents how sick she'd been, how stressed and tired she was, how I'd been playing up, how she was worried about money now she was a single parent without a job. She said that phrase a lot – *single parent* – and I saw my grandparents look at each other. There was an elephant in the room, and eventually Granny addressed it.

'What happened, Josephine, if you don't mind me asking?'

'Your son chose his job over his family,' Mother replied. My father didn't have a name anymore, or any connection to Mother; he was just someone else's son, someone else's father, it seemed.

'Yes, Clive told us he'll be coming back as soon as term finishes,' Granny said impatiently. 'But what … what made you want to leave so suddenly? Without him? I thought you were happy there?'

'Don't you know?' Mother said, her eyebrows shooting up her face.

'Clive won't tell us,' Granny admitted, and a brief expression of triumph flashed across Mother's face.

'Well, I'm not surprised,' she said smoothly. 'The story doesn't paint him in the best light.' She paused for a moment. 'So, he didn't tell you anything, about what happened with the police?' My heart began to quicken. Surely she wasn't going to tell them the truth?

'The police?' Grandad said, in obvious surprise.

'Yes,' Mother said, one eyebrow still raised. 'You really don't know. Well, I'll tell you.'

She did tell them, but it wasn't a story I'd heard before. I sat in silence as she spoke, my mind spinning. This is what she told my grandparents.

In Martinique, Mother had worked for an artist's showroom, painting and making vases. She was the biggest-selling artist by far – her work flew off the shelves – but the showroom owners, Elodie and Nicolas, were jealous of her talent. Mother knew they resented her but she was professional, as she always is, and tried to ignore it. But one day, she became concerned. Elodie and Nicolas hired a young local boy to glaze their pottery, and he became very sick. Mother began to do some research, and she discovered that the glaze the boy was using contained toxic chemicals. She rushed to tell Elodie and Nicolas and urged them to use a different glaze, but they refused. Why would they spend three times as much, they said. There was no proof the boy was sick because of the glaze, anyway.

Mother did everything she could, but no one acted. Even Clive, who should have supported his wife unconditionally, told her to leave it. The boy recovered for a while and returned to glazing pottery, despite her best efforts. She spoke to him herself, even offering him money from her own pocket if he stopped glazing, but Elodie and Nicolas had poisoned his mind and he refused. Soon he got sick again, and this time, sadly – so, so terribly sadly – he died, poisoned by toxic chemicals in the glaze. Mother was outraged, of course, and took to the local newspaper to expose Elodie and Nicolas, but to divert the blame, the disgraced couple accused her of stealing from them and selling her art illegally! The police were sent to bring her in – *her*, as if *she* was the criminal! They soon realised their mistake, of course, and were enormously apologetic, but it was too late. There was no way Mother would stay on an island where a boy's tragic death would have no consequences, where greedy, immoral people like Elodie and Nicolas would never pay the price for their crimes, where Mother's good reputation would suffer the ignominy of being accused of *stealing*. Perhaps other people could tolerate this, but not her. She had her morals and she would stick to them, thank you very much, even if it meant losing everything. That's just the kind of person she is.

Granny and Grandad listened in stunned disbelief while I listened in fearful, indignant confusion. I didn't understand how Mother could tell such stories. I knew it wasn't true – that wasn't the reason we left – but she told the tale so convincingly I wondered if she knew that herself. I watched her as she spoke, her earnest expressions and the nimble way she controlled the narrative, and she was so convincing, I almost believed her myself.

Maybe there's something wrong with her memory, I thought. *Maybe she doesn't mean to tell such stories*. But two things stuck out to me as I listened – and I later learned it was the same for Granny, too. The first was that it wasn't enough for her to be absolved of any wrongdoing; she had to become the hero, the one everyone should have listened to. The only one in this sorry tale who wasn't in the wrong – unlike the rapacious liars Elodie and Nicolas, or my disloyal and apathetic father, or the misguided, impulsive police. Only Mother escaped unscathed, only she was a martyr.

The second thing was how she looked as she told it. There was a righteous anger in her eyes as she spoke of how her name had been besmirched, shock and pain on her face as she revealed the devastating truth of what happened – of how the boy she'd tried so desperately to save had died. It was mesmerising, watching her face as she spoke; the corners of her mouth turning down, the fleeting quiver of her lip, tears brimming. And then, when Granny and Grandad went into the kitchen afterwards, there was the look she gave me as she leaned back in her chair and propped her head on her fist, cocky and proud, like she was saying, 'How do you like my story?'

That look scared me more than her lies ever could. I thought about it in bed, later that night, and I dreamed of it too: the bold raise of her brow, the arrogant curve of her mouth, the cold gleam in her eye.

PSYCHOPATHY SYMPTOM #6

Pathological lying

Psychopaths lie effortlessly, glibly and with authority. They lie in order to control others, to elicit sympathy, to avoid condemnation and to present distorted images of themselves. Unlike normal people who feel shame when they lie, psychopaths actually revel in their lies. It feeds their desire for domination and provides them pleasure; this is called 'Duper's Delight'.

7

FRAUD

*'Psychopaths lie effortlessly, glibly,
and with authority.'*

Reuniting with Granny and Grandad wasn't the only wonderful thing that happened in my first month in Lewes. I also made my very own best friend. I met Amelia on my first day at school. She was a year older than me and we were in different classes, but the school was so small everyone knew everyone. I noticed her at lunchtime, playing with her friends across the schoolyard. She was a tall, beautiful girl with long blonde hair, and to me she seemed impossibly glamorous. I felt drawn to her almost instantly, but I was too shy to say hello. I shuffled as close to her as I dared and then stood there, an awkward smile fixed on my face, trying to act like I belonged. She looked at me, whispered something to her friend and marched over.

'I'm Amelia,' she announced. 'What's your name?'

'Olivia,' I mumbled, wishing I had an ounce of her confidence.

'You're new,' she said, and I nodded. 'Where are you from?'

'Um …' I hesitated. I wasn't quite sure where I was from, we'd already moved around so much. 'Well, we lived in Martinique before we came back to England.'

'Martinique?' Amelia frowned, her hands on her hips. 'Where's that, then?'

'I dunno,' I said, stupidly. She laughed at me, though not unkindly, then beckoned me to walk with her. On one side of the playground was a small pond where pupils learned about nature and newts and watched frogspawn grow into frogs. There were lilies in the pond, pink and pale yellow, and around the water's edge was a border of large white stones.

'Do you like our pond?' she asked. I nodded that I did. 'Loads of water animals live in there,' she said. 'You can poke them, if you're careful. Go and have a look.'

As I stepped forward to the edge of the pond and looked over, I heard a faint giggle behind me, then I felt her hands against my back. She shoved me – not too hard, but hard enough – and I staggered over the white stones and into the pond. Cold green water rushed into my shoes, weeds wrapped round my ankles like fingers, and I lurched out, sliding on the wet stones. I looked at Amelia breathlessly, my heart racing. Her hand was over her mouth, hiding the smile I could clearly see in her eyes.

'I'm so sorry!' she gasped. 'I don't know why I did that!' She giggled again, and I laughed back uncertainly. She walked over to me and I blinked, unsure if she was coming to push me in again. Instead, she put her arm around me. 'I really am sorry,' she said. 'I don't know why I did that ... I must have thought it would be funny. Are you okay?'

'Yes!' I said, not wanting her to think I was a sissy. 'I'm fine. It *was* funny!'

She glanced down at my sodden shoes and dirty trousers.

'Oh dear, your shoes are all wet.'

'That's okay, they'll dry,' I said, trying to sound nonchalant. I was already dreading what Mother would say when she picked me up – she hated dirt, hated clumsiness. In my head I was already trying to think up an explanation.

'Your mum will be angry,' she said, and I glanced at her. 'I'll tell her it was my fault,' she said grandly. I shook my head at once. I liked Amelia and wanted her to be my friend; I couldn't have Mother thinking badly of her. But she was resolute. When school finished, she strode over to

79

where Mother was leaning against the wall, standing away from the other parents, peering at me over her sunglasses. I trailed behind, my heart thumping.

'Mrs Lacroix?' she said. 'I'm Amelia, I'm in Year Five. I'm so sorry, but I fell over at lunchtime and knocked Olivia into the pond. She's all dry now but her shoes and trousers are dirty. I'm so sorry. I wanted you to know it was my fault, not Olivia's.'

I watched Mother's face carefully. I could see she was interested in this confident girl who'd marched up to her. Her eyes flickered over Amelia, then over to me. I shuffled my feet. There was a little pause while she thought what to say. Then she smiled.

'Don't be silly!' she said with that lovely lilting laugh of hers. 'These things happen. A little bit of mud never did anyone any harm.'

I remembered how she screamed at me when I tracked sand into the house in Martinique, and said nothing.

'Phew!' Amelia said with a laugh. 'I was worried you'd be angry.'

'Why ever did you think I'd be angry over a bit of mud?' Mother said. She was still smiling but her voice had that edge to it now. I knew Amelia wouldn't have noticed, and I began to fidget. 'It's no problem, really.'

Behind Mother I could see a woman approach us, and from her blonde hair and bright smile I guessed she must be Amelia's mother. 'Hello!' she said to Amelia. She had a warm voice, a faint accent and her eyes crinkled when she smiled. 'Didn't fancy saying hello to me today then?' Amelia grabbed her mother's hand with a relaxed confidence I envied.

'I was just saying hello to my new friend Olivia's mum!' she said. 'I accidentally knocked Olivia into the pond earlier, so I wanted to say sorry.'

'Clumsy girl!' Amelia's mother said affectionately. She smiled at me, said hello, then turned to Mother. 'Hi, I'm Sigrid. You must be new here!'

I knew without looking at her that Mother had noticed Sigrid's foreign accent, that her interest had been piqued. She smiled back at her, that big, winning smile of hers that showed all her teeth. 'Hi, I'm Josephine. Yes, we moved here last week.' She tucked her hair behind her ear, her dimples in full force. 'Do I detect a continental accent?'

'Yes, I'm Swedish,' Sigrid said, and I saw Mother's eyes light up.

'I'm French,' she said instantly, as I knew she would. 'It's lovely to meet another European!'

Mother was drawn to the fact that Sigrid wasn't a dry, stuck-up Brit as she said Granny and Grandad were, but I could see she also genuinely liked her. She was intelligent, funny and confident; pretty, too, which never hurt in Mother's eyes. Mother didn't look up to anyone – no one, whoever they were, was more interesting or dynamic than she was – but Sigrid at least was worthy of her friendship.

* * *

With more people in our lives, Mother returned to her usual self. She rented a studio in an artists' residence in town and started her own arts and painting business. She sketched portaits and daubed paint and shaped pots, singing along to The Beautiful South as she did so and insisting I sing along with her. She played the album *Blue Is The Colour* on a loop that year; I still know every word to it.

She visibly perked up, taking pride in her appearance, pinning her hair up with brightly coloured scarves and headbands. She became a chameleon again, and it fascinated me to watch the way she created and then discarded her personas at will. The beleaguered single mum wasn't someone she wanted to be for long – it wasn't glamorous enough, or interesting enough, or fun enough – though it was useful for a while. But being a gutsy, self-sufficient artist who'd ditched her no-good husband to start again with her little girl was a much better role to play. She painted my father as a villain – when she spoke of him at all – and people congratulated her on her strength and independence.

'It's good that you left him,' I heard Sigrid say one afternoon as they had coffee in her garden. 'You've come so far in just a month, you don't need him. Men like that never change.'

Men like what? I wondered. *What stories had Mother been telling?*

'That's true,' Mother sighed, wrapping her hands around her coffee cup and biting her lip. 'I just wish I had acted sooner. If I had, maybe that little boy would still be alive ...' Her voice cracked and she looked down. 'I just feel so *guilty ...*'

'Stop it,' Sigrid said. 'You did everything you could.' She leaned forward and rubbed Mother's arm. 'I think you're a hero.'

Mother laughed quietly and wiped a hand across her eyes. 'Well, I wouldn't go that far ...'

I felt heat rising in my face and looked away. That night I wrote in my diary: 'It's all LIES. Lies lies lies. I KNOW they are lies. But I think she believes them'. She didn't, of course, but that's how convincing she was: even though I knew these stories were false, I still felt that she believed them. The painful catch in her voice, the way her big grey eyes brimmed with tears, the way she let her chin tremble, just for a second, before taking a deep, calming breath and raising her eyes skyward; she was masterful in her manipulation. But I still didn't really know it, then.

I missed my father terribly, but from that first day at school, Amelia and I were like peas in a pod, which made me feel better. She looked after me like a little sister. She put her arm around me when we walked, told jokes when I felt sad, plaited my hair, told me I was pretty and funny.

After school we went to Amelia's house and had picnic parties in the garden, where we sat around a wooden table and talked about the things that mattered: Furbies and Pogs and The Spice Girls. We traded toys and painted each other's nails and ate enormous bowls of cherries covered in mountains of squirty cream. Shrieking with laughter, we spat the pips at each other. I thought about my birthday just a few months before, where I'd sobbed in my bedroom, lonely and humiliated. How I'd ached to have a friend. It felt like a very long time ago.

'Your mum's weird,' Amelia said one day through a mouthful of cherries. My heart fluttered.

'What do you mean?' I said, but she shrugged.

'She's just weird,' she said. 'She looks at you in a really weird way, sometimes. Me as well. I don't think she likes me very much.'

'She does like you,' I said. 'She told me so.'

She hadn't, but I wanted to protect Amelia from Mother, from what had happened before. Mother was still mean to me sometimes, but in the few months we'd been back in England she'd been nicer than ever before. I didn't want to think about the bad times – I wanted to draw a line under it, to use one of Mother's expressions. Things had changed, Mother had changed. Maybe it wasn't her fault or my fault, maybe it was Martinique's fault. Maybe we were never meant to go there. Maybe my father really was selfish not to come back with us. Maybe it *was* his fault. But I wanted to draw a line under it, and so in my mind I did so. I imagined myself back in Martinique, standing on the beach in front of the lagoon, facing towards our house on top of the cliff; I had a long stick in my fist, and I scored it through the sand, slowly, purposefully, and as the line emerged, that was it. That was the end of all the bad stuff – gone, forgotten.

'I don't think she does like me,' Amelia insisted, lining cherry pips along the table and flicking them, one by one, into the flowerbed behind her. She hesitated for a moment, then snickered. 'Do you know who she reminds me of?'

'Who?' I asked.

She glanced at me slyly, then laughed again. 'You know the Grand High Witch in *The Witches*?' I put my hands over my mouth. I was obsessed with Roald Dahl books, and Amelia and I had watched the film together a few days before. It thrilled us both, but when the Grand High Witch slowly peeled off her pretty face to reveal the beast underneath, something clenched tight around my heart. 'Not because they look alike!' Amelia added hurriedly, seeing my face. 'But sometimes she's so nice to you, so kind and sweet. And it's funny, because it doesn't always seem real. Yesterday, when I came over for tea, you spilled your drink and she said it was fine, remember, but her face looked weird, all stiff, or like it was a mask. I half-expected her to pull it off and her to be an ugly witch underneath!'

I laughed, unsure what to say; I wanted to confide in Amelia but I was afraid to. I was afraid she wouldn't want to be my friend if she knew how Mother could be, and I was ashamed of myself, too, for being such a disappointment, for making Mother so cross. And yet, somewhere beneath the fear and shame was another feeling, of protection and loyalty to Mother. I couldn't betray her, but there was a desperate burning in my stomach. I needed Amelia to know something – a small thing, just a little slice of the truth.

'Sometimes she gets really cross,' I mumbled. 'Usually because I'm naughty. But sometimes ...' I didn't know how to put it. As I thought about it, an emptiness swelled inside me and for a reason I couldn't understand, tears pricked behind my eyes. I felt awkward, embarrassed. I picked up the can of squirty cream and sprayed it into my mouth, holding my finger down on the nozzle until frothy white cream came drooling down my chin. I don't know why I did that; maybe to plug up the empty feeling inside, maybe to buy myself more time, maybe to stop myself saying something I shouldn't. But somehow, though she was only ten, Amelia understood. She leaned across the table and squeezed my hand.

'Don't cry,' she said. 'I'm sorry I said that, I was only joking!' She looked at me for a moment, then laughed. 'You look like a crazy person, foaming at the mouth!' Then she picked up the can of cream, aimed it at her own mouth and sprayed until cream dribbled down her chin. 'There, now we can be crazy people together!'

* * *

As if making a best friend wasn't wonderful enough, having Granny and Grandad back in my life was the icing on the cake. Three days a week Granny picked me up from school while Mother worked in the studio and I spent the evening at their cottage. I loved the cottage – the smell of old paint and cracking leather, the undercurrents of age and dust, the lace curtains bobbing in the window, my grandmother fussing over me, my grandfather's soft grey beard. I came to see it as my safe place, and even now when I look back these memories are cast in a different light; they seem to glow gold, or maybe sepia, like nostalgia. Either way it was my haven, and I wished I could spend every moment there. Sometimes Amelia would come too, and we'd dig around in the garden with Grandad, or bake biscuits with Granny, or just lie on the sofas in the living room, chatting, trying to do headstands, crashing into the coffee table.

I have no doubt that the reason Mother reconnected with Granny and Grandad was because she needed their help. Without my father around, someone else had to share the parental duties and my grandparents were the perfect candidates. Mother could palm me off to them as much as she liked, knowing they would never complain. They were terrified she'd cut off contact with them again; when we lived in Martinique I wasn't allowed to speak to them on the phone or return their letters. She was nice to them when she came to collect me, acting pleased to see me and thanking them with one hand over her heart, but in the car driving home she let rip. She called them 'The Twits', like the horrible couple in the Roald Dahl book, and told me horrible stories about them: how cruel they'd been to her in the past, how Granny should leave Grandad as he was a wicked man, how they complained to her about looking after me, how disappointed in me they said they were ... I tried not to believe her.

* * *

One July afternoon I arrived at the cottage after school to find a surprise waiting for me: my father, sitting in the kitchen, a bashful smile on his face. I burst into tears, racing towards him as I had done in my dreams, throwing my arms around him and squeezing him tight. I remember this so well: the way he hugged me back, the way his arms were heavy on my shoulders, the way he cupped my hot, wet face, the tears that glittered in his eyes, the way Granny hovered in the doorway, a sad smile on her face.

'You're back!' I exclaimed, not relaxing my grip. 'You're really back!'

'Of course I'm back,' he said. 'I said I'd come back as soon as term finished, didn't I?'

'Are you back forever?' I said, and he nodded.

'Of course I am, my little Olive.'

'Does Maman know?' I asked.

He glanced at Granny before he looked back at me.

'No ... it's a surprise.'

'Maman doesn't like surprises,' I said.

'Well, your mother won't answer his calls,' Granny said. 'So, if she doesn't like the surprise, there's not much we can do about it now.' There was a bitterness in her voice that shocked me, but when I looked at her, she smiled. 'It will be alright.'

I wasn't sure it would be, but I said nothing. When Mother arrived to collect me that evening I could tell she was shocked to see my father, but she quickly smothered the look.

'Clive,' she said coolly, and the hopeful smile died on his face. She shot an accusing look at my grandmother. 'I should have known you'd be colluding behind my back.'

'Josephine, no one's colluding with anyone. Clive's just got back and had nowhere else to go. He's our son, of course we'll give him a place to stay.'

Mother sniffed. 'Come on, Olivia. Get in the car.'

My father stood there uncertainly, then touched Mother on the arm.

'I'm … I'm coming too, aren't I?'

She blinked at him, her face blank. 'Why would *you* come?' she said. 'We're separated.'

'But not really,' Father said, glancing from Mother to me and back again. 'Not *really* separated. Come on, don't do this. You know I want to be with you.'

'Not as much as you wanted to finish the term,' she shot back, her mouth all twisted.

'That's not fair and you know it,' Father said, and he sounded firm this time. I couldn't bear to see him diminish before her the way he always had, and I hoped with all my heart that he'd come back stronger, tougher, more resolute than before. I hoped he'd been hardened – I needed him to be impervious to her. 'I told you I'd come back as soon as school finished, now I'm back.'

'Great,' Mother said, looking at him like she hated him. It hurt my heart to see. She put her hand around my shoulders and began propelling me out of the house. 'Come on, Olivia, let's go.'

'Wait!' My father followed us out. 'Wait!' He touched her shoulder again, gently, tentatively. She looked at his hand in disgust and he dropped it. 'Look, just tell me what you need me to do. Tell me what you want.'

'What I want?' Mother echoed, like he'd said something stupid. She thought for a moment, her head on one side, her right hand still draped around my shoulders. It felt heavy on my neck, and I wanted to shrug it off, but I didn't dare. 'I want you to work for it,' she said suddenly, her face hard. 'Fight for me. Fight for me the way I deserve to be fought for!'

So he did fight for her, as she knew he would, as we all knew he would, and she relished every moment. He sent huge bouquets to the house – pink and red roses, frothy white flowers like lace, purple blooms with dark, glossy leaves – and depending on her mood, she arranged them in vases or tossed them in the bin. 'Flowers, how original!' she sniffed, but when she was gone, I rushed over and lifted the lid. I looked at the unwanted bouquet and my heart bled for my father. Sometimes I plucked a single blossom from the bin and hid it in my bedroom; that way it was as if my father wasn't rejected or cast aside: he was hiding here with me, safe in my room, away from her.

Sometimes, when she was giving him the silent treatment, he turned up unannounced and begged her to take him back – she was always dreadful when he did that. I was in the bath one evening when the doorbell went.

'I wonder who that could be,' Mother said, patting her hair in place as she left the room.

It was Father, as she knew it would be, and I sat still, wishing the water would stop sloshing around as I strained to hear. I could hear his voice, flat and despondent, as she screamed and swore at him – he was a fucking bastard, a waste of space, and what was he thinking to bring more shitty flowers to her when she'd made it clear she wasn't fucking interested?

I stood up in the bath and pressed my face against the little window in the roof, peering out as far as I could. I could see him, his sad face and the flowers in his hand pointing hopelessly towards the floor. She started pushing him then – hard, mean shoves in his chest – but when he didn't react, she snatched the flowers from his hand and started hitting him with them. It almost looked funny, but it wasn't. She stepped backwards then and I couldn't see her anymore, but I could still hear her, and the words she used to hurt my father hurt me too. They were cruel words, and I didn't have to understand them to know that they were designed to hurt: *sad fool. Sick prick. Ugly cunt.* When I went outside the next day there were petals scattered across the ground – soft pink peonies, my favourite – and they were dirty, wilting in the sun. That also hurt to see.

It took a month before Mother agreed to take him back. She drew up a contract that he had to sign before she would even entertain the idea of a reconciliation – she needed to know she could trust him, that she'd always be his priority. She wouldn't stand for coming second best to anything, whether it was work or his parents or even me. I didn't quite know how I felt about it all. Part of me was thrilled my father was home, but another part was scared, and I watched him move into our tiny attic flat with a gnawing unease in my gut.

My father was cheery; he shot me a triumphant grin as he threw his case onto the table, and I smiled back, but there was a bitter, metallic taste in my mouth, a flutter of apprehension in my stomach.

Years later, when Granny and I reconnected after nearly a decade, she told me that she'd thought for a while that it really was the end. My father – for the first time in his life – had spoken to her honestly about his relationship. He said then that he thought the marriage was truly over.

'Perhaps it's for the best,' Granny told him. 'Maybe this is the way it has to be.'

But then he would look agonised. 'But if I don't fight for her, I won't see Olivia again. I know I won't, she'll make sure of it. She'll take her to France and that'll be it. What can I do? *What can I do?*' And he wrung his hands together, and Granny looked at him and couldn't believe this man was her son.

'If you don't know what you should do, Clive, I can't help you,' she told him.

I believe that he fought for Mother for me: because he loved me, because he knew he couldn't leave me alone with her. But I wish he hadn't bothered. He could have escaped her, if he hadn't stayed. He could have unfurled himself from her grip before it was too late, before he became a willing pawn in her games. And if he'd gone, if he'd escaped her clutches, perhaps I would have realised it was possible. Perhaps I could have escaped her too, and we could have gone away together, my father and me, to start a new life away from her. But he must have thought staying with her would protect me. He must have.

* * *

As soon as my father moved back in, Mother changed again. For a few months I'd been her ally, her confidante, and Father was the enemy, but now our roles swapped. I became a disappointment again; a failure, a disaster. 'Clive, what's *wrong* with her?' she asked him, whenever I spilled my drink or forgot to do a chore, or didn't notice her new haircut. Father would look down, mutter 'I don't know,' and then when Mother left the room, he'd glance up at me and give me a small, sheepish smile. I felt betrayed and would turn away, but I could never stay angry at him for long.

The attic apartment was too small for the three of us, so we moved into a new house, an old country cottage just outside Lewes. Instead of renting, as we usually did, my parents bought the house, and I was glad. I wanted to stay in our Lewes cottage forever. It was small but sweet, with a bright, cosy kitchen, a rickety staircase and an open brick fireplace. There was only one bedroom, but my father converted the basement into a bedroom for me. It was dark and in winter it smelt damp, but I didn't mind, because in the fields behind the cottage horses roamed, and behind that were overgrown fern woods, where Amelia and I would crawl through and pretend we were explorers.

Our garden was big and overgrown, and one weekend, Father and I dug out a little pond, lined it properly, filled it up with the hose then went off excitedly to the garden centre to buy fish. I loved the pond; I spent hours poking around, trying to catch tadpoles or newts, stroking them gently before returning them to the water, or rummaging in the undergrowth, catching frogs or insects and bringing them over to the pond – to this lovely new home I'd made for them.

'You'll be happy here,' I said.

I hoped more than anything they would.

* * *

One day in September Amelia came to sleep over, and Mother took us to pick the last of the season's strawberries. This is the most vivid memory I have before the age of ten, and even now, I can still recall it with a disturbing clarity – every sound, every smell, every taste. It was late afternoon on a hot, sticky day, and the air smelled of hay and honeysuckle, earth and sun cream. Amelia and I marched through the fields of fruit, little green punnets over our arms, stuffing more berries in our mouths than we dropped into the baskets. My mouth tasted of strawberries, Amelia's chin was stained red. Our hands were sticky with juice.

The punnets were small and the farm was big, so every time the strawberries began overflowing from the sides we had to traipse back to the stall, have the berries weighed and set aside, and return to pick more. Mother had made it clear she wanted lots of berries – she liked making jam, and she made jars and jars of the stuff while we were in Lewes. She gave them to people as gifts, tying gingham cloth over the lids and securing it with brown string. It was a new role for her to play: the creative country wife, who not only made beautiful ceramics and paintings, but also was a dab hand in the kitchen. Wasn't Clive a lucky man? 'Not to toot my own horn, but my jam has won awards,' she'd tell neighbours as she pressed a jar upon them. 'I have a knack for it. I knocked this one up yesterday!' She didn't mention all the times she effed and blinded over the stove because the bloody jam wouldn't set. That was never her fault: it was mine, for not picking the right berries, or my father's, for buying the supermarket own brand sugar rather than the fancy stuff she wanted. It was a serious business, this strawberry picking, and after the third time we plodded through the fields to empty our punnets, I had an idea.

'Amelia, let's squish our berries down into our baskets!' I said. 'They're going to be squished anyway, and this way we'll be able to fit more in!'

Amelia agreed that it was an excellent idea, and we began picking berries with renewed vigour, filling them to the top of our punnets and then squishing them down until juice dribbled down the sides and our hands were stained scarlet. We ran back to where Mother was waiting by the stall, chatting to the lady who sold the fruit. Amelia and I were breathless, flushed in the face, grinning from ear to ear. I remember looking at her and feeling so content, gazing at my beautiful friend who glowed in the golden light, smiling at her so widely that my jaw ached. I looked over at Mother and waved, holding my basket aloft triumphantly. She raised her head, slowly, and I could see her looking at me carefully, her eyes lingering over Amelia and my interlocked arms, my jubilant smile, my exultant stance. She smiled back, but it was one of those tight smiles I'd learned to fear, and I dropped my basket to my side. It was still hot, but the breeze that circled around my shoulders and neck seemed icy cold.

'Look, Maman!' I said as we approached her. 'Look how many strawberries we fitted into our baskets!'

Mother looked into our punnets at the fat red strawberries flattened down, red rivulets staining the sides. 'That's not a very nice way to treat the lady's fruit,' she said in a flat voice, and the fruit lady laughed.

'Oh, it's no problem. Rather an ingenious way of getting more berries in your basket!' she said to me. 'I just hope no one else thinks of the same idea, or I'll be out of business!' She weighed up our final basket, packaged up the fruit and waved us a cheerful farewell.

Mother nodded towards the car. 'In!' she said, and Amelia and I scuttled towards it. Not a word was spoken as we drove home, but I knew something was coming. My chest felt tight, my heart ticked like a clock. Our sweet day of berry picking had turned sour, and I couldn't bear to look ahead as Mother drove to find her eyes looking at me in the mirror. I stared out the window at the meadows that raced past and twisted my sticky fingers together in my lap. Eventually we pulled up outside our house, and Mother turned around and smiled at Amelia.

'Come on, out you get!' she said in her lovely light voice. She looked at me. 'Stay,' she said, like I was a dog. So I stayed, looking away from Amelia so I wouldn't have to see the apologetic look on her face as she climbed out. I waited in the backseat for five minutes, ten minutes, 20 minutes. Half an hour stretched into an hour, and tears filled my eyes as I looked out onto the street, watching a few solitary cars drive by. For something to do I started picking at my left arm, digging into the base of each tiny hair with my nails and tearing them out. Afternoon faded into dusk, and from the backseat of the car, I watched the sky change colour. Buttery gold rays turned to a rosy pink light; it fell onto the road, trembled for a moment, then dimmed and was gone.

After about two hours Mother returned to the car. I could tell by her walk that she was boiling with rage, and I shrank back in my seat as she opened the door. Without a word she grabbed my right arm and pulled me backwards out of the car. I screamed as I tumbled out, as she dragged me towards our front door. I craned my neck as I tried to look for my father, to see if he was home, to see if he could protect me.

'Please stop, Maman!' I sobbed, but still she said nothing. I stumbled on the front step as she yanked me over it and along the hall. She opened the door to my little basement bedroom, shut it quietly behind her and began dragging me down the stairs. My tailbone, my ribs, my spindly legs knocked against the cold stone, every step a jolt through my body. When

Mother reached the last few steps, she pushed me down them. I fell head over heels, my jaw scraping on the carpet as I landed, arms splayed in front of me. She stepped over my legs and I cringed, waiting for the hit, but it didn't come. Instead, she pushed me against the wall and leaned forward so she was only inches away. I remember thinking then, quite distinctly, quite absurdly, how she reminded me of Miss Trunchbull from *Matilda* – only scarier, so much scarier.

'You stupid cow!' she spat from between clenched teeth. 'You disrespected the woman's fruit, didn't you? Walking back like a little bitch, like you owned the place. You disrespected her and her fruit!'

'No, Maman!' I said, my hands over my face. 'I didn't mean to, I'm sorry!'

'I've never been so embarrassed in my life. I'm ashamed of you. You're a disgusting, greedy, arrogant girl. I am mortified.'

'I'm sorry,' I sobbed. 'I just wanted to get more fruit for you!'

'Oh, so it's my fault, is it?' She laughed, and it was a thin and bitter sound that made me shudder. 'Well, guess what? *You* put these feelings here! *You* made me feel like this, I didn't make myself feel like this.' She pushed me back again until my head knocked against the wall. 'What a shame you had to ruin your sleepover with Amelia! Now, I have to ring her mother to tell her how naughty you were. Now, she'll have to come and pick Amelia up early. How embarrassing for you!' She rocked back on her heels, like she was finally satisfied, then turned and trod lightly up the stairs. At the top she paused and looked back at me. 'Don't you dare turn your light on, you can sit in the dark and think about what you've done.' Then she opened the door, and light from the hall flooded into my room. She stood there, silhouetted in the doorframe, her curtain of hair flickering. 'Nighty night!' she snapped, and then she was gone.

I sat in the dark for a while, sobbing into my knees, then crawled across the floor and fell onto my bed. It was a warm evening, but I was shivering uncontrollably, so I wrapped myself up in the little patchwork quilt that Mother made when we were in Martinique. I loved that quilt, even though the material was scratchy and the threads were coming apart at the seams. It was made up of floral squares in the most beautiful colours – dove-grey, lilac, sea-green, azure blue – and it reminded me of the evening skies in Martinique. I traced the outlines of the flowers to calm myself, and as I looked up through the window over my bed, at the small square of midnight blue sky, I wondered why I'd thought things could be different here.

After a while I heard a car pull up, and Sigrid's friendly voice, and Mother's warm greeting. I scrambled to my feet, wincing as I did so, and pushed the bottom of the window up. The scented air that flowed into my stale room was a relief, but the sound of Amelia's voice was sweeter.

'Can't I go and say bye to Livvy?'

'I'm afraid not, Amelia,' Mother said. 'She's been incredibly naughty this evening. When I spoke to her about being more respectful of other people's property she threw a fit. She was violent towards me, it was quite shocking!'

'Violent?' Sigrid asked, and I heard the surprise in her voice.

'Yes, she bit my arm. See?' Mother said, and I heard a gasp as she ostensibly extended her arm. Dread shuddered down my spine.

'Ouch!' My father's voice – I hadn't realised he was there. 'Jose, why didn't you say?'

'Gosh, that looks painful,' Sigrid said. 'Do you think you should get it checked out?'

'No, I'm sure it'll be fine,' Mother said briskly. 'I don't want to make it into a big thing. But Olivia needs to learn to control her temper, so she's staying in her room tonight.'

'Are you sure Olivia did that?' Amelia's voice sounded doubtful, and I loved her for it.

'Of course she did! What else do you think, I did it myself?'

That laugh again. I couldn't bear it, I couldn't believe it. I hadn't bit her, I hadn't, I hadn't. The idea I would dare bite Mother was absurd, laughable, but there she was, showing off her wounded arm to appalled gasps and concerned sympathy. Mother's arm must have looked bad, but how? The obvious answer – that she'd bit herself to have a wound to show off – hung in front of me, but it was somehow elusive. I knew that was what happened but I couldn't comprehend it. Why would she do this? Something like a scream began building in the back of my throat, and I pressed my hands over my face to stifle it. I didn't understand.

I wanted to be up there with them, telling Sigrid about the strawberries we picked, how Mother would make jam with them, how Amelia and I would sell it at the annual village fair. I could still hear their voices; I imagined the four of them chatting under the stars on this warm September evening, the way Sigrid's eyebrows would have contracted when she heard about my naughtiness, my father's disappointed face, the look of shock in Amelia's eyes. And then I saw myself, with my snotty, soggy face and my balled-up fists, the blanket draped over my shoulders like a bitter old lady, and I suddenly hated myself.

I knew that I was being punished, but I didn't know why. I didn't understand why Mother was so cruel to me. What had I done? I knew it was something I had done because she was so nice to Amelia; she was nice to almost all other people, apart from my father at times, and sometimes Granny and Grandad. I heard Amelia giggle from upstairs, and I finally realised that I must be a horrible person, a truly terrible girl, for Mother to treat me like this, for my father and Sigrid to believe that I had done such a vicious thing. I must deserve to be down here, in the dark, by myself, while they laughed under the late summer stars above.

When Amelia and Sigrid finally left and my parents had gone inside, my stomach twisted. Between billowing sobs, I threw up the strawberries, and they were shockingly red on my clean white sheets. I was disgusted with myself, and I remember thinking how angry Mother would be. I tried to sleep on the floor, but my body ached from being dragged down the stairs and I couldn't bear it. Too tired to do anything else, I lay on my bed and curved myself away from the shiny red puddle. As I listened to the faraway sounds from outside, I picked at my arm, knowing I deserved the raw, stinging pain. I felt the heavy thudding of my heart, beating in my ears, and I breathed in the scent of my own vomit – sour, yet sweet, just as the berries had been.

PSYCHOPATHY SYMPTOM #7

Cunning and manipulative

Psychopaths are extremely adept at manipulating other people, using flattery, guilt or sympathy to get what they want, and executing it all in a poised, effortless manner. Psychopaths don't experience true emotions towards others, but they are very good at mimicking people and present themselves as sincere and empathic. Those around them often have no idea they're incapable of genuinely caring for others.

8
DECEIT

'Psychopaths are extremely adept at manipulating other people.'

It began to dawn on me that in Mother's eyes I needed to maintain an acceptable level of happiness. She didn't want me miserable – sitting alone in my room reading a book, or digging in the flowerbeds, pretending I didn't need friends because I had a garden – but then neither did she want me to be *too* happy. Perhaps 'happy' isn't the right word. Maybe it's confidence, or assurance, or any sign of strength in myself. She built me up until I met her contentment quota, praising me, lavishing me with gifts, but then when I was in danger of becoming complacent, she knocked me down in a furious frenzy. I needed to be fulfilled, but meek; satisfied, but small.

When I look back now I can see why she attacked me on Strawberry Picking Day. It was because she saw I was growing in confidence. I was getting older, I had friends, I had my grandparents too – though I was seeing them less and less, to my confusion and dismay. She could sense that perhaps there was a time when I wouldn't eat out of the palm of her hand, I wouldn't be intimidated or susceptible or malleable in the ways she wanted me to be. And it was that, more than anything, that scared her, because above all, she craved control. She could sense the beginning of her dominion slipping from her fingers and it scared her. As I grew older, what would happen? If she hit me, would I hit back? If she pushed too hard, would I dig my heels in, or would I run away to a foreign land, as she had done, never to be heard from again?

But for now, the problem was that I was getting too big for my boots. But what was the solution? For a long time after, Mother wasn't as brutal as she'd been on Strawberry Picking Day. I actually think she may even have felt bad about it, though common sense tells me this is unlikely. At any rate, she didn't do anything too harsh for the next few months, but the problem I posed was not going away. Her solution was to move again, to drag me away from everything I loved, but this time my father put his foot down. They battled over it that autumn and winter, and for a while I really thought Father had changed. I'd never heard him deny Mother anything, certainly not for a sustained period of time, and I listened to their rows with a strange glint of pride burning in my belly. My sweet father, I loved him so much.

'We're not moving,' he would say. 'Olivia needs stability, and she loves it here, going to school with her friends, running around in the fields. I'd have done anything to grow up in a place like this.'

'Yes, but this house is too small,' Mother would reply. 'It's poky and dark. And your parents are too close, they're interfering all the time. Plus, it's not good for Olivia, being stuck down in the basement. It's not good for her lungs, she'll get sick. Don't you care about your daughter's health? Look at her, look how pale she is,' she insisted, waving a hand over at me and ignoring the fact I'd always been pale.

But my father stuck to his guns. It wasn't just about me; he'd only just started teaching at Brunswick, a prestigious boarding school half an hour away. 'I need to have some longevity in my job,' he said, sometimes even raising his voice so Mother couldn't butt in. 'Moving isn't an option now, Jose. You know that.'

So, Mother changed tactics. She picked a fight with our neighbours, Janet and Bill, whose daughter Jenny I was friendly with. Mother never really liked Janet, ever since I'd told her that she'd let me watch two whole hours of cartoons with Jenny. 'Far too much TV for a child,' she'd sniffed, but that was it. Then one day I came home from school and my father was already back, Mother sobbing in his arms. There were droplets of blood on the kitchen floor and shattered glass, and my father looked very distressed. Janet, Mother asserted, had attacked her with a milk bottle after they'd had a disagreement when Mother hadn't wanted to lend her any money. She'd cut Mother's arm, and poor Mother was so traumatised, she rang my father up at work and begged him to come home because she was so afraid. Father confronted Janet, who denied even setting foot in our home, let alone attacking Mother. I remember her appalled, furious face as she hissed at my father, 'Your wife is a psycho! A *psycho*!' I didn't know what a 'psycho' was, but it sounded very bad. I couldn't imagine Janet getting angry, let alone hurting someone, but Mother's arm was all bandaged up and there was blood on the floor, so it must be true.

Mother declined to press charges – 'I'd only be punishing poor little Jenny, and she's already suffered enough, with that witch for a mother,' she said gallantly – but she began to say she didn't feel safe. 'I'm scared to be here, Clive,' she insisted, and she looked it too, with her hands clasped together and wrinkles on her forehead. I couldn't conceive of her being scared of anything, let alone plump, smiley Janet from next door, but she maintained that she was. Surely being attacked by nightmare neighbours was a reason to move?

Yet still my father was resolute. 'It was a one-off,' he said. 'Trust me.'

But Mother was used to getting her own way. One morning in December, I went out into the garden after breakfast, as I usually did. Amelia would be calling over in a few minutes, and we'd do the short walk to school together. I hopped along the path, my shiny school shoes crunching on the gravel. It was a lovely winter morning, with crisp air and an icy blue sky, and I tramped down the path to my pond.

But my pond wasn't there. The clear, rippling surface was covered in a thick white substance. At first I thought it was snow, but when I raced forward I saw that it was foam. A frothy carpet of suds blanketed the surface of my pristine pond. Unable to process what I was seeing, I fell to my knees and began scooping at the foam, clawing it into my arms, desperately trying to clear it so my beloved fish could breathe. As I swept up armfuls of suds, coughing at the chemical scent of lemon, the surface of the pond was unveiled. Finally, I could see my lovely fish: they were floating upside down, the pale winter sun reflecting off their underbellies, shimmering ghostly white in the green water. I screamed and Mother rushed out, stumbling on the gravel path in her haste to get to me. She stopped when she saw the pond and my poor dead fish.

'Oh no!' she said. 'Oh no, Olivia! Whoever would do such a thing? My poor little Olive!' And she wrapped her arms tight around me and rubbed my back as I sobbed into her chest.

I was inconsolable. My pond, that I'd spent all summer perfecting, gone. My fish, whom I'd loved, my fish who my father and I had carefully chosen, dead. I'd created personalities for them, made up elaborate backstories. Mother even helped me pick names for them, and we'd chosen French names, in honour of her. There were my common goldfishes, Jean-Paul and Claude, who'd escaped the sewers of Paris after being flushed down the toilet by a spoiled rich boy; then there were Louis and Pierre, the big old kois, who thought they'd never escape the garden centre and were thrilled to finally have a home; and there was the comet goldfish Celine, my favourite fish of all, who had beautiful white spots and a long flowing tail. Now, they bobbed upside down on the surface of water, so undignified in death, so unseemly. I knew their last moments would have been awful, that they would have suffocated as toxic soap seeped into their gills; they would have thrashed about in the lather of suds, hopelessly trying to find some fresh, clean water before their little bodies gave up. It hurt me deeply, in a sharp, raw way that tightened my throat so it was hard to swallow. A bitter seed had lodged itself inside me; no matter how much I gulped, it wouldn't go.

When I got home that day, after Amelia and Sigrid walked me back in quiet sympathy, my father was already home. That was strange. Grim-faced, he was pacing in the kitchen, his fingers linked behind his head. Mother sat at the table, slowly stirring a cup of tea. I thought Father would come over and hug me, but he didn't. Instead, he said, 'Olivia, I'm sorry about your fish.' Then he said, 'I think we need to think about our future. I'm afraid your Mother's right. Whether it was next door who put soap into your pond or not—'

'Of course it was,' Mother interjected.

'Whether it was or not,' Father continued, 'we need to think about whether we want to stay here after what has happened.'

'I want to stay here!' I said, panic rising inside me. 'I don't want to move again, I want to stay here. I love it here, I feel safe here.'

My father looked at me pityingly. His expression, and the way his glasses had slid down the end of his nose, made me cross. 'Olivia, someone poured washing-up liquid into our pond,' he said, slowly, as if I was stupid. 'They deliberately killed your fish, this wasn't a mistake.'

'I know!' I said. *How could he say that as if I didn't know, as if I didn't care?* 'But I still want to stay! I'm not moving ... I won't go, I won't!' My voice was shrill, rising to a shriek, and my father stared at me. I'd never spoken to either of my parents like this, never refused to do anything I was told; never even offered much resistance.

'Look, no decision will be made yet,' he said eventually. 'Let's see how things go for the next few weeks. But you should know, we *are* thinking of moving.'

I remained silent, not trusting myself to speak. I could tell by Mother's face that she was furious my father had, in her eyes, 'backed down', but she said nothing. After dinner, I dried the dishes as she washed up. She'd been quiet all evening, which was curious; she usually dominated the conversation, either telling us all about what she'd been up to, or demanding to know every detail of what we'd done that day. Suddenly she stopped washing up, shook her hands free of water and glanced over her shoulder at me. I remember this moment so well, thinking about it makes me sweat, even now.

'Oh dear, we're all out of washing-up liquid,' she said softly, flicking the yellow plastic bottle with one long, slender finger. 'So strange ... I only bought it the other day.'

It took a moment before I understood what she was saying. Bristles of horror began to creep over me, and though I didn't want to look at her, my whole body turned to face her, like she was pulling me with invisible string. I remember her expression so well – every bit of her posture, her demeanour, unnerved me so completely. She looked inquisitive, alert: her head was tilted, just a little, her eyes wide and blinking. She wasn't smiling, but she was, really; the corners of her mouth curved up, and they were twitching, quivering like a bow – like she wanted to laugh but knew she shouldn't. It was barely perceptible, but I could see, I could tell. It was an expression I knew, and I hated. *I know you know*, she was saying with those wide, fluttering eyes, those rounded lips. *But what are you going to do about it?*

What could I do? What could I say? 'I hate you' is what I wanted to say. 'You're evil, and wicked, and I hate you.' But I didn't say that; I didn't say anything. I looked down at the cloth in my hands and began wiping it over the plate. It was already dry, but if I staying looking into her eyes I knew I would scream, or cry, and I was scared once I started, I would never stop. Over and over, I wiped the plate, my hands shaking. I could feel tears stinging behind my eyes but I couldn't let them fall, I couldn't let her see.

And then I felt her standing right behind me, and I could smell her, jasmine and orange and that sweet, nameless powdery scent, and I started to tremble. 'I think that plate's dry now,' she said. Her voice was very low, barely more than a whisper, but the words buffeted into my ear, her warm breath shivered down my spine, and my whole body started convulsing. I flung the towel down, dropped the plate on the counter, and ran downstairs to my little basement bedroom. I'd thought I would burst into tears as soon as I was alone, but as I flung myself onto my bed I felt another feeling, a burning rage that rocked my whole body. How could she do this? I couldn't believe she could do such a thing. My fish, whom I loved, whom we'd named together – she killed them. *She killed them*. My little pond I'd spent all summer working on, my pride and joy, she destroyed it. It seems so obvious now – why hadn't I realised immediately? – but it just wasn't in my child's brain that someone could do such a thing, even my own mother.

I was learning, though – just not fast enough.

* * *

That spring Mother started to get sick. For most of the year she hadn't been in the best of health, but those irregular colds started to become more frequent, and she became tired and snappy. She normally exuded health and vitality: you only had to look at her, at her luminous skin and thick hair and clear bright eyes, to see that this was a woman on top of her game. Strong and powerful, she was blazing with energy, and when that started to erode she crumbled.

Sniffling into tissues, a cardigan over her shoulders, rubbing her cold hands together, she languished on the sofa. She still tried to boss my father and me around, demanding we bring her hot drinks or snacks or another pillow for her head, but it wasn't the same. Her voice sounded strangled, cottony, and though I pretended she was the same as before, we both knew she wasn't.

Local doctors referred her to London specialists, and the hospital visits became more and more frequent. She returned home exhausted, ashen faced, with bandages around her arms. 'I've had so many needles in me, I feel like a pin cushion,' she grumbled. 'What is it with the doctors in this country? Why does it take so long to get a bloody diagnosis?'

Sometimes I came to London too, but usually I didn't. I begged to stay at my grandparents' but my father shook his head silently, and I was dropped off at Amelia's house instead. With a slight stab of guilt, I pushed Mother from my mind, pushed away all thoughts of sickness and blood tests and hospitals, and played without a care in the world. It was a relief to have her gone, a comfort to be safe.

And then finally her blood tests came back and there was a diagnosis. Leukaemia, they said. And they were so sorry, but the prognosis wasn't good. My father explained to me what leukaemia was, but I didn't really understand. I was given leaflets and fact sheets about the disease, and I read them all, writing about it in my diary, trying to process this new information.

When you have leukaemia it's cancer. It starts in the tissues that make blood. This is usually bone marrow, this lives inside our bones. The cancer means that normal white blood cells turn abnormal. This is bad because white blood cells are part of the immune system, and that defends your body against infection.

That's what I wrote in my diary. I'd copied out sentences from the leaflets in the hope that I would understand, but I still didn't, really. The words floated in front of me and they were meaningless. I couldn't grasp what blood cells were or what they did. I didn't know what tissue was, other than it was what Mother was snivelling into all the time.

I knew that she was very sick. I knew that germs were bad for her, that she might die. She and my father visited countless specialists, hoping and praying there'd be one who'd say, 'Aha! I know just what to do. This is a case for me!' but they never did. One doctor told her that sadly, there just wasn't much they could do at this point; she should go home and enjoy the time she had left with her family. Mother didn't like that one bit. Four months later they flew to Belgium to see a leukaemia doctor there, a specialist considered one of the best in Europe. But she returned home sobbing, and when she saw me, she flung her arms around my shoulders.

'He wants to keep me in a special room,' she wept, wrapping her thin arms around me. 'You'd only be able to visit me from behind a glass window. I don't want that. I won't be able to touch you, inside this glass room. I don't want that, I want to be able to hold you.'

But you don't, I thought, as her tears dripped onto my shoulder. *You never want to hold me. Are you different, now that you're ill? Now that you might die?*

She got paler and sicker, drooping in front of our eyes like a wilting flower, draping herself across sofas with rattling sighs. When I look back at this time now, it's murky. It's harder to recall than the years before, which is strange, but maybe I didn't want to remember. I still wrote in my diary, but after a while I grew tired of writing about how sick Mother was, how sad my father looked, how the doctors shook their heads. I remember some things very clearly, but they are feelings more than events, moments as opposed to days. I remember feeling terror: terror for Mother, for what might happen to her, but also terror for myself, because for all her flaws, for all the times I wept and screamed and hated her, underneath it all she was still my mother.

She was passed from doctor to doctor until finally, someone offered her hope. I remember this meeting well – parts of it, anyway. We were at King's College Hospital in London, and the doctor was Indian; he was tall with a short beard and full lips. I don't remember what he said to Mother, but I remember one thing very clearly. He looked at her and his face was kind. 'Do you want to see your little girl grow up?' he asked. I heard Mother gasp, or maybe it was a sob. I glanced across at her and her eyes were shining, her mouth open.

'Yes,' she breathed, '*yes.*' And then she looked at me, and there was a burning in her eyes, a look I'd never seen before. She reached across and clasped my hand, squeezing it gently in her own. 'That's what I want more than anything in the world. To see my little girl grow up, to be there for Olivia. *My* Olivia ... my little Olive, whom I love.'

And then her face crumpled, like a child's, and I felt sad but also embarrassed, to see her so diminished. I didn't question that she meant it. I knew, in that moment, with every ounce of my being, that she meant those words: in that moment, she loved me. In that moment, she would have done anything to be there for me, to see me grow up.

'Right,' the doctor said briskly. 'Let's get to it then.'

* * *

Of course, it was anything but a brisk process. She had chemotherapy, round after round of it, and she grew thinner and thinner, month after month. She was fragile, floppy like a rag doll, and sometimes it was hard to look at her. In a certain light, when shadows fell across her face and hollowed her eyes and cheeks, she looked like a skeleton, and it scared me, to see her skull beneath her skin. Then all her lovely hair started falling out, and she whimpered as clumps sailed to the ground in golden wisps. I whimpered too, because her fear was contagious and in spite of everything, I loved her.

My father took a leave of absence from work and spent much of the week in London while I spent more and more time at my grandparents' house. This was no problem for me, as I'd missed them terribly over the past year and couldn't understand why I wasn't allowed to see them anymore. But Father started rubbing his face and sighing whenever he dropped me off.

'This isn't right,' he'd say, more to himself than to me. 'You shouldn't be here so much. This isn't right, you shouldn't be seeing them as much.'

'They like having me here,' I'd reply with confidence – they told me so enough – but he'd only stare at me wordlessly and shake his head. And then one day he dropped a bombshell.

'I'm sorry, Olivia,' he said suddenly. 'I'm sorry, but you need to go to Brunswick.' I stared at him. Brunswick was the school he taught at, a private boarding school half an hour from Lewes. I'd visited once last autumn, after my father got the job, and it looked like a manor house straight out of the classic children's books I adored. It was a Victorian red brick building with turrets and enormous windows and a swimming pool and a chapel. A school that other children went to, rich children with double-barrelled names. Not kids like me, with only one surname and scabs on my knees.

'No!' I said. 'Please, no! I want to stay here, in Lewes with Amelia and Granny and Grandad. I won't go there, I won't go!'

'I'm sorry,' he repeated as I burst into tears. 'It's happening. I've spoken with the school. They've very kindly offered us a bursary, what with your mother being sick and me teaching there. This is a wonderful opportunity. It's an excellent school, a wonderful chance for you to get the best education. You remember how much you loved it when you visited.'

'But I liked it to *visit*, not to stay!' I sobbed, but he just shook his head.

'I'm sorry,' he said again. 'It's the right thing. I'm not around enough for you right now. You can't live with Granny and Grandad, it's not fair on them. They're your grandparents, not your parents—'

'They like having me!' I wailed, but again he shook his head.

'They love having you, but not almost every night. I won't ask that of them. You need structure and stability. With Maman in hospital, I can't give that to you now. This won't be forever, my little Olive,' he added, stroking my wet cheek, 'but it's the right thing for now.'

I cried and I screamed and I protested every way I knew, but he wouldn't budge. Behind my sorrow at leaving Lewes School, where

I was happy, there was another feeling of bitterness, of resentment for Mother. Because now she'd won, hadn't she? Even though it had been months since she'd squirted washing-up liquid into my pond, her end goal had been achieved. Her aim – to remove me from what I knew and loved, to stifle my confidence – was realised. Even though she lay sick, possibly dying, in a hospital bed an hour away, she still managed to beat me.

But in the end, I loved Brunswick. The first week was terrible – I missed Amelia, the familiarity of Lewes School, the little library with the red chairs where I would curl up and read – but after a week or so, something changed. It was hard not to get swept away in the freedom Brunswick offered; not just literal freedom, in the sense that the grounds were enormous – acres of landscaped gardens and gently swaying fir trees – but in the attitude of the school and teaching itself. I felt like I could be myself. Though I loved reading and writing, I'd always struggled with spelling and comprehension, and the teachers at Brunswick soon realised I was dyslexic. They gave me extra lessons with a special education teacher who was kind and patient and didn't make me feel stupid. I made friends quickly, and while there was no one who could replace Amelia, the other girls were kind and welcoming.

My absolute favourite thing about Brunswick was its grounds, because it had its very own secret garden. Well, perhaps 'secret' isn't the word, but it was a walled garden, and there were small plots of soil we could 'adopt' and make our own for the year. When I excitedly told my father about it, he drove me to the garden centre one weekend and bought me dozens of packs of seeds. As summer approached I spent hours in that garden, kneeling in the dirt and poking around, but only one of my plants actually flourished. It was a mint plant that grew to about two feet tall, and every day at lunchtime I rushed over to my little plot of land and picked a bunch of leaves. I gave them to my friends and I chewed them myself, spitting out the dark green mush once all the minty flavour had gone. The garden, like Brunswick itself, was my own, something I didn't have to share with Mother or even my father.

When school finished for summer I was devastated – I didn't want to go back to our sad, neglected cottage. Father went up to London to see Mother every other day, and though sometimes I came too, usually he'd drop me off at Amelia's. When I asked why I couldn't also spend time with Granny and Grandad, he shook his head mutely. Sometimes, very occasionally, we went to my grandparents' house for dinner. It was never as fun as before, because my father was quiet and withdrawn and the mood sombre. I felt like I had to be sombre too, so I thought about sad things as we sat around the table: puppies with nobody to love them, abandoned kittens mewing in boxes; my father, sitting alone in Martinique, looking forlornly out the window.

One day that autumn I remember very well. It was a Saturday, and as usual we'd taken the train up to Victoria, then got the Tube to the hospital. I hated going there. I dreaded seeing Mother – this sick, drooping woman who lay limply in bed – but mainly I hated the hospital, the very idea of this huge building where sick people came to live, or to die. I knew there were dead bodies in the hospital, and though my father insisted they were kept somewhere else, I became terrified I would open the wrong door and come face-to-face with a corpse. As we walked through the endless corridors I looked at the doors that were shut and wondered, *Is this the room where they keep the dead people?* If I turned the handle and stepped inside, what would I find? Piled-up bodies, rotten and festering and forgotten? I knew that after a person died someone cut them open to see what killed them, and I began to wonder what they did with all the body parts. When nurses walked past, pushing hospital trolleys I felt certain they were hiding trays of foul-smelling, wobbly organs, quivering like red jelly in bowls.

After we'd seen Mother, Father liked to go to the hospital canteen for a snack, but I could never eat. I looked at the spaghetti Bolognaise and knew that really, it wasn't spaghetti at all – it was boiled entrails from someone who'd died that day, and the tomato sauce was their blood, clotted and curdled in the heat of the kitchen. The only thing I could ever manage was a Slush Puppie, and it became the highlight of each visit. I loved all the flavours – blue raspberry, strawberry, cherry, orange – and I mixed them all up in one drink while my father waited patiently behind.

This day, the one I remember so well, the one that came to define so much of my relationship with Mother, started like any other. I remember that I was wearing my new purple trainers, and they rubbed at the back, but I couldn't say anything to Father because I'd begged and begged him to buy me them. We walked along the same corridor, like we'd done so many times already, but when we got to the room this time it was different, because the woman lying in bed didn't look like my mother at all.

Her skin was greyish-white, like she'd been shut up in a dark place for a long time, and the shape of her face was different. Since she lost her hair I'd never seen her without the colourful headscarves she wound around her head, and without them her head looked smaller, skull-like. Her cheeks were sunken, and there were purple circles under her eyes tinged with yellow. I stepped closer to her, and her eyelids looked paper-thin, tiny dark mauve veins creeping over them like motorways on a map. I was scared to go over to her, but my father nodded to me.

'Go and speak to Maman, Olivia. I'm going to get a coffee, I'll be back in a minute.' He smiled at me, though it was more of a grimace, and closed the door behind him. I knew he didn't really want a coffee, that he just wanted Mother and me to have some time together, and I wished he hadn't gone. I didn't want to be shut up in the room with her, but I took a deep breath and I tiptoed over.

'Maman?' I said, hovering by the side of the bed. 'Maman, it's me. It's Olivia, your little Olive.' Her eyelids fluttered open, and when she saw me, she smiled.

'Livvy,' she said. Her voice sounded weak, but she raised her spindly arms to me, and I leaned forward and tried to hug her as best I could. It was hard, because I couldn't get my arms underneath her, and I was scared of hurting her, but I stroked her shoulders gently and pressed my face into her collarbone. At once I wished I hadn't, because she didn't smell like Mother anymore. There was always a freshness that clung to her, a spring-like dew, like the smell of roses after rain or wet grass in the morning. But that day there was a different smell, and it was dry and heavy and stale, like some ancient dusty book, thick with time and decay. I was scared to pull away, so I kissed her instead, on her hollow cheek. And I remember feeling sick then, because she even felt different now. Her firm skin had lost all its resistance, and it felt mushy, pulpy, like sodden paper about to collapse. I was afraid that when I pulled away her face would disintegrate beneath my lips. But it didn't, and when I leaned back from her, I saw that tears were falling from her eyes.

'Olivia,' she said, her mouth trembling like a baby's. 'My darling girl, I'm going to die.'

'No, you're not,' I said, though I knew it was a lie. When I touched her spongy skin it felt like there was no blood running through her at all, and I couldn't believe she could look that way and still be alive. 'You're going to live.'

Tears spilled down her cheeks and she shut her eyes. I could see her chest rising and falling underneath her hospital gown. 'I *am* dying, my love,' she said. 'I wish it was different. My sweet little Olive, how I wish it was different.' I stood there awkwardly, shifting from one foot to the other, not knowing what to say. She put her hand gently on mine. 'You are mine, and I am yours,' she said. 'And it will always be so. But you need to promise me something ...'

'What?' I asked. My stomach was throbbing; I remember feeling a desperate urge to wee.

114

'You need to let me go. I can't do this anymore. I can't, it's too hard.' She stretched out her arm, smoothed my hair, stroked my forehead. 'Can you do that for me? Please, my darling girl? Will you let me go?'

I stared at her. I didn't know what to say. I knew what she was saying, but at the same time I didn't, not really. So many times I'd wished she would disappear, that she would go away forever so it could be just my father and me, yet now it was happening, I wished it wasn't so. But I could see that she was hurting and I wanted to make her pain go away so I stroked her hand again, though I couldn't bear to touch her, and I said, 'Yes, Maman, I will let you go.'

They were fateful words, though of course I didn't know that then, and once they were out of my mouth, something changed. The line of her mouth twisted down and her thin hands twitched towards me, like she wanted to grab at me but didn't have the energy. Her nose wrinkled, her jaw clenched.

'Just what I thought,' she rasped. 'You evil, wicked girl! You can't wait for me to die, can you? You can't wait! You evil, sick girl! You horrible, hateful thing!'

Her sunken eyes were like caverns in her face, and I was terrified to look into them, to see the darkness that lay beneath. I wanted to look away from her but I couldn't, so I did the only thing I could: I retreated, walking backwards, our eyes locked all the while, until I felt the door behind me. I fumbled for the handle, twisted it down, then staggered down the corridor to find my father.

* * *

I don't know if it was that same night, but this was when the nightmares started. I began to see Mother as dead. In my dreams she was drowned, floating beneath the surface of a still, dark pool. She was wearing her hospital gown, and though her hair was gone, in my dreams it was restored, and it floated around her head like a halo. I stood above her on dry land and I looked over her, waiting for her eyes to flicker open. They never did, but the fear that they would consumed me. In those dreams she looked like Mother but also not; like a wax figure of Mother, but her fine features were blurred, her face was hazy.

After a while the dream switched, and it was me who was drowning. I receded into the depths while Mother rose up like a ghost, and I sank through the water until I hit the ground at the bottom, then I sank through that, too. Even though I was buried I could still see Mother, floating above the surface of the pool. Her eyes stayed shut, but I knew she was alive, because through her robe I could I see her heart, clenching, then unclenching, like a blood-red fist.

PSYCHOPATHY SYMPTOM #8

Early behavioural problems

Most psychopaths display problematic behaviour at an early age, and this usually includes lying, cheating, bullying, stealing or premature sexuality. While some of these behaviours can be seen routinely in non-psychopathic children, in a psychopathic child they are persistent. Spiteful, savage behaviour towards other children – including their siblings – is often one of the first signs of the psychopathic child's inability to feel empathy.

9

VICE

'Most psychopaths display problematic behaviour at an early age.'

I turned ten, and Mother stayed sick. Her parents, whom she barely spoke to, moved over from France to be with her while she was in hospital. I knew them as my *Grand-mère* and *Grand-père*, and while I had a few vague memories of visiting them before Martinique, I hardly knew them. They were lovely, but more formal than Granny and Grandad, to whom no one could compare in my eyes. It was strange, seeing their dedication to Mother, because whenever I'd asked her in the past why we hardly ever saw her parents, her mouth became taut and I could see the muscle in her jaw twitching like a heartbeat.

'My parents were terribly cruel to me when I was growing up,' she'd said eventually, tossing her head. 'They didn't care about me, they only cared about my older brother and sister. I was an outcast, their mistake. They didn't understand me, they didn't appreciate my creativity. They raged at me for the smallest thing, particularly my mother. They threw me out of the house as soon as they could. I was 17 when they cast me aside, a baby. But leaving them was the best thing that ever happened to me. I escaped them, their manipulation and cruelty. That's why I'm so independent today. I should thank them, really.'

But I soon discovered that I loved *Grand-mère* and *Grand-père*: they were patient and kind, and because they were both linguists, we could speak in English. Sometimes they stayed in our cottage on the weekends I was back from school; they had my parents' room while Father slept on the sofa, and on Sundays, *Grand-mère* took me for walks along the beach. We collected pretty shells – pearly ones that curled like baby's ears, or iridescent, shimmering cones – and lined them up on the kitchen table, where they gleamed in the light. *Grand-mère* taught me to make paper flowers, and we arranged them in jars on the table.

'Maman would like this,' I said, knowing it would make *Grand-mère* happy. It wasn't true – Mother hated fake flowers – but *Grand-mère* beamed at me. I couldn't imagine her ever flying into a rage, as Maman had said. Perhaps she had mellowed in her old age.

'What was Maman like when she was young?' I asked one day.

Grand-mère looked at me. 'What do you mean?' she asked slowly.

I shrugged. 'What was she like? Was she naughty? Because she says …' Here, I hesitated for a moment. 'She says you were mean to her, growing up.'

Grand-mère smiled faintly. 'Your mother always had a problem with the truth.' She paused, like she'd said something she shouldn't, then closed her mouth and looked away. But I wanted to know more.

'She said that you threw her out, and that's why she had to run away to England.'

Grand-mère sighed heavily now. 'You're a big girl now, Olivia. I will tell you some things about your mother, but you must remember that she was a different person then. People change when they grow up, and your mother has changed more than anyone I know. The person she was then isn't the person she is today. Can you understand that?' I nodded. 'We loved your mother very much,' she continued. 'We always did, we always have. But she was a strange child. A difficult child. She could be very cruel to her sister and brother. She was the youngest, our third child, yet her older siblings were scared of her, because she did such terrible things. One minute she was wonderful, our brilliant, intelligent daughter ... She was so clever, you know. She was fluent in English and German by the time she was 12, it was astounding. But the next moment ...' She trailed off and looked away from me. 'It was hard for us, because she told lies about us. Terrible lies.' She shook her head, her hand over her mouth, and I saw there were tears in her eyes. I wanted to know how terrible those lies could be, for her mother to still cry so many years later, but I was afraid to ask.

'But you threw her out of the house,' I said. There was loyalty there still, for Mother, who was sick in hospital and couldn't defend herself.

'We never threw her out,' *Grand-mère* said wearily. 'But at that time she was living a lifestyle we couldn't support. She was only 17, but there were so many men. *So many men.* Sometimes she would bring them home, but when your *Grand-père* forbade it, she would disappear, for days sometimes. We were scared for her. We didn't know if these men were making her do these things, things she didn't want to. She was ... she was getting into trouble, and we couldn't deal with it, with the constant worry, the way she didn't listen to us, this new lifestyle, this revolving door of men. Her anger towards us. We told her she must stop, and if she wouldn't, then she could no longer live with us.'

'So, she left?' I asked slowly. 'You never threw her out?'

'No, we never did.' She swallowed, once, twice, like there was something stuck in her throat. 'She didn't communicate with us for ten years after that. We didn't even know if she was alive.' A sob suddenly escaped her throat, and its loudness, its rawness, startled me. I reached for her hand, and it was smooth, soft like a baby's and not an old woman's. *Grand-mère* smiled at me.

'But then one day she called us up, right out of the blue. She told us she was married now, that she'd had a baby, a little girl, and that she was a successful artist, and that we'd be proud of her.' *Grand-mère*'s mouth was trembling, but she was still smiling. 'And we were. We visited you all – you were a little baby, you won't remember – and she was a different person than before. She was such a natural with you, the way she held you and kissed you and was so patient. And I realised this must be her calling, she has found herself. All the erratic behaviour before, maybe it wasn't just part of growing up, maybe it was frustration, because she didn't know what she was meant to be. But when she had you, she knew: she was born to be a mother.' She reached out and cupped my cheeks with her soft baby hands. 'She is a good mother to you, isn't she?'

I stared at *Grand-mère* silently. She looked very old in the bright light from the window. I gazed into her grey eyes, like Mother's only paler, and I saw hope there, I saw kindness. Suddenly I felt desperately sad. 'She's the best mother in the world,' I said.

Grand-mère closed her watery eyes and I saw the relief shudder through her body. 'I knew it,' she said softly, holding me to her. 'I knew it would be so.'

* * *

That autumn there was a breakthrough. Mother's older brother Richard – the nasty bully she'd told me about ('I still have the scars, see? Here and here') – saved her life. He gave her a bone marrow transplant. No one else was compatible, but her big brother was, and one day he flew over to England, went to the hospital and part of his body was removed from him and put inside Mother. I liked Uncle Richard very much, and when I imagined the transplant, I saw it like one of those adverts for heartburn: inside Mother's body it was fiery red, sizzling with pain and searing with fury; but then a cooling silver elixir was poured into her, and that was Uncle Richard, and it soothed Mother, it extinguished her anger and dampened her disdain. It softened her like I wanted her to soften.

We were told the transplant was successful, though Mother was still very sick and it was touch-and-go for a while. I didn't know what I thought, other than I was confused. I didn't know who this thin woman with the bald head and no eyelashes was. I didn't know whether she would live or die. I didn't even know what I wanted. The hardest thing was that although she terrified me, even as she lay there in that hospital bed, there was more to her than that. There was more to our relationship than fear or oppression or manipulation. There were moments of intimacy between us, moments that seemed genuine; moments I felt even Mother couldn't fake.

I knew by this point, at ten years of age, that Mother liked playing games. That every time I reached rock bottom and truly hated her and she could see it on my face, she took pleasure in reeling me back in. I didn't understand why, or even how she managed to do it so seamlessly, but that was what she did. But was it always deliberate? Because there were times, even looking back now, when I don't think she was playing.

As she slowly began to recover, I sat on the side of her bed and told her about my new school – we always called it my 'new school' even though I'd been there a year and a half by this point. I told her about the friends I'd made, about our dorm rooms and bunk beds and the countless times we watched *Titanic* on VHS, about the dark wooden corridors and old creaky floorboards that made me think of Misselthwaite Manor from *The Secret Garden*. I told her about my own secret garden, where I grew mint plants almost as tall as I was, and once or twice I even picked her a few sprigs. I told her about our train journeys to see her, and how by the time I got back to school everyone else was asleep, and I'd sneak back into the room and pretend to be the dorm mistress, hushing the girls loudly if I heard them whispering. She laughed at that – the first time I'd heard her laugh in a long while – and pride swelled inside me, that I'd made my sick mother laugh.

When she had the energy we would paint together, watercolour paintings on A5 canvases. She worked painfully slowly, daubing the paint with all the effort of manual labour, and if she couldn't finish hers in time, she posted it to school later that week. In the package there was always a present she'd bought from the hospital gift shop, and I knew that she'd walked there herself, gently shuffling in her robe and dressing gown and her slippers. I knew she'd stood there, holding herself up by her IV pole as she thought what to buy me, and I was touched. It was usually a miniature game, a tiny noughts and crosses box or a mini pencil and pad for Pictionary, and I loved opening the packages and seeing what treasures she'd sent that week. I taped her finished paintings to the wooden slats of the bunk bed above me, next to the posters of kittens and puppies I'd torn from magazines; that way, I could fall asleep looking at them. I told her that too, and she looked choked.

When she finally came home that spring there were moments there too. Times when she was watching a film in the living room, wrapped up in her big blue dressing gown, and as I walked down the stairs, she called for me. 'Olivia, won't you sit with me and watch this film? I think you'll like this one, it's a funny one. Or we can watch a video? Whatever you want.'

And I'd look at her, at her pale face and her pitted cheeks and the way she was hugging her knees, suddenly old, suddenly wizened, and I felt sorry for her. I knew she was vulnerable, and I also knew that she didn't know how to be. Maybe it was that, more than anything else, that made me sit beside her, but I think she was grateful. She would smile at me and shift a little closer, and after a while she would gently lean her head on my arm. Once, when I got up when the film ended, she touched my hand lightly. 'Thank you,' she murmured. I didn't know what she was thanking me for – sitting beside her, forgiving the past? – but I felt that she meant it.

Did she? I won't ever know, but I clung to that belief for a long, long time.

* * *

Mother was weaker than I could ever have imagined. I used to peek through the bathroom door while my father bathed her like a child, his hand hovering over the puncture wound in her back, where they'd injected Uncle Richard. Yet I was still scared at the idea of being under the same roof as her again. I was grateful that I went to Brunswick, and even though Father said I didn't have to board anymore now Mother was home, I insisted I wanted to stay.

Mother curled up in chairs like an old cat, feeble and sluggish, and I knew she wanted me back home, but didn't have the energy to argue. She just looked at me with those wintry eyes as I played my winning hand. 'I need stability,' I said to my father, parroting his own words back to him. He nodded gravely like I'd said something profound and agreed that I should stay on.

That spring, shortly before my eleventh birthday, Mother came to visit me at school. I was happy that she was finally well enough to leave the house, but I remember hating the fact that she'd come to Brunswick. It was my place, my safe place away from her, and I didn't want to share it. She made me take her to my secret garden, and I resented her for that. I made up every excuse possible not to go – it was too muddy, my plants had died, I had a tummy ache – but she insisted, and I trailed after her bitterly, kicking the soil as she wandered around, exclaiming at all the budding flowers.

She brought sweets for my friends, bags of Jelly Babies and Wine Gums and Hubba Bubba in all the best flavours – Atomic Apple and Seriously Strawberry and Crazy Cherry – and I watched my friends see how many pieces they could cram into their little mouths. I felt sour as I watched them chewing Mother's gum, their cheeks packed and swollen like hamsters as they blew bubbles as big as their faces. I knew it was churlish but I burst every one I could, poking my index finger in their faces, trying to pop Mother's presence away. When the bubbles burst, the gum stuck to their faces and my friends moaned. 'It won't come off,' they snapped, as they tried to peel the tacky residue from their lips and hair. 'Ugh, Livvy!' they grumbled, as they picked at the gluey substance stuck to their skin. 'It just won't go!'

Now you know how I feel, is what I thought. 'Sorry,' is what I said.

* * *

What I didn't know about this time, and even the year before, was that while she was lying listlessly in hospital, Mother was a busy little bee. She'd decided, before she got so sick, that my father should cut his parents, my Granny and Grandad, out of our lives once and for all. That was why I'd seen so little of them the year before she got ill. She'd asked to borrow a large sum of money from them; she and my father had just reunited after Martinique, they needed a bigger place to all live together and they were tired of renting. Surely all reasonable parents are happy for their children to borrow money for important things, like forever homes?

But Granny and Grandad refused. They didn't have the money, also they had three other children who'd never asked them for a penny and so it wouldn't be fair. This was when Mother decided that was it: she was done with them, and that meant my father and I were done too. He was forbidden to talk to his parents or write to them. Any letters Granny did send to our home, Mother intercepted.

I didn't see my grandparents for almost a year, even though they only lived 20 minutes away. It wasn't until Mother started spending more and more time in hospital that my father caved and started letting me see them again. Not because he felt he ought to, as their son, but because he had no alternative. Not because it was right, just because he needed them.

Mother stated that he must choose between us or his parents. Instead of questioning why it was an either–or situation, Father went along with it, just like he always had. I knew none of this until my early twenties, when Granny and I told each other everything and she showed me the letters she'd saved for over a decade.

Why had she saved them? For evidence, she said. Just in case.

* * *

18 September 1999
Lewes

Dear Jean and William,

I received your letter that you sent my husband yesterday. You want to know some facts about our lives so you can inform others? Well, here they are:

– We bought the house outside Lewes. My parents <u>sold their house</u> so we could all benefit from the money. I invested half my share in the house and the other half I invested [in] Olivia's future, so we can <u>help her when she asks for help</u>.

– Olivia loves her new home, she has a big basement bedroom and Clive made a pond for her outside, which she has filled with plants and fish. You'd love to watch her 'messing' in the garden, as you called it. She's growing so quickly. It's a shame you're missing it!

– My parents and I are in regular contact and they're looking forward to seeing the house. We're very close and have always been honest with each other – never stabbed each other in the back, like your family. It's the opposite of your 'relationship' with Clive. He never had a relationship with you, so when I showed him how it could be, he chose me, and he always will.

– It's a shame it has to be this way but I'm afraid it's payback time now, dear Jean. Clive is MY husband and you'll have to live with it. You're only hurting yourself by contacting us, so please, leave us alone. None of us want to hear what you have to say. Go and look after your other sons, because the three of us won't ever be sitting around your table again, I can promise you that.

With love, Josephine

25 September 1999
West Sussex

Dear Josephine,

Thank you for your letter. The letter of mine you mention I actually wrote to Clive, so I was hoping for a reply from him. You state in your letter that Clive never had a loving relationship with his family. Well, there you are quite wrong and I think it's both cruel and presumptuous of you to even suggest it (not that you would know anyway). Perhaps he had something you never had: everyone adored him.

While we are comparing relationships, I would say that ours with Clive has been very calm when compared with the stormy relationship you've had with your parents over the years. Remember what you told us at the beginning? You spent hours regaling us with stories about your truly terrible childhood – were they true, I wonder now? You had not been on speaking terms with your parents for years. At the time I persuaded you to get some help from a counsellor, as I felt I was the wrong person for you to be divulging your family secrets to. I also encouraged you to get back together with your parents – you called them on the phone from our house, remember?

Yes, Clive is your husband but we're not competing with you! Relationships between husbands and wives are not like those of parents and children – you must know that, you have a child yourself. But the fact remains that he is still our son. You made him choose between us, was that fair? If you don't like us I'm sorry, but should you stop Clive from seeing us? Or Olivia, our beloved granddaughter?

We don't want to take him away from you; it's not a battle, he is yours. I was hoping by now we could be friends again, but from the extremely hostile tone of your letter I realise there is little possibility of that (on your side, anyway).

It's good news about your house. We're sorry we couldn't help you, but we couldn't afford it, and sadly, we do not have a second house to sell. I hope that your parents are well.

Our love to Olivia and Clive.

* * *

9 November 2001

King's College Hospital

Dear Jean and William,

During the darkest days of my treatment, as I lie awake, fighting against my disease, I am often visited with memories of my past. Sometimes I'm taken back to our difficulties and the arguments we had, and then I try to relate that to all I am going through: my misfortune in getting leukaemia, the necessity to have round after round of chemo, and in their wake all the misery, pain, nausea and anxiety, the constant fear that I might die.

So I wondered why my in-laws couldn't even show the least bit of interest in my condition, why they only extended such a shallow offer of help to Clive and Olivia, who are obviously utterly distressed at my ordeal and the thought of losing me. I am extremely disillusioned about being rejected and disregarded by you.

As I am about to turn a page in my own life, I fear that neither your names or your memories will ever more figure on the remaining pages. Between us there is nothing left. Your total lack of human kindness and sympathy has done its work. From now on I shall thrive on my own parents, and Clive and Olivia's love, which is helping me pull through.

Goodbye!

Josephine and Clive

West Sussex

22 November 2001

Dear Josephine,

We were glad to receive your letter, but found the contents hurtful and disturbing. Please do not think we haven't been thinking about you and praying that you will make a full recovery. I have been phoning Clive from time to time to see how you are getting on. I would have liked to do more but you made it very clear almost two years ago that you did not want anything more to do with us. This made it very difficult for us to know what to do. For a year we didn't see any of you, or even know where you were living.

This business has broken our hearts. It was not of our choosing to lose you, but if, as you have implied many times, we were putting a strain upon your marriage, that was the last thing we wanted. As to why we were coming between you I cannot say, because you never told us. We welcomed you into our family. I know you found William difficult to understand; you used to spend hours telling me what a terrible man he was! Not the most tactful thing to do considering you knew I loved him very much. I now wonder if you were not trying very hard to break us up.

I found Clive's complete indifference to the situation very hard to understand as well. When I received your letter, I phoned Clive to try to find out what exactly you meant – as he had also signed it. He said you were just getting a few things off your chest. So here

I shall do the same. Perhaps we can start by considering a few questions about your letter.

1. *Were you turning the knife in our wounded hearts for pleasure?*
2. *Were you just confirming the fact you want no more to do with us?*
3. *Do you just enjoy a good row and felt like starting it up again?*

The thing is, Josephine, I had an idea this would happen eventually, that's why I've kept all your letters. I was sure that although you were the one who broke off the relationship, you would eventually blame us for it. You literally drove us away, so perhaps you can give us an idea of what we should do next? When Clive finally told us you were ill, without giving us any detail, I wrote to him, offering help, an olive branch. The result? A hurried, whispered phone call from him while you were upstairs, and a hasty mid-sentence ring-off when you came into the room.

I know this situation gives you a great feeling of power, something you obviously enjoy. You like to manipulate people. I know you are an extremely intelligent woman, but you're playing a dangerous game.

We are happy to hear that your treatment has been successful so far. I'm sure your determination and true grit has helped. We admire your courage greatly.

With love, and I mean LOVE, to you all.

* * *

Something seemed to thaw in Mother in the year after her recovery. I always assumed she softened towards me because she'd been so ill; because it took glimpsing death, or even staring it in the face, to realise how much she had in life, to appreciate that she had a husband and a daughter who loved her, in spite of how hard she made it. Now I know what was going on behind my back, I know that wasn't the reason.

Mother loved having a victim. It was more than that; she *needed* to have one, someone she could control and manipulate, intimidate and isolate, and then later, cajole back into her warm, forgiving embrace. That was what she craved more than anything else. What I presumed was her warming to me after leukaemia melted her icy heart wasn't warmth at all, it was merely indifference, because her attentions were aimed elsewhere.

That summer, when I turned eleven, Mother was well enough to start planning our next adventure. Ex-communicating my grandparents wasn't enough for her by this point, she wanted to punish them by leaving the country. I didn't know that at the time, of course. For me she had a different story, a different reason why we had to move again.

'My love, it's time for a fresh start. I've beaten leukaemia – a miracle, when you think about it – and it's time to move on somewhere new and fresh. Somewhere more exciting! I'm tired of the boring, dreary people here. I need to recover somewhere more vibrant, more creative. It's time to move!' When I protested that I didn't want to go and would miss my friends, she kissed my forehead. 'This won't be like before, my little Olive. We won't be going all the way to Martinique! We'll just be a few hours away, on the continent. You can come back and visit your friends every few months, and they can come and visit us, too. You'll love it! A wonderful new adventure! Not many eleven-year-olds will be as sophisticated and worldly as you, I can assure you!'

So, we put the house up for sale, packed up our bags, bade farewell to our friends, and just like that, we ran away to Berlin.

PSYCHOPATHY SYMPTOM #9

Failure to accept responsibility

Psychopaths very rarely accept culpability for their own actions. They tend to either rationalise their behaviour ('I only did it because …'), blame another party ('I did it because X deserved it') or deny responsibility altogether ('X is to blame, not me'). Psychopaths do not honour commitments, reject responsibility and attempt to manipulate people through their denials, twisting the truth to avoid any blame.

10

REPRIEVE

*'Psychopaths rarely accept culpability
for their own actions, twisting the truth
to avoid any blame.'*

I felt sick on the flight to Berlin, and I made up my mind that I would hate the place. Tired of being uprooted, I sat next to Mother seething with an animosity I'd never felt before. I leaned my head against the window and swallowed. My throat felt tight, dry, and there was a strange taste in my mouth. I was sure that I could taste the plane itself, the metal and plastic, the warm soggy food and sticky body heat. My stomach heaved. I turned to Mother to tell her I felt sick, but when I looked over at her, she was already staring at me, smiling. She looked like she'd won a prize; her eyes gleamed like wet stones, her pale cheeks were flushed. She was excited, and when I looked into her eyes, she laughed jubilantly, that beautiful, terrifying laugh. Her laughter seemed to rise inside my eardrums, and with it the steady droning of the plane and the rush of the air conditioning and some nameless, ceaseless thumping sound, pumping in my ears until I could hardly stand it. I put a hand over my mouth to stifle my nausea and looked away, out the window, where I wanted to be. Falling 30,000 feet and splatting on the ground would be better than this.

We arrived in Berlin on a rainy, miserable day in July 2002, and I looked down on the city as we descended, this enormous, colourless urban sprawl with dark rivers cutting through it. *If Mother wanted to leave grey England, why had we come here?* It was sunny when we left, a beautiful summer's day, but we left all that behind us for this dreary granite city, with dark, ugly buildings and a darker, uglier history. I didn't know much about Berlin, but I knew it was the city of Nazis and bombings, of bloody wars and concrete walls, and I knew I would hate it – I was determined to hate it.

We moved into a rented top-floor apartment in Kollwitzkiez, in the Prenzlauer Berg neighbourhood. The apartment was old and ornate, cream coloured, with a big balcony where I discovered, to my reluctant delight, boxes of overflowing pink peonies. It was owned by a family friend of *Grand-mère* and *Grand-père*, and I was told it was only a temporary measure, until we found a place of our own. The rooms were big and airy, with shiny wooden floors, sparsely furnished with old-fashioned easy chairs, heavy brocade curtains and dark wood bureaus. It was nice, I supposed, but it didn't seem like somewhere we should be living. More like someone else's house, as though the owner would march back at any moment and exclaim in horror at our presence.

I'd never lived in a city before, apart from those few weeks Mother and I stayed in London after Martinique, and Berlin overwhelmed me. It was easy to hate initially; it rained and rained those first days. Mother was still too weak to do much and the journey exhausted her, so she retreated to bed while we waited inside. I remember looking out the window, arms folded, at the fat raindrops that caged me in, as bitterness burned inside me.

After a few days the sun emerged, and my father and I left Mother to explore our new home. Our neighbourhood had quiet cobbled streets, pretty buildings and interesting shops, and little cafes selling ice creams and cakes that made me drool through the windows. There was also colourful street art, burnt-out old cars, tatty armchairs and broken TVs left on the street. It was a strange, curious place. We ventured out further, exploring the different districts and visiting museums and art galleries, always bringing Mother back postcards or books so she felt included, so she'd know we'd been thinking of her. We went to markets and bought her bright scarves for her head, artsy jewellery and bottles of perfume, to try to get her feeling like herself again. She took the gifts with a dismissive sniff, unwrapped them slowly, and held them in her hand for a long time before she spoke. 'Rather gaudy,' she'd say, if we bought her a patterned silk scarf. 'Did a street child make these?' she said about some long turquoise earrings I'd chosen. But she wore them all the same, and as I looked at her, wearing the scarf and jewellery I'd picked out, I felt proud – I was helping her recover, in my own small way.

Sometimes, when Mother had the energy, she came out to stroll with us along the river, though we always walked slowly and stopped at cafes so she could rest. 'Isn't this great?' she said, gesturing at the river and the people cycling lazily past. 'Isn't this so much better than stupid Lewes?' I didn't think it was very fair to compare a Sussex town to the German capital – surely London was a better comparison? – but I nodded vigorously all the same and said, 'Yes, Maman. *So* much better! Thank you for taking us here.'

She closed her eyes in the sunshine, and I could almost see the vitamin D infusing her skin. *Make her well*, I thought, squinting up at the glare of the hot sun. *But not too well*.

* * *

I grudgingly began to like Berlin. It was different to anywhere I'd been before. There were houses and walls sprayed with bullet holes, and I poked my fingers into the jagged craters and felt awed at all the things that had happened in this city not so very long ago. There were people with green hair and big heavy boots and no one looked twice at them, and I found that I liked the idea of being anonymous, a tiny, insignificant person in a huge, indiscriminate metropolis – a place so different to

Lewes or Martinique, where nobody would care about the pale English girl or her strange, scarf-wearing mother.

September started, and I enrolled at the international school. My father would be teaching there too; he'd had a phone interview before we'd even left the UK, and found out he got the job that August. This was my first year of secondary school, and although I pretended to be excited and was glad my father would be there with me, I felt like there had been a mistake – I didn't feel old enough to go to big school, I still felt like a little girl. I still wanted to dig around in the garden and crawl through fern woods. The good thing about going to school in Berlin was that I didn't stand out. Being such a big city, there were tens of thousands of expats, and I made friends from all over the world – Russia and Brazil and Spain and Canada. It didn't matter that I couldn't speak German because here everyone spoke English.

But I missed Amelia. We wrote to each other every week and I treasured her letters. Her bubble writing sparkled in purple glitter pen, and she dotted every 'i' with a heart and wrote 'I MISS YOU!!!!' in capitals at the bottom of the page. My father bought me some fancy writing paper and fragranced gel pens in exotic scents like honeydew melon or lime and coconut, which I was very excited about, and I wrote page after page, pouring my heart out to Amelia. I also wrote in my diary. I wrote about my new friend from school, Charlotte, who'd recently discovered she was adopted. She was struggling to come to terms with the fact her birth mother hadn't wanted her. I wrote in my diary that autumn:

I told Charlotte that it's a good thing she's adopted, even if she doesn't think so, because now she knows that her parents really did want her. They wanted a baby so much they didn't care if it was someone else's to start with. I told her that sometimes your real mother isn't the best mother you can have. I wish I could be adopted.

For that first year, things were quiet in Berlin. Mother loved being 'back on the continent', as she called it. She felt at home, even though she didn't go out much, and she took delight in comparing how much more cultured these 'real' Europeans were compared to the bland Brits. She was fluent in German and she enjoyed introducing my father and me to things that were closer to her own culture, or translating things for us when we went to restaurants, rolling her eyes at the waiters in real European kinship.

But she still wasn't well. After so many rounds of chemotherapy she'd developed liver disease, and often she seemed just as sick as before, pale and clammy and hanging limply around the house. She didn't paint, she didn't draw, she didn't read; she just sat in front of the TV, watching German soaps or the shopping channels with a remote look upon her face. Sometimes I studied her while she slouched in her chair, slack-jawed and expressionless. It unnerved me, because she didn't look like she was there anymore. She looked like she'd been extracted from her body, and all that was left was this empty shell, this hollow husk.

On the days she felt better she seemed to enjoy playing housewife. My father and I came home from school and dinner would always be on the table – proper German dinners like schnitzel with potato pancakes and sauerkraut, or beef rouladen with dumplings and red cabbage. She had nothing to do in the day apart from cook and clean, so the house was always spotless. When our possessions arrived from England she began making the house look like a real home, even though we knew we'd only be there a year. She hung up all our family photos and arranged flowers around the house, and when Father and I came home she'd show us what she'd done proudly and we'd have to make all the right 'Ooooh!' and 'Aaaaah!' sounds and tell her what a good job she'd done. At dinner she'd ask us about our days – every minute detail. What had we eaten for lunch? What did I learn in class? What did my friends' parents do for a living? What was the art teacher like? Was she pleased with my progress? What colours had I used to paint? What kind of red? No, but which shade, specifically?

No matter how much I told her, it was never enough. Though dinner always started off pleasant enough, it ended sourly, with Mother spearing food on her fork as though she wanted to hurt something, her lip curled like there was a bad smell at the table. The was a heavy feeling at dinner time, a thick resentment that hung over our heads, and I knew that really she hated us being out of her sight, hated us having new lives she wasn't a part of.

But there was something else she hated more. Mother had never been vain, exactly. She certainly wasn't the type to spend hours putting on make-up before she went out. But she was proud: she needed to be considered desirable by men, she needed other women to see her as a threat. But after leukaemia, after so much chemotherapy, she just lost her looks. It was unbearable for her. Her hair never did grow back properly, and the thick, golden curls I'd envied so much were gone forever. When her hair finally started to come back it was mousey brown, brittle and wiry, sprouting from her scalp in wild tufts. She tried to grow it out, covering it in conditioner and special oils that cost a fortune, but it never grew longer than a few inches. My father tried to protect her from all the money-spinning scams that promised new hair growth, but Mother wouldn't hear it. She said he was being his usual cheap self, that he just didn't want her feeling confident again. But then whenever this magical hair growth failed to materialise and she was left crushed, she accused him of not protecting her, of not stopping these terrible companies from capitalising on her pain – it was his fault.

'It'll grow back,' I said one day, seeing her stroking her fluffy head in the bathroom and looking dismal.

'I know it will,' she snapped.

'You just have to give it time.'

'Oh, what the fuck do you know?' she said, whirling round to face me. 'Are you a cancer doctor now? *What's my diagnosis, Doctor? Can you help me?*' Her voice was mocking, her face contorted and ugly, so I backed away and said nothing. I felt sad for her, for the way she looked now. Her skin had changed, too. It used to be firm and youthful, so clear that when she did wear make-up, it was only ever mascara and a slick of lipstick. She never needed to put anything on her face; she literally glowed. But now, when I stood close to her, I could see that the skin under her eyes had turned thin and crêpey, her face was mottled and blotchy. She had aged, a decade at least, and the skin around her mouth was withered like a dried apple. Sometimes I could still see her former lovely face behind this new alien one, and my heart ached for its familiarity.

If that wasn't enough, her metabolism was shot to bits. She'd always been slim, and during her illness, she looked positively skeletal. As she recovered she regained the weight, but she didn't stop there. The pounds crept on, and the funny thing was that she didn't seem to notice for a long time. She developed a taste for German cakes and desserts, and while my father and I were at school, she sat in front of the TV, stuffing her face. She loved *bienenstich*, a cake filled with vanilla custard and topped with caramelised almonds, or Black Forest gateau, with its layers of chocolate cake and whipped cream and cherries. Her favourite was *spritzkuchen*, those sugary fried pastries like doughnuts, and at one point she was eating them every day. Once my father made a jokey comment about her growing a sweet tooth in Germany, and she flipped out, throwing plates and glasses at him until he locked himself in the bathroom to escape. He never said a word about it again.

But even though she kept eating, I could tell she was unhappy with her weight. I knew because she started taking it out on me. One day, shortly after Christmas, she came into my bedroom while I was getting changed. She marched up to me and grabbed my stomach, twisting the skin until I cried out.

'What's this?' she asked, as I backed up against the wall.

'It's my tummy,' I said unnecessarily.

She stared blankly at me.

'I know that. But why's it so fat?'

I looked at her and then down at my stomach. It had never occurred to me that my stomach was fat – I'd always been a slim girl, with long, skinny arms and legs, but my stomach was softer, slightly rounded. I stroked it like I was suddenly aware of it for the first time.

'It's okay,' Mother said. She was smiling in a strange way; I think she meant it to be benevolent. 'I'm not cross, it's normal for young girls to have weight insecurities. I'm going to help you.'

But I don't have weight insecurities, I wanted to say. I'd never really thought about my body that way before. I was only 11, I had barely started puberty. 'Thank you,' I muttered. I pulled my shirt on quickly, desperate for her cold eyes to stop running over my body, which I now instantly hated.

She was serious about helping me. A week later, I got home from school and she greeted me with open arms and a big smile. 'I'm the best mother in the world!' she announced. 'Look what I bought you!' She threw a package into my arms and I opened it. Inside was a big grey pair of shorts, but they weren't like any shorts I'd seen or felt before. They were made of rubber, thick and inflexible; they felt like a yoga mat. When I looked at her questioningly she sighed. 'I bought them from the Shopping Channel,' she said, as if that explained it. 'They'll help you lose weight.'

I held the rubber shorts in front of me. They looked like elephant legs. 'How?' I asked. 'I won't be able to do anything in them, they're too thick.'

She rolled her eyes like it was a stupid thing to say: *stupid, fat Olivia.*

'You don't wear them for exercise, you wear them to bed.' When I looked at her blankly, she sighed again. 'They'll elevate your body temperature. You'll be so hot and sweaty in the night that you'll sweat out so much salt and the weight will fall off. See?'

I nodded that I did see, and that night I duly went to bed wearing my yoga mat shorts. I didn't lose any weight from them, but I did lose plenty of sleep. I tossed and turned and sweated, grabbing my stomach like Mother had done and kneading it like pizza dough. As sleep slipped away from me and the room slowly lightened, tears of frustration spiked behind my eyes.

Every month there was a new 'gift' she bought me from the Shopping Channel, and I had to be grateful and thank her as if it was something I'd asked for. There were sticky plasters I stuck to the soles of my feet that Mother said would draw out toxins from my body and help me lose weight; there were rubber toe rings targeting specific pressure points to trigger weight loss. Every week Mother asked me how I felt about my body: Did I feel more confident? Had I cried recently about my tummy? She'd scan my body with that steely stare and I hated standing there while she assessed me. My child's body was awkward; thin and willowy in some parts, soft and fleshy in others. It was beginning to change, and I wanted to keep it my secret – I didn't want to have to share it with her too.

When she wasn't eating or assessing my weight or watching TV, Mother sometimes wrote to Granny. She'd announce that she was doing it – 'Clive, I'm writing to your mother. *Someone* in this family needs to keep the communication going' – and though I begged her to let me include my own letter, or at least add in a personal message at the bottom, she always refused. Father and I knew we were forbidden to have any contact with Granny or Grandad, yet Mother always made the point that she was the only one who ever made the effort. We sat silently while she wrote the letters, a faint smile on her face, like she was telling Granny a funny story. She never included our address or phone number, so Granny couldn't reply, but she usually enclosed some photos of me and my father, which I thought at the time was nice of her. Years later, I saw some of the letters she sent to Granny.

19 May 2003
Berlin

To Jean

I thought I should remind you of your son's family life here in Germany with <u>his wife</u> and <u>his child</u>. We are having the most wonderful time here, among the worldly and sophisticated Europeans.

It's such a shame you missed your granddaughter's birthday last month. Olivia was heartbroken Granny couldn't be bothered to send her a present, or at the least, a card. It's lovely that my parents are around to spoil her. She's forged quite the bond with them, it's heartwarming to see.

I've enclosed a few pictures to introduce you to our happy family life here:

1) Here's Olivia, now 12, sitting on our balcony among the flowers. She's inherited her mother's green thumb.
2) Olivia and her friend Katie from school. Look how tall she's getting!
3) Clive, your son, and me, enjoying the warm sun. We're having quite the May over in Germany! Hope it isn't raining too hard in Sussex.

It's a shame you're missing all this. I fear Olivia no longer even remembers your face.

With love, Josephine

When my twelfth birthday arrived, Mother had a surprise up her sleeve. I'd been begging for a pet since we arrived in Berlin, some warm-blooded furry animal to cuddle, to make our unfamiliar apartment feel like our own, like a home. Mother said the apartment wasn't pet-friendly, but perhaps, if I was a really good girl, she'd think about getting me a cat once we moved. But on my birthday, my parents got me a puppy – a gorgeous white Maltese, who bounded around merrily and licked our hands and wagged her little stumpy tail. I loved her immediately.

'I chose her,' my father said, beaming at me. 'She reminded me of the puppy in *Tintin*.' Father adored the *Tintin* comics as a boy, and we'd been reading them together for years. I loved reading with him, curled up together on the chaise longue, taking turns to do the voices of Tintin and Captain Haddock and Professor Calculus. We named the puppy Snowy, like the dog in *Tintin*, and for a short time she became part of the family. Mother took her on short walks while Father and I were at school – she enjoyed getting out of the house and feeling useful. When I got home, Father and I would take Snowy for a second walk along the river, and it was the best part of my day. I watched her trot along, tail wagging, tongue lolling, and I knew she was happy, and that made me happy too.

But it wasn't to last. Mother became irritated with Snowy's liveliness. She didn't have the patience to train her, to take her outside every time she needed the toilet. We'd come home to puddles on the wooden floor, dried-up faeces in the corner of the room. 'Clean it up,' Mother would say, waving an arm in the direction of the mess. 'She's your puppy!' I cleaned it up without complaint and took Snowy outside, burying my face in her fluffy white fur, whispering pleas to her to hold it in until I got home. I prayed she would somehow understand me, but she was just a puppy.

When Snowy was around five months old, I came back from school to find Mother sitting alone in the living room, filing her nails.

'Where's Snowy?' I asked. Tiny grains of nail floated around her in a haze.

'I had her rehomed.' She didn't look at me; she looked at her nails as she filed them, holding them out in front of her to review the shape. Her hands were dirty, stained muddy brown, like she'd been working with clay.

'Why? Where?' My heart was thumping. How could she have rehomed Snowy so quickly? She barely left the apartment, she didn't have any friends.

'Never you mind,' she said, inspecting her fingers, filing some more. I swallowed; I wanted to ask more questions but something was caught in my throat. It was as if I was suffocating in her cloud of nail filings. In my mind were images of ghostly white fish floating, frothy piles of soap, the sharp scent of lemon, and I knew I was afraid but I didn't know why.

I never found out what happened to my sweet puppy. My heart ached for weeks, thinking of her soft little body, her fluffy white hair, her stumpy legs, her big bright eyes.

* * *

After Snowy had gone, Mother needed a new distraction, something else to take her mind off the monotony of TV and housekeeping. She still wasn't well enough to get a proper job, but one evening, she called up the headmistress at the international school, and a week later she had a new part-time job. That was how good she was.

It was a strange position, and it was clear the role had been created just for her. Every morning, for one hour, she looked after the children of teachers, who arrived at school much earlier than the other students. These unlucky kids were taken to the school gym, where they could play on the equipment or read in the corner, or just chat among themselves. It wasn't what Mother wanted to do, but it got her foot in the door and got her out of the house. It also offered her the one thing she'd desperately been missing: control over others.

She ordered and scolded with renewed vigour; it was like a medicine to her, a life-giving tonic no doctor could prescribe.

Being a child of a teacher myself, I had to go along to this strange crèche-like environment. I snuck off to the quietest corner of the gym and tried to lose myself in a book, but always I was drawn back to her presence. I listened to the way she talked to the other children, to the authority in her voice, to her brisk, business-like manner. I looked at the way her hands fluttered as she talked, the way she clapped for order, the expression on her face as she laughed, and I realised something was different. Her voice, her pattern of speaking, the way she dressed, even the way she laughed, it all changed in the gym. It was like she was mimicking someone – maybe someone she'd seen on TV, maybe someone she'd met – and her display in the gym was a performance, an imitation.

I liked going to school, even though I dreaded that first hour with Mother. At home I was quiet and cautious, but at school I let loose. I laughed, I shrieked, I was silly, I linked arms with my friends and whispered in corners, I braided hair and passed notes and drew rude cartoons. My best friend was Sarah, a kind, shy girl whose friendship I treasured. In our dynamic, I was the stronger one: she looked to me for approval, she laughed at my jokes, she asked for advice. What was great about Sarah was that Mother liked her too – or rather, Mother liked Sarah's mother Enid, a glamorous, rich American. Enid was confident and stylish, with dark auburn hair she pinned up with barrettes. She wore lots of gold jewellery and smart outfits in bold colours: olive green dresses with navy blue blazers, or flowing coral skirts with teal sweaters. She was animated when she talked, waving her ringed hands around like an Italian, and she had a low, throaty laugh that swayed her whole body. Soon after they met Mother began wearing lots of rings and bright colours and gesticulating when she talked. Her tinkling laugh deepened and became guttural, and I realised that it was Enid she was emulating, those early mornings in the gym. I started looking away from her whenever she did it – I didn't want to see the new rings glinting on her fingers, the way her body weaved and danced when she laughed, the way she played pretend.

But that summer there was terrible news: Sarah and her family would be moving back to the US. I was devastated at the loss of my friend, but there was a silver lining: Sarah asked me to come with her to summer camp in Canada. Her family had been going for three generations, she said, and she just knew I would love it. There was no point asking Mother, I knew that – three whole weeks out of her sight, there was no way she'd allow it. But one day, shortly before they moved back home, Enid asked Mother if she'd let me come. The camp would help me develop key social skills, she said, and it would be a fantastic opportunity. To my surprise, Mother agreed that I could go.

'Let's be honest, Olivia needs all the social help she can get,' she said, laughing throatily and waving her hands around.

So that July I boarded a plane with my friend and her family and flew across the ocean. Those three weeks were the best of my life. We did all the traditional camp things I'd only read about or watched in films, like toasting marshmallows and singing songs around the campfire. We slept in wooden huts with ten other children and two counsellors, and we whispered and giggled until we were hushed. In the mornings we washed in the lake with special biodegradable soap that smelled like green apples. We hiked through the forest, we swam in the lake, we skimmed across its surface in bright coloured canoes. It was freedom like I'd never felt before; three whole weeks away from Mother, but without the guilty burden of her illness weighing me down.

I knew, when Mother allowed me to go, that she'd punish me when I got home. But while I was in Canada, I didn't care. I tried not to think about her in the day but at night, in the hot, stuffy cabins, I saw her in my dreams. She threw her head back, arching her spine and swaying her body and clapping her ringed, delicate hands, but her fingers were dirty, caked in earth and soft white fur and something dark red and dried. She laughed as she danced, huskily and sensually, but her face was blank, mask-like, her cold eyes watchful.

PSYCHOPATHY SYMPTOM #10

Juvenile delinquency

While psychopaths generally display behavioural problems as a young child, this tends to escalate during their teenage years. From the ages of 13–18 most psychopaths showcase behaviour that involves hostility, aggression, manipulation, or an uncaring, vindictive strong will. Criminal behaviour is also commonly seen among juvenile psychopaths, although this is by no means ubiquitous.

11

DEPRAVITY

'From the ages of 13–18 most psychopaths showcase an uncaring, vindictive strong will.'

I felt different when I came back to Berlin. It felt like I had been on the most astonishing, life-changing adventure; that I had grown in some indistinct, yet crucial way. I felt a distance from Mother when I returned, a detachment. Something had been severed. It was as if we were sitting in the same room but I'd drawn an invisible curtain between us. She couldn't see it, but it was there all the same and I was safe behind it.

She was cold when I came home. My father waved from behind the barrier at the airport and I waved back brightly, pretending I was pleased to be home, pretending I'd missed them. Mother stood rigidly beside him, arms folded, a distant smile on her face, as insincere as if she'd painted it on. I knew something was going to happen. I sat in the backseat of the car and braced myself for it: I could handle it, whatever she was going to do.

The first thing I saw when we got home were the boxes. I knew we would be moving soon – our lease in the apartment was only for a year – so I wasn't surprised, but I also knew that Mother was waiting for my reaction. I kept my face impassive as I spoke.

'Where are we moving to?' I asked.

'Lake Müggelsee,' Mother replied, her eyes on my face. I swallowed; I didn't know where that was – it wouldn't surprise me if it was in a different country.

'Where's that?'

'It's about 40 minutes from the city,' my father chimed in, not noticing the glare Mother shot at him, 'so don't worry, you won't need to move schools again!' Relief coursed through me, but I tried not to let Mother see how happy I was. 'We sold the house in Lewes,' Father continued, 'so we've bought this house!' He was excited, his face glowing with pleasure. 'You'll love it, Livvy, you'll love it! It's right on the lake, so you'll be able to swim and sail in the summer months. It's gorgeous, wait till you see it.'

'That sounds nice,' I said. I didn't care where we lived as long as I didn't have to change schools again and leave my friends behind. Besides, living by a lake sounded like it could be fun. I could tell my measured response wasn't what Mother wanted. She'd hoped for resistance, anger, tears, but I wasn't going to give it to her.

'I'm bored of Berlin,' Mother said. 'I want to be somewhere more tranquil, somewhere I can breathe fresh air and get well. Properly well. This city is exhausting, I'm sick of it.'

'Okay,' I shrugged. 'When are we moving? Shall I go and pack?' I had my back to her, but I could still feel her eyes on me. I knew she was angry with me – angry that I'd gone to Canada, angry that I wasn't reacting how she'd hoped. Angry at my very existence.

'We're not moving until next week, there's no real rush,' Father began, but Mother shushed him hotly.

'Why don't you take Olivia's case to her room?' she said. Father recognised his dismissal, and as he walked out of the room I turned to face her. She ran her eyes over me and I knew it was coming then, whatever it was: my punishment for breaking away. 'You need a haircut,' she announced. I touched the end of my ponytail. I'd had an inkling this was coming; ever since her own golden curls had failed to materialise, Mother had become funny about my hair. If I absently played with a few strands, looping it around my fingers, she slapped my hand away. 'Stop it, You look like a bimbo! Tie your hair back.' She started to mock women who dyed their hair: 'Ridiculous vanity! Spending hundreds of euros to turn your hair nicotine yellow? Ridiculous!'

'I like my long hair,' I insisted. 'It's easy to manage, I just put it in a ponytail.'

'It looks like a rat tail,' she said, tugging on it so my head jerked back. 'You're a big girl now,' she added mockingly. 'You need something more grown-up.'

'I like it long,' I repeated, but she made a scoffing sound in her throat.

'Why? It's dreadful.' She pointed to the chair behind me. 'Sit!'

It was only then that I realised she was going to cut it herself.

'Let's go to a salon,' I said, trying to stay calm as she dug around in the kitchen drawers for some scissors. 'Please, let's go to a salon.'

'It's a waste of money,' Mother replied, pushing me down into the chair. 'Besides, we're too busy packing to go to a salon.'

'But you don't know how to cut hair!' Panic was beginning to wash over me. I knew what she was going to do, and school started in two weeks. The idea of turning up with a tufty crop was more than I could bear. 'Please, Maman! Please, let's go to a salon!'

'I've cut hair before,' Mother said firmly. A smile darted across her mouth as she propped a mirror in front of me. She brandished the scissors with a flourish, working them like castanets. 'How hard can it be?' She smiled at my reflection, not even trying to hide how much fun she was having. In the mirror I saw my father walk back into the room, timidly, like a guest in his own home. He looked at me, at the tears beginning to glisten in my eyes, then he turned around and sloped back along the hall. I closed my eyes – there was no point doing anything else – and listened to the dull, heavy snip as the scissors clipped close to my ear. I could hear Mother humming.

When I opened my eyes I cried, properly then. I had what can only be described as a nineties bowl cut. 'Please, Maman,' I sobbed. 'Please stop cutting! Everyone will talk about me, everyone will laugh. I'll be the stupid English girl with the terrible hair. Please, Maman!' Begging was my only option, because this wasn't about my hair, it was about control. If I showed her that she'd hurt me, that she'd won, perhaps she would relent. I could see her thinking in the mirror: a bad haircut on me would reflect badly on her, and she couldn't have that, could she? 'Please, Maman!'

She sighed. 'I'll soften it a bit,' she said. 'But that's it.' She began snipping into my blunt fringe, but I had a cowlick so my hair fell away in curtains around my face. Mother leaned back now and then to examine her work, but as chunks of hair fell away from my face I discovered that I rather liked the way I looked with shorter hair. My face looked different than I remembered: my green eyes were bigger, my features more defined. I looked like Mother, but also, I didn't: I looked like me, and I decided I liked the new me. I looked older, and now that the sun-bleached ends had been snipped away, my hair was darker, too. For the first time in my life I could be considered a brunette – I liked that idea.

Mother finished cutting. She hovered behind me in the mirror, waiting for the backlash, for the drama she so craved, but I wouldn't give it to her. I drew my invisible curtain between us, stood up wordlessly, wiped the tears from my face and walked stiffly to my room.

* * *

That summer there was a clear beginning, middle and end. It began in Berlin, when I sat in Sarah's garden and drank peach iced tea and sucked ice lollies while paddling in their pond. The middle was in Canada, where I'd had the time of my life, swimming and sailing and singing around a fire, like people did in films. And summer ended at Lake Müggelsee when we moved to our new home – our new 'forever home', as my father fancifully called it. But that summer, something shifted in me: I didn't know what it was, but I felt that I was stronger for it. Lake Müggelsee would be a new beginning, and I was ready for that. I felt different, grown-up. Perhaps things would be different here, now that I was different.

Our new home backed onto the water, and though I tried to be stoic as we pulled up, excitement shot through me when I glimpsed the lake. A blue shimmer gleamed from behind our white house, and through the kitchen window I could look across to wooded walkways and sandy beaches, picnicking families and nodding boats. It was easy to imagine that we could be happier here, particularly in that moment, when the sun was bright and the air was warm and my parents smiled and joked while they unloaded boxes from the car. I looked at the tall willow tree just past our house and I could imagine Mother sitting under it, enjoying the shade and the warm air, the late summer sun thawing her chilliness. I could see myself sitting beside her, but in my mind's eye I looked older, my short hair a chic pageboy cut. I sat next to her companionably, my legs propped up against the canoe that after Canada, I could handle like a pro. I saw myself and my father growing plants and flowers in wooden trays, and I saw Mother painting them, and as she painted, she sang. I saw us not as happy, for that would have been foolish, but content. Perhaps here Mother would find what she was searching for, whatever it was. Perhaps she would be satisfied with her new home, with her husband and her daughter, who followed her around the world, loyal and loving, like dogs.

* * *

We moved into our new home and school started again. I was close to three other girls, Katie and Claire and Morgan, but there was still no one who compared to Amelia. We still wrote to each other, but I thought I could sense a faint distance in her letters. She told me about her life and she asked about mine, but sometimes, when I re-read her letters in moments of despair, it felt like she was writing to her grandparents to thank them for a gift rather than to her best friend; obligation rather than desire. I hoped I was wrong. I knew our lives had taken different turns. Amelia was hundreds of miles away now, like Granny and Grandad, like my old life that had seemed so terrible at the time but now beckoned to me with its easy familiarity.

Mother's health declined again that autumn, and I fought to stop the relief showing on my face: I didn't want her dying, I didn't want her sick, but also, I didn't want her to have the energy to shout and scream or berate me about my weight. Her shattered liver flared, and whenever she ate or drank, she ballooned like she was six months pregnant. She pressed her hands over her belly and wailed in pain while my father fussed over her. I tried to feel sorry for her, but her cries were distant from behind my curtain.

She'd started working at my school in the mornings again but only lasted a few weeks. I thought she'd quit because of her health, but I later learned there were complaints about her behaviour. I knew then that she'd got sloppy; that in her pain and frustration she'd let her mask slip. It was one of the only times where she lost control in public.

She receded back to the house, or when she was feeling up to it, the shed, which my father converted into a painting studio for her. He even bought her a kiln so she could make pottery, and in that stuffy shed, she tried to rekindle her talent.

That year, for the first time in my life, I felt older than the other children in my class. I was used to feeling young and silly, but now I felt seasoned, remote. Not in an aloof way, like I thought I was better than them, but an obscure, separate way. School felt like a sea we were all trying to keep afloat in, but while they splashed and laughed in the surf, I sailed ahead, silent, vigilant. I wanted to join them, but something kept me back. It was almost like the invisible curtain I'd drawn to keep Mother out had enclosed me too; people could see me, yet no one could get in.

Every day after school I stood in front of Mother and told her what I'd done, what I'd learnt, what I'd eaten. She watched me impassively while I spoke, but behind those empty eyes I knew she was hunting for reasons to chide. She ran her gaze over me, searching for laddered tights or loose seams or one of those stray pimples that had started appearing on my face. If there was nothing she could say about my looks, she thought of something else – I wasn't good enough company, I wasn't pulling my weight in the house, my friend who stayed for dinner didn't thank her enough, I hadn't bothered to phone *Grand-mère* and *Grand-père*, I didn't sound excited enough to talk to them.

That year, I started on the school swim team. Mother deemed it 'a nice sport for a girl' and besides, it would help with my weight issues. She was annoyed that I hadn't lost any weight, but it didn't seem to occur to her that I was still growing. I was getting tall – at 13, I was only a couple of inches shorter than she was – and everything on my body seemed to be either getting longer or wider. I didn't see how it was possible to lose weight until I stopped growing, but I swam like my life depended on it, every single morning before school, sometimes after school too. Our swimming coach made us do length after length, no stopping until he blew the whistle. The other kids groaned and moaned but I jammed my goggles over my eyes and kicked off against the wall like I was itching to go. And I was. It was quiet, under the water. I could hear nothing but my own breathing, the frothy sound of bubbles streaming from my mouth, the wash of the water as my arms chopped through it. As I swam I thought of nothing but my own timing: three arm strokes, turn the head, open the mouth, breathe. *Stroke, stroke, stroke and breathe. Stroke, stroke, stroke, breathe.*

* * *

Winters were miserable in Berlin. It was freezing, much colder than England – far too cold for Mother to work in her painting shed, even if she put her big green coat on and wrapped up in scarves and hats. She needed her hands to be nimble, and in the freezing German winter, they were stiff and slow. So even on the days when her liver wasn't playing up, she was bound to the house, where she simmered in a quiet rage until I came home.

The Christmas I was 13 started pleasantly enough. Mother gave me presents with a grin on her face – wonderful presents, like Scarlett by Cacharel, my first bottle of grown-up perfume, and beautiful boots in buttery brown leather – and she looked pleased when I threw my arms around her in thanks. She made a real effort that day. She'd spent all Christmas Eve cooking, and though Father and I had offered to help, she shooed us away with a tea towel. 'This is our first Christmas by the lake,' she said, wiping her pink face on her apron. 'I want it to be perfect, I want to do everything myself!' I knew that she did want it to be perfect; that it really meant something to her, to play the part of the German *hausfrau* hosting a magical lakeside Christmas for her family. It was a traditional dinner: we ate roast goose with plump bread dumplings, braised red cabbage, stewed kale, and we drank spiced wine and nibbled on molasses and ginger cookies. Just for this day Mother didn't raise her eyebrows when I reached for seconds, or make biting comments when I seemed to be enjoying my food. We raised our glasses and toasted our new home by the lake, our happy life in Berlin. In that moment, we were happy.

But that Christmas I received a big parcel from England. There was no return address on it so I opened it eagerly, thinking it was from Amelia. But it was from Granny and Grandad. I'd had no contact with them for three years, not even letters or phone calls. After plenty of sleuthing, Granny had managed to find our address, and she sent me three years' worth of birthday and Christmas presents. She sent the *Harry Potter* books, fun science packs with tweezers and test tubes and experiments, little sets of bubble bath and body lotions, fountain pens with fancy calligraphy nibs and different coloured inks. She didn't know what I liked. She didn't know me anymore.

As I opened all her lovely gifts a strange sadness crawled over me, this realisation that Granny was hurting too, that she wanted to make me happy but didn't know how to anymore. I blinked my tears away before Mother saw, then laughed when I saw the card: *Merry Christmas, Olivia*, she'd written, *With love from your evil grandmother*. Mother snatched the card away and read the note. She glanced up at me, slowly, and I tried to rearrange my features into a solemn expression.

'She just won't take the hint, will she?' she said, an odd smile on her face. 'She just won't leave us alone.' I made a small noise in my throat, like I agreed with her, but when I looked back up a moment later, she was still looking at me and I knew she was livid. Not because Granny had discovered our address and sent me presents, but because in her card Granny was laughing at her. And I was in on the joke, I was complicit. If there was one thing she hated more than being ignored, it was being laughed at.

'Go to your room,' she said quietly. I looked up at her, and her serene face stared back at me. She looked flat and cold, like the lake that gleamed behind her. My heart began to throb.

'Why?' I said. She said nothing. I glanced at my father, but he was studying his hands. 'It's Christmas.'

'Go to your room,' she repeated, still in that low voice. I hesitated for a moment, but a moment was too long. She stood up, and the sudden movement sent terror flooding through me. I jumped to my feet and bolted for the door, tearing up the stairs and running to my bedroom. That was all it took: one look. I was like a beaten dog, only more pathetic because I should've known better. Humiliation rolled over me. I hated myself for making it so easy for her, for not being stronger. Most of all I hated that I still cared: that I still loved her, that I wanted her to love me. Because I did, desperately so.

Tears swelled in my eyes. I tried to be tough, to shut her out with the curtain inside my head, but that day I couldn't do it. I searched, desperately, through thick sobs I tried to stifle, for strength within myself – strength I *knew* was there – but I came up empty-handed. Shut up in my room, I seethed at myself, in fury, in frustration; in fear I couldn't imagine not feeling.

That was when I really started to pick at my arms. I'd done it on and off for several years, ever since Mother locked me in the car after I disrespected the strawberries. I didn't know why I did it, but as soon as I was in my room, I rolled up my sleeves and started picking. I had these unsightly little bumps on my arms from where the skin had grown over hair follicles, and I found a way to deal with them: I gripped my nails around a hair, then dug right down into the skin to where the root was and ripped it all up. If I did it well, I'd be able to see the white hair root, as well as the skin that came up with it, and there would be a tiny red pit in my arm. If I pressed it, blood bubbled to the surface, a delicate crimson pinhead.

I tried to hide the raw red marks on my arms. When I swam, I jumped straight into the pool from the changing rooms before anyone could get a look. When Mother was inspecting my body, as she continued to do, I crossed my arms over my chest and hugged my biceps like I was cold, but I couldn't hide them for long.

'What are these?' she asked one day, pulling my hands away from my upper arms.

'I don't know,' I said stupidly.

'Did you do this?'

'No.'

She looked at me in that penetrating way of hers. 'Why have you done this?'

I shrugged; I couldn't answer her, I didn't know why I did it.

Mother tried to help me, in her own way. She'd decided she didn't like German doctors – they were all 'quacks' – so she made up her own remedies. She went to holistic shops and bought tea tree oil and lavender cologne, and she created homemade solutions and rubbed them on my arms every evening. The oils stung my cut skin and she wasn't gentle: she rubbed vigorously until my arms went white with pressure and the angry red spots stood out even more. She did this for a month or so, but when she saw no improvement, she gave up.

'You can pick yourself to death for all I care,' she announced, throwing the special oils she'd bought in the bin with a crash.

I carried on picking my arms, but only in private, when I was in my room; only after we'd had a fight. It was a private thing, my picking. Why would I stop? It was a release, like the way you'd pour yourself a glass of wine after a hard day, or the way you step into a steaming bath when your muscles ache. You know it's too hot, but you sink into it all the same; it stings and it scalds, but something in the searing pain also soothes.

* * *

Summers in Berlin were better. If Mother was able to work in the shed or sit in the garden and paint, then her mind was occupied. She always sang as she worked, and I remember at this time she was listening to M People. I could hear her singing from inside the house, and occasionally, she would shout over to my father and me, who she always seemed to assume were listening with pleasure. 'I could give Heather Small a run for her money!' she'd yell, and Father and I would glance at each other and smile. Mother couldn't sing half as well as she thought, but I came to love hearing her tuneless crooning; it meant that she was busy and wouldn't busy herself with me.

We had some good times on the lake, too. One day, in early summer, we went to a butterfly garden. Mother was in a good mood; I remember she wore a wide-brimmed straw hat, and a chunky gold necklace, and loose white trousers that swirled around her legs when she walked. I told her she looked nice. 'You do, too,' she said generously. She sang in the car as we drove and it felt like old times, those times years ago when she sang special songs to me and looked at me in the rear-view mirror and squeezed my leg. Something in my brain was nudging me, telling me those weren't happy memories, but it was a beautiful sunny day and I didn't want to listen.

We strolled around the butterfly garden like any other family. My father was excited, exclaiming at the different species, nudging me when he saw a caterpillar. 'Isn't it amazing?' he said, pointing at a chrysalis hanging from a tree branch. 'Isn't nature just spectacular?' He had a gentle, childlike way of looking at the world, always seeing the best in people and drawing me in with his keen eye for beauty. I looked at the chrysalis, at the way it extended from the branch like a stubby cigar, and I agreed that yes, it was amazing. I couldn't get my head around it: how a stumpy, fat caterpillar could wrap itself up, go to sleep and emerge as a whole other creature, one more beautiful and elegant than it could have surely anticipated being. For a long time I stared at the chrysalis, transfixed, wondering what stage the creature inside was: was it closer to butterfly or still a caterpillar? When I turned around, Mother was looking at me. She smiled, winked, shot out an arm and gently twisted the chrysalis off the branch. As my father wheezed in shock, she popped it into her sunglasses case and carried on walking as if nothing had happened. Father shuffled off to the gift shop, mortified, while I followed Mother in a daze. They bickered in the car all the way back – Mother said she was 'teaching me about butterflies' – but I said nothing, thinking of the chrysalis in her case and hoping it was unharmed.

When we got home, Mother took the chrysalis out and put it on the kitchen table. Her hand hovered over it and for a wild moment I thought she was going to squash it. But then she disappeared, and when she came back, she was carrying the big potted plant that stood in the corner of the living room. She went out of the room again, and on her return this time she was carrying a box of dental floss. I watched her silently as she attached the chrysalis to the branch of the plant, winding the floss around it so neatly it looked like it had always hung there. She placed the plant in a sunny corner of the kitchen and that was that: I had my very own chrysalis.

About a week or so later, I was having my evening bath when I heard Mother call me. The butterfly was hatching! I hurtled downstairs, a towel wrapped around me, and she and I peered at the chrysalis as it rocked gently on the branch. It slowly emerged, its soft wings folded against its tiny body, a perfect black and white butterfly, more delicate and beautiful than I could have imagined. Mother said it was too weak to fly so we must look after it for a day or two. We fed it sugar water, and I watched it drink with a smile on my face. I was so proud of my lovely butterfly. A couple of days later, we took it out to the garden and placed it on the wall. We watched as it gently beat its wings up and down, and after a while it tried to fly. It seemed to hover at first, skipping like a stone across the wall, then took off in earnest, fluttering across our garden: my butterfly's maiden flight! Caught up in pride and delight, I reached for Mother's hand; she smiled at me and squeezed my fingers, and we watched the butterfly until it disappeared. This is one of my happiest memories.

But still, the arguments were constant. During this period Mother's preferred mode of punishment was locking me away: in my room, in the house, in the car. The car was the worst. She instructed me to 'think about what I'd done wrong and how I was going to apologise' and there was nothing else for me to do but lean my head against the window and pick at my arms. I was only ever locked in the house when she went out with my father, and I was left strict instructions to clean every room before they returned. She threw the cleaning products at me, cans of polish and bottles of bleach and dusters and brooms, and said if the house wasn't 'pristine' on their return, there would be trouble. She took away the TV and DVD remotes so I couldn't watch anything, but I still had the radio. I turned it up as loud as I dared – not so loud I wouldn't hear the car return – and got to work. I always started with the top shelf of the bookcase in the living room; this was where my father kept the liquor. I took a swig out of each bottle as I dusted the shelf, and even though they tasted disgusting, I smacked my lips together like it was delicious. Mother would be furious if she knew.

These punishments were the latest form of breaking me. Before, I'd broken easily; a single look, a shove, even the silent treatment, had been enough to make me tremble and beg. But I was getting older, things were different now. Mother had to work harder to break me, whether it was standing in my face screaming until she was purple or dragging me up the stairs and locking me in my room. After a while, no matter how hard I tried, I always broke. My bluster crumbled, my face collapsed, and it was like I was a small child again, gazing at her silhouette through a glass door and wishing she would come to me. It was usually the exhaustion that got me, the endless nights crying from fury and frustration, from the sheer unfairness of it all; I just wished she would stop.

When I finally broke it was cathartic, for Mother. I cried and sobbed and told her I was sorry, and she listened patiently before explaining to me why I had been so wrong, why I had mistreated her so terribly, why I should be ashamed of myself. I reiterated my apologies again and again while she nodded through them. Yes, I had been incredibly selfish. Yes, I did have a short temper I needed to curb. Yes, I should be more respectful of my poor mother, who has faced enough adversity as it is.

Once she broke me, she got out the family photos, those happy snapshots that hung on our walls, on the shelves, on the fridge. 'Remember this?' she said, waving a photo in front of my face.

Yes, yes, I remember.

Our fights developed a pattern and we stuck to it for years. They unfolded like a ritualistic dance: she punished me until she broke me; when I was broken, I atoned; before she forgave, I must remember.

'Remember this? Remember when we went to the school fair and you sold my jam and won best prize? Remember?'

'Yes, Maman. I remember.'

'I'm the best fucking mother in the world, aren't I? Aren't I just the best?'

There was no point arguing it. Why would I?

'Yes, Maman. You're the best mother in the world.'

PSYCHOPATHY SYMPTOM #11

Poor behavioural controls

Psychopaths have very weak inhibitory controls. While normal people are able to regulate their behavioural responses, psychopaths are hot-headed and highly reactive. The smallest affront is enough to overwhelm them, and they are easily offended and frustrated. While they often react with disproportionate anger or aggression, these extreme outbursts are usually brief, and they are quick to act as if nothing untoward happened at all.

12
FURY

'Psychopaths are highly reactive. The smallest provocation is enough to overwhelm them.'

When I was about 14 Mother didn't seem to know what to do with me. I was stuck in a curious in-between stage – too old now to be treated like a child, but far too young, and far too weak, to be respected. She worked harder than ever to keep our dynamic going, to honour the cyclical nature of our relationship: the control, the fights, the punishment, the peace making, the bonding. The control again. Our rows escalated to the point we were having explosive, sometimes physical, altercations once a week. I'd long since given up hope that my father would step in; he just sat there idly, a disappointed look on his face as he stared at the floor. I never shouted back at Mother, never disrespected her, but my face must have said it all; sometimes all it took was the wrong expression to set her off. At least once a week I cried myself to sleep, locked in my room, trying to tell myself I didn't care. I might be crying, I might have picked my arm until it was a raw and speckled mess, but *deep down* I didn't care. I *didn't* care. I didn't, I didn't.

Sometimes my affirmations worked. Sometimes I really, genuinely, didn't care. By 14 I knew, deep down, there was something inherently wrong with Mother, something that couldn't be my fault. Something poisonous was inside her but I could disengage from that, from the very fact she was my mother. The older I got, the more I was able to detach from her, even if those moments were fleeting. For short flashes of time I could reject the idea we were connected in an important way. Who was Mother, anyway? Who was she to me? She was just a nasty woman I happened to live with. That was it. She could have no effect on me; she had nothing to do with me.

Other times disconnecting from her was impossible. Bad blood flowed through her body, I knew that – but I was her child, so didn't it flow through me also? If there was something wrong with her, was there something wrong with me? We were mother and daughter; I was tethered to her. We were once fastened together, body to body, and even now we were bound by ties I couldn't break. The truth was, I didn't want to break those ties. I wanted her to love me, and even more than that, I wanted her to be proud of me. Because she was my mother. Because I was hers and she was mine, like she'd always said. Nothing she or I did could destroy how we were linked, and every time I glanced in the mirror I was reminded of her: in the set of my jaw, the line of my brow, the glint of my eye, Mother looked back.

Still, I reluctantly admired her. Not for her cruelty or indifference or the way she lied with such ease, but the way she didn't care. Her strength, her conviction, her inability to admit she was wrong – it was all so different to me. I apologised if someone stood on my foot, I wrung my hands at the slightest rebuke. I was weak, and I knew it, and I hated it. I wanted to be strong.

My friend Katie from school was a Christian. Around her wrist she wore a 'WWJD' (What Would Jesus Do?) band. Sometimes, if I was at school or alone and something happened that made me scared or uncomfortable, I thought about Mother: What Would Mother Do? If teenage boys whistled at her and yelled, What Would Mother Do? She wouldn't flush or drop her bag, or fumble around with books on the ground. She would march over, eyes blazing, fists clenched, and the boys would flee in terror. If a girl at school made a catty comment,

What Would Mother Do? She wouldn't duck her head and pretend she hadn't heard as her cheeks flushed red. She would destroy the girl with her mean, mean mouth, and everyone would hear it, everyone would know.

As our battles became more and more climactic, so did our reconciliations. When we were in the making-up phase, Mother started taking me shopping – or as she called it, 'Mother and daughter bonding'. She drove us to the most upmarket shopping centres, linked an arm through mine and said, 'Let's get you some treats, shall we? You deserve them.' It was like she'd read an article on how to bond with your teenager and was ticking them off as she went: clothes shopping, check. Gossiping, check. Manicures, check. On those days, money was never an issue. She spent hundreds on me, sometimes thousands, buying me things I neither wanted nor needed. I was still never allowed to get my hair styled or cut, but when it came to clothes, it was a whole other ballgame. Ignoring my suggestions to go to the mainstream stores where my friends shopped, she dragged me into fancy boutiques where the clothes were overpriced and uncool. She picked out the outfits she liked and made me try them on for her. I stared at myself in the changing room mirrors – I looked like a 14-year-old middle-aged woman.

'I don't like it,' I said, emerging from behind the curtain and plucking at the heavy skirt that swung around my ankles. 'No one my age wears things like this.'

'Why do you want to be like everyone else? You should want to stand out. It's good to be different! Trust me on this. I have excellent taste, everyone says so. Feel the material, feel how well made it is. Feel how soft it is.'

'Yes, it's soft,' I said, dutifully rubbing the fabric between my thumb and index finger. 'But I'm not sure it's my style. It doesn't look nice – on me, anyway.'

'Don't be so precious,' she said. 'You should be more grateful. Most girls your age would give anything to be treated like this.'

Mother took it as a personal insult when I rejected the clothes she suggested. They might be different, but *she* was different; why didn't I want to be different like her? Didn't I want to be just like her? To avoid arguments, I pretended that I'd changed my mind, and actually, on reflection, I really did like the brocade skirt with the diamond patterns, or the blue linen kaftan that made me look shapeless and frumpy. But I knew they weren't clothes for me; they were for her. They were her outfits, outfits she liked or wished she could wear. In her eyes, I wasn't my own person, separate from her. I was an extension of herself, like an extra arm or leg. I belonged to her. I was hers, yet she wasn't mine.

Sometimes I glimpsed our reflections in shop windows as we strolled along, arms entwined, strides aligned. I stared at us, at our coordinated outfits, our expensive shoes, our short haircuts, our rigid, steady mouths. I was just like her, I realised. There might have been nearly 30 years between us and more than 50 pounds, but there we were, two peas in a pod. Reflected back in the glass, it was indisputable. Sometimes the sight made my skin crawl, other times it pleased me in a strange, unknowable way. In those times, I wound my arm tighter through Mother's and leaned into her gently. 'Thank you for my new shoes, Maman,' I would say. 'I love them so much.'

* * *

Even after her health recovered, Mother didn't return to teaching while we were in Berlin. Instead, she started another art business, this time specialising in sculptures. She sold them to popular homeware shops in Berlin and her work even featured in *Homes & Gardens*. From this, she got what she craved most for her talent: recognition. It was confirmation that she really was unique, she really was special. No one else's art was as passionate and personal; no one else's work was as inspirational as hers; no one else had overcome so much adversity to then achieve so much success.

With Mother out of the scene, school became my refuge. It was the only time in my week I could try to erase her from my mind, to forget about our issues and just be normal. But even from a distance, she made her presence known. When I opened my lunchbox there was always a little surprise. Every month there was a new fad diet Mother wanted to try, but this one stuck: she read that you should only ever have carbs or protein in a meal – never the two together, heaven forbid. So that's how I ate, for an entire year. I opened my lunchbox to find nothing but cheese cubes and a few slices of ham, usually with notes attached. '*I want you to feel slim, confident and beautiful,*' she'd write. '*Remember how you'll look in your swimsuit this summer!*' Other times, when she was cross with me or I was being punished, her notes were more cutting. '*You'll never get skinny if you keep on eating,*' she'd warn. Every lunchtime I read her notes, rolled them into little scrolls so no one else could see and placed them back inside my lunchbox. I ate my food mechanically. There was no pleasure in it; it was a means to an end.

'What are those notes in your lunchbox?' Katie once asked. 'Are they from your mum?'

'Yeah.'

'What's she saying? Can I see?'

'No, sorry. They're personal, they're just little notes. To make me feel better.'

'Like affirmations?' she asked. 'Like, "I'm so great!" Or "I'm going to have a really productive afternoon!"?'

I smiled at Katie, at her sweet naivety. I thought about telling her. Not the whole truth, but a shade of it. But when I looked at her, I saw her cool, choppy bob, I saw her big, trusting eyes. I saw her rosy cheeks, her dimples. Well-fed, well-loved, she would never understand. She couldn't be trusted.

'Yeah, kind of like that. Just notes to make me feel confident.'

'Aww,' Katie said. 'That's so lovely!'

'Isn't it?'

I tucked Mother's latest note into the empty Tupperware container, closed it and chewed my ham slices in silence.

'*Do not reward yourself with food. You're not a dog.*'

* * *

One blazing summer afternoon when I was 14, I went over to Katie's house in the city. It was a Saturday, and Mother let me get the train by myself. 'Be back by seven,' she'd said, 'or else!' She laughed then, like it was a joke. But I planned to be home much before then; I was going to surprise her with my maturity, and I sat back on the train as the city rushed towards me. I felt very grown-up.

We never did much at Katie's house – we usually lay on her bed and talked and listened to music, but that day I remember we were in the living room. It was early July, a hot, drowsy day, and the living room had big French doors we'd opened all the way. The sofas were brown leather, old and cracked, but cool against the backs of our legs as we sprawled across them. Katie turned the TV onto a music channel and we lay there, damp- faced and sticky, idly watching music videos.

'Ugh, Cher!' Katie muttered as the next video came on. 'Mum loves her, she didn't stop playing this song when it came out.' I made a non-committal noise. I didn't know anything about Cher, I certainly had never heard the song that was playing – 'Strong Enough' – but I remember this moment vividly: lying on the sofa in a patch of sunlight, one arm flung across my face to shade my eyes, feet propped up on a pile of cushions, listening to the lyrics with a strange feeling in my chest.

I knew, as I lay there listening, that this Cher was singing about a romantic relationship. The song was about being strong enough

171

without a man, but as I listened, I thought of Mother. Something in the song resonated in me, there was something that connected. Behind my closed eyes I imagined myself saying those words to Mother, telling her that I was strong enough, that I could live without her, that she'd never see me cry. The message of strength, of refusing to let someone see your pain, reverberated through me long after the song was finished. Katie laughed at my new devotion to Cher, but later, when I turned to leave – much later than I'd planned – she gave me a CD.

'You can borrow this,' she said. 'It's *Cher's Greatest Hits*. It's my mum's, and she'll want it back, but at least she won't be able to play it on repeat for a while.' I threw my arms around Katie and squeezed her, and for the next hour, as I sat on the train back to Lake Müggelsee, I listened to the album on my Walkman. I knew Mother was going to punish me for being late, but I tried not to care. I'd been dealing with her for 14 years now, I could handle it: I was strong enough.

I could tell she was angry as soon as I came through the front door. She had an apron tied around her waist, a scowl on her face. 'You're late,' she said.

'Just 15 minutes,' I said, before adding, 'Sorry, I had to wait for the train.'

'You should have left earlier, then. That's not an excuse.'

'I'm sorry,' I repeated, trying to sound earnest. 'I won't be late again.'

'No, you won't,' she said in a low voice. Then she pointed to the kitchen table. 'Set the table, then tell your father dinner's ready. It's probably ruined now, we've been waiting so long.'

'Sorry,' I muttered again as I lay forks and knives on the table while trying to look contrite. Dinner was quiet; *too* quiet. Every time I glanced up from my plate Mother was looking at me, one of those cryptic looks on her face. My father was silent – he knew a storm brewing when he saw one. As soon as we'd finished dinner, he said a quiet thank you, got to his feet, made a great show of stretching like he was relaxed, and shambled out of the room.

A slow retreat, as always.

'It might be nice if you could clear the plates without that look on your face,' Mother said. 'I don't know why you're looking so disgusted, it's *your* food.' Silently, I stacked the plates in my arms, placed the cutlery on top and walked to the sink. 'Why did you leave so much food on your plate?' She couldn't bear not getting a reaction. 'Why are you so spoilt? People are dying of hunger all around the world.'

'You wanted me to leave the food,' I said, scraping the leftovers into the bin.

'I said no such thing.'

'You didn't need to,' I said, turning to face her. 'You were giving me the "*Olivia is so fat*" look.' Mother rarely needled me about food or my weight in front of Father, but she was an expert at silent reproach. As I held a fork up to my mouth she pursed her lips, raised her eyebrows and quietly inhaled. My father never seemed to notice, but of course I always did, so my fork would be lowered and the food pushed around my plate until everyone else had finished.

'What are you talking about?'

'Never mind.'

'I *do* mind.' She was calm on the surface, but a vein by her temple flickered. 'I've had just about enough of your attitude. You think because you're 14, you're all grown-up? You think you know better than me? You think you can talk to me in this way? Rock up home whenever you want? Is that what you think?'

'No,' I said. I turned my back on her and began rinsing the plates under the tap.

'Oh, but it is, isn't it?' Her voice was soft now, smooth and silky. The hairs at the back of my neck started to prickle. 'You stupid cow! You stupid, fat cow!' My heart began to jump in my chest but I didn't turn around, I didn't say anything. I didn't have to say anything: I was strong enough, I *was* strong enough. 'Do you have any idea what it's been like for me? To survive cancer, to have my health destroyed, to work harder than you can ever imagine to get well again, just so I can be there for my daughter, only to have her turn into an ungrateful, disrespectful brat?' She was getting into it now, salty barbs tripping off the tongue with ease. 'Do you know what it's like to think your cancer has come back because your health is being ruined? By all the worry? All the concern for your spoilt, stupid daughter? Do you know what that's like?'

'No,' I said again, turning to face her. I didn't like having my back turned when she was this close. 'I don't know.' I kept my expression vacant, my tone measured, and her nostrils flared. I'd never spoken to her like this – matter-of-fact, as if I didn't care.

'I lived for *you*,' she spat, stepping forward so I could see myself reflected in her shiny grey eyes. 'I did it for *you*. I do everything for you, and this is the person you've turned into?' She waited for me to speak, but I didn't. I simply watched her, as if she was something of no concern that had wandered across my eyeline.

She shoved me then, and I lurched backwards against the sink. 'You're not worth living for! You're not my daughter! You're a disappointment, a disaster! You're worthless!' She spat out the words and they sprayed me like bullets. I felt every one – pricking beneath my skin, stinging like needles – but I gritted my teeth and didn't look away. I looked at her expectantly, like I was waiting for something. I thought of Mother's face, that nonchalant, arrogant expression she wore when she'd told a big lie and everyone had eaten it up, and I aligned my features accordingly: the oh-so subtle raise of the brows, like I pitied her; the soft, relaxed mouth, like I was smothering a smile. I could see that terrible anger swelling inside her, but when she spoke, her voice was a rustle.

'Do you know what you've done wrong?'

It could have been one of many things. It could be that I was late home, that she didn't like my tone. It could be that she didn't like my face, seeing her own blank mask reflected back at her. It could be that she hated me.

'No,' I said. 'I don't.'

I was strong enough, I'd said it.

But then I was too strong, and in a flash, Mother thrust me backwards. My spine arched over the sink, my head knocked against the taps. She snatched the bar of soap from its little white bowl and tried to ram it into my mouth. I sealed my lips up and shook my face from side to side but she became more forceful, jabbing the soap in my face, in my eye, in my neck. It was like she was stabbing me with it, and the force, the sheer ferocity behind it, terrified me. I twisted my head and tried to scream for my father, but that just gave her an opening. She smashed the soap inside my mouth and I gagged on its perfumed waxiness.

'What did you fucking say to me? We need to wash your mouth out, you little fucking madam!' I could feel the soap breaking apart in my mouth as I struggled, its slick detergent taste trickling down the back of my throat. I would choke if I swallowed it, I would, I *would*; I could already feel my neck tightening. I pushed her away blindly and spat out the soap. It trickled from my mouth, white and lumpy like cottage cheese. I coughed and spluttered into the sink, slippery chunks of soap behind my teeth, the chemical taste all over my tongue. As Mother pulled me up to face her, I could feel the hatred emanating off her: 'Is your mouth clean now, you little fucking madam?'

I felt weak and dizzy, as though I might faint at any second, but as I met her gaze something steely washed through me. *You'll* never *see me cry.* I could feel hatred for her burning through my body. I looked at her, right into her eyes, and I knew in that moment she could see it on my face, she could feel it, how much I hated her.

'No,' I said. My voice was loud, defiant, and seemed to echo in the room; it seemed to hover there between us for a moment. Then she hit me round the face. A half-punch, half-slap, it was right on my cheekbone. My head lolled back but before I knew what I'd done, I'd slapped her back, as hard as I could, right across her left cheek. There was a moment of silence, of heavy expectation, then an awful guttural growl from her, as if she was feral. She grabbed me by the hair and swung me to the floor, and we grappled like wrestlers on the kitchen tiles. I felt her fingers round my neck, the tug and tear as my shirt tore, the rip of my hair as she pulled. In my mouth I tasted blood and soap. As her hand tightened around my throat I brought my knee up. I hit something soft, she grunted, and I flipped myself over and started crawling across the floor. I needed to get out, I needed to get away.

'You fucking bitch!'

From behind me I could hear her, the smack of hands on tiles as she pushed herself up, the scrape of shoes as she stood, and I staggered to my feet and ran. I ran through the kitchen, down the corridor, out the front door, down the road, along the path that ran along the lake. It was getting dark now, the holidaymakers and day trippers long gone, just a few young people sitting in small groups on the beach, drinking and chatting. I could hear their music, their laughter, their jubilant shouts. As I ran, I sobbed.

After 20 minutes or so I stopped running. There was pain in my chest, on my face, on my scalp. As I collapsed onto a bench and gasped for air, I thought what to do. I couldn't go back into Berlin; I'd left with nothing, no money, no purse, no jacket. There was no one around the lake I could stay with. But I'd be damned if I would go home. I would stay out, all night, like the little fucking madam I was. Let her worry, let her panic. Let her heart pound and her cancer come back. I *was* a little fucking madam, how many shits did I give? None. No shits at all. I wiped the tears from my cheeks and tried to quiet my breathing. In my head I sang Cher songs.

Night fell – gently, at first, then quickly and coldly. I rubbed my arms to warm them. I was wearing only little shorts and a sleeveless shirt, and I could feel goosebumps rising on my skin. But I couldn't spend all night on a bench so I pushed myself to my feet and wandered around the lake until I reached a public toilet block. I walked in slowly, trying not to notice the thick, sharp stench of urine and bleach. I checked each empty cubicle – for what? Monsters? Bad men? Mother? – and then sat down in what I thought would be the cleanest bit of floor; underneath the mirrors where people dried their hands. I leaned my back against the wall and hugged my knees.

I didn't know why Mother hated me so much; I didn't understand her games. But I knew, finally, the importance of being strong: I *was* strong enough. I'd won, this time. Then I lay down on the cold stone floor, curled myself up into a ball, folded my hands beneath my head and tried to sleep. I dozed fitfully, jerking awake every half-hour and wondering where I was. When I dreamed, I dreamed of Mother.

I woke just as it was getting light. My whole body ached, right down to my bones, and I when I tried to stand, my legs shook. I pulled myself up by the sink and studied myself in the mirror. The sun wasn't fully up, but it was light enough to see the purple bruise that loomed on my cheekbone, my bloodshot eyes, pale, staring face: I looked soggy, undercooked. I touched my bruise gently – it didn't hurt.

I splashed some water on my face, then washed my hands. I remember this so clearly; looking down at my fingers, my hands, turning the tap on, squirting soap from the dispenser. I remember drying my hands under the dryer, turning them over, rubbing my palms and the gaps between each finger and the grooves on my knuckles. I remember holding my hands out in front of me and thinking how thin and pale my fingers were, how when I made a fist I could see the bone pressing tight at my knuckle. I wondered how much it would hurt, if I slammed it into Mother's face. I remember looking at my nails and thinking how ugly they were; they looked like crescent moons, bitten right down to the tip, ragged skin around the edges. As I held my clean hands to my face and inhaled I could smell the perfume of the soap, but beneath it, I could smell bleach, urine, vomit, and another smell that made my stomach churn. I swallowed down my nausea and rushed outside. The sun was rising across the lake, and I walked to the water's edge. I lay down on the grass and breathed in the clean, fresh air, feeling how soft the earth felt beneath my back – I should have slept out here instead.

Hungry and tired and sore, I didn't know what to do. I wanted to go home but I was afraid to. In the cold light of day my dread was unveiled and I didn't feel strong anymore; I didn't feel like I'd won, I felt weak again. My gaze fell back to my tattered nails and I began to pick away thin splinters of skin, stripping them back until blood bubbled to the surface, wincing at the sharpness of the pain. I wanted food, and a bath, and my own bed. But I couldn't go home, I *couldn't*.

I don't know what I did for much of that day. There's a gap in my memory from when I got up from the grass and late afternoon – I think I walked around the lake. I may have sat for a while on a bench. I might have paddled my feet in the clear water; I may have walked through the woods, along the sandy paths that wound around the trees. But when the sun started to sink low in the sky and my shadow lengthened in front of me, I knew I couldn't face another night away from home. I'd been gone 24 hours, my parents would surely be worried. Yesterday's animosity would surely have thawed.

I walked home slowly, thinking what to say to Mother, how I'd get in if they were out. When I got back, I could see her in the kitchen at the front of the house. She was cooking something at the stove – I could see the circular motion of her arm as she stirred – and my stomach twisted with hunger. I ducked behind a bush and crouch-walked to the back of the house. I tried the door, which was always open when someone was home; Mother was in and out of her work shed. But this time the door was locked. I rocked back on my heels, uncertain what to do. Then I heard a noise from the shed. My father was packing Mother's kiln for her, and I watched him for a moment, seeing how meticulous he was, the way he held each pot or vase so carefully. It angered me, to see how much he cared.

'Can you let me in the house, please?' My voice sounded small. I knew he heard me because I saw his back stiffen, but he didn't say anything. I watched him for a short while. Just as I was going to ask again, he spoke from inside the kiln.

'You're not going back in until you apologise to your mother.' He didn't turn around, he didn't acknowledge me. I felt foolish standing there, ignored by my father who found a clay oven more interesting. Willing myself to stay strong, I marched back to the house.

You'll never see me cry.

I tapped on the glass. My tap sounded meek, so I knocked harder, then cringed as it echoed through the glass. After a moment Mother came to the door. She said nothing, just looked at me from behind the glass. Her expression was vacant, almost polite, like I was trying to sell her something and she was waiting to politely decline. But behind her smooth face there was fury; I could almost feel it, like heat waves, rising from her skin.

'Yes?' she said, like I was a stranger asking for directions. There was no relief that her child was safe, no concern that something might have happened to me. Just a cool, sneering indifference.

'Can I come in, please?' She cocked her head to one side like she was thinking. 'I'm sorry,' I added, thinking of my father's words.

'What are you sorry for?'

'For running away, for hitting you.'

'Have you ever heard of a child who hits their mother? I never heard such a thing!'

'I'm sorry.'

'What else did you do? Why else are you sorry?'

'I'm sorry I had an attitude, I'm sorry I was late.' She watched me through the glass with cold apathy, and tears bristled behind my eyes. I tried to blink them away but I was crushed by the weight of it all. She stood in front of me, blocking my way home. 'I'm sorry if I looked at you funny!' I tried to remember that I was strong but my voice was rising to a screech, a high-pitched keening, the sound a baby would make. 'I'm sorry I cleaned the dishes with a bad look on my face, I'm sorry I answered back, I'm sorry...' Tears were streaming down my face but I didn't have the energy to wipe them away.

Let her see I was hurting. She'd like that. That's what she wanted, after all.

I heard the key turn in the lock. Mother opened the door wordlessly, and still whimpering, I stepped inside. As I walked past her I flinched, expecting her to hit me or pull my hair, to pick up where we'd left off when I'd crawled across the kitchen. But she didn't. She stood very close to me, close enough that my skin prickled, and she didn't say anything at all, and that made me nervous. She followed me along the hall, and I turned to her expectantly on the stairs.

'Go to your room,' she said. So, I did. I wanted to eat something, I wanted a long, hot bath, but I was afraid to leave my room. I fell onto my bed, wriggled under the covers and cocooned myself up like a chrysalis. Maybe when I woke up I would step out of bed a whole other creature; something stronger, more majestic, something more beautiful and dangerous than before.

As I lay in my bed weeping, I remember feeling like I'd been violated. Mother's contempt and disdain, her utter indifference to me was like a knife in the chest; I felt exposed, torn open. I didn't think I would ever feel this pain, this guilt, this quiet, aching sadness; I didn't think I could be ripped open in such a way. It was like she stuck a knife in me so quietly and so carefully that I barely noticed, but then she slashed it across my chest with such rapid force that I was torn apart, I was broken. I could feel parts of myself shuddering away from reality, recoiling from the shame, folding in upon themselves like shrivelling paper in flame.

PSYCHOPATHY SYMPTOM #12

Sexual promiscuity

Psychopaths regularly engage in promiscuous sexual behaviour. This is not because they love the act of sex so much, it's more about elevating their ego and attaining power – or escaping from the boredom of everyday life. Sex can also be used as a tool to gain quick access to other people, and even when psychopaths haven't had numerous affairs, they still take enormous pride in discussing their sexual exploits. Sex is not viewed as an intimate or private act, but one to flaunt and brag about.

13
LUST

'Psychopaths regularly engage in promiscuous sexual behaviour.'

Time passed, and Mother and I fell back into our old cycle. At times I hated her so much I could actually feel it; it burned in my chest, an awful, fiery pain. I tried my best to switch off. I played Cher on my Walkman, blaring the music so loud there wasn't room to think of anything else. I couldn't bear to think of Mother, but sometimes she crawled into my mind no matter how hard I tried. In my thoughts she was always smiling, and thinking of her grinning face made my head pound. In those moments all I wanted was to look into her stony eyes and to break her; to smash her into pieces, to shatter her the way she had shattered me. But these were just thoughts, daydreams – I knew I would never dare.

Other times, when she was affectionate and tolerant and took me out for 'mother and daughter bonding', I tried to enjoy it. Drinking coffee together in fancy cafes, I savoured her attention: the way she laughed at my jokes, the way she stroked my arm like she loved me. I wasn't sure what I thought about it all anymore. I knew I still loved her, but the love jostled alongside the hate. I could only feel one or the other; they couldn't exist together. I tried my hardest to forget what happened in the bad times, because there was no point remembering. I found I had a talent for forgetting, for brushing things aside, for disengaging from the truth.

Pictures of myself, smiling, gap-toothed, Mother's arms around me, hung from every wall in our house. It was easy to look at those pictures and create memories around them; to cast aside reality and create a happier, harmonious alternative. Who wants to face the truth when the lie is more comforting?

It was exhausting, being jerked around by her like a puppet. But that was just the way it was. I couldn't change her any more than I could escape her so I had to accept her.

When I was younger I used to think of Mother as having 'moods'. *Careful, she's in a bad mood today, I should watch out*, or *Great, Mother's in a happy mood today, maybe she'll let me go out to play*. But as I grew older, I realised they weren't moods and her behaviour towards me was premeditated and controlled. She disguised it with a duplicity that astounded me, and this was the worst thing. To her friends and acquaintances and strangers she'd just met, she was a different person. No one would believe it.

I once asked Mother why she only ever had one glass of wine and no more. 'Because I don't want to lose control,' she said. 'More than one glass and the wine is in control. I want to be the only one in control of me.' She was the epitome of calculated control – at all times, even when she seemed to have lost it. It was only behind closed doors she showed her true face; no one else saw the other side. Only my father and I did. It was our little secret, and I felt swollen with it, with the words I wanted to speak but knew I never would.

* * *

What else happened that year, the year I was 15? Back home in Sussex, my grandfather died. He'd been having heart attacks the past few years, and Granny tried desperately to let my father know. His brothers tried too, sending letter after letter to our home, but Father never read them – Mother got there first. Once, my Uncle Peter managed to phone him at the school, and he came home that day, quiet and withdrawn. Mother asked him what was wrong.

'My dad's sick,' he said in a low voice, like he thought I couldn't hear. 'I'm not sure what to do, I should probably go home.'

'Oh Clive!' Mother sighed, rubbing his arm gently but looking at him in exasperation. 'You'll never learn. You know this is just your mother trying to manipulate you. She wants you to feel bad and get in touch with her, that's all this is.'

'You're probably right,' he sighed. 'But what if he really is sick? He's old, you know. It sounded serious. It sounds like they're worried he might ... well ... pass.'

'Of course it sounded like that,' Mother said. She was using her soothing voice and her face looked pained. 'Because that's what she wanted it to sound like. You know what she's like, my love. You know how she manipulates. Don't fall for it.'

So he buried his head in the sand, and a few months later, Peter phoned the school again and this time my father learned that his father was dead. He was guilt-stricken and devastated; Granny hadn't been trying to manipulate him after all. Spurned by regret, he decided that his family needed him, and this time nobody, not even Mother, was going to tell him otherwise. When he came home from school that day his defiance surprised me. He shook his head mutinously as Mother at first cajoled, then demanded he stay. I was glad to see that he did have a backbone after all, though it was sad to think this was what it had taken for him to realise it.

'I'm going,' he said. 'That's final. Don't press it, please. He's my father.'

'But *why* would you go?' Mother asked. She looked like he'd said something crazy. 'So what that he's your father, what has he ever done for you? He always hated me! He would've been pleased if *I* died when *I* was sick. He wouldn't have come to *my* funeral, I tell you that.'

'This isn't about you,' he said, and Mother actually recoiled. 'I'm going, Jose. I'm going, and I think you and Olivia should come too.'

Mother shrieked with laughter. 'I'd rather slit my own throat,' she said.

'I think we should be there for my mother.'

'Your mother? Why?' Her eyes were hard and shiny. 'Really, Clive, tell me why? Your mother wasn't there for me when I needed her, remember? When I was ill, she couldn't have cared less. So, why should I be there for her? Tell me why!'

'It doesn't matter whether or not you think she was there for you when you were sick. I want you to be there, isn't that enough?'

'Of course it's not enough,' Mother said. 'We're not going. Not me, not Olivia.'

'I'd like to go to my grandfather's funeral, please,' I said quietly.

But they both ignored me.

* * *

When my father left for England Mother ranted and raved for days. She said he was a terrible husband and father, that he'd abandoned us, that we'd be better off without him. For that week I became her best friend, her confidante, and it all reminded me of another time, that time back in London years ago, when it was just Mother and me and my father had been the enemy. I nodded silently when she cursed his name, I made soothing sounds as she wept in fury, I patted her hand while she told me what a selfish fool he was. She rang him constantly while he was away, saying her liver was playing up, she was sick, she was scared. She demanded that he return, or else. There was never anything at the end of that sentence – just the vagueness of whatever 'else' meant.

In the end, Father didn't even stay for the funeral. Mother kept prodding him to find out what we'd been left in the will; it had been a week since my grandfather had died, why hadn't the will been made public? What were his siblings and mother trying to hide? They were trying to swindle my father out of his rightful inheritance, and Clive couldn't sit back and allow that to happen! So, my father suggested they read the will before the funeral. His family refused. He pushed, harder and harder, and in the end, Peter said that if he wanted to hear the will, he should have the decency to stay for the funeral. But my father didn't stay. This was the point, I later learnt, that his family gave up on him.

My grandfather left everything to Granny anyway. When she learned this, Mother was more incensed than I'd seen in a long while. She stalked around the house, hands balled and shoulders squared, trembling with rage. She couldn't believe that my grandfather wouldn't *want* to leave her something – a token, at the very least, for the love she'd given his son, for the granddaughter she'd raised so tirelessly. But no, nothing. It was just as she'd always thought: her in-laws were devious and cruel, and we were better off without any of his family in our lives.

But after the shock settled, Mother started thinking about Granny. What would happen when Granny died? Would she cut us out, too? There was money now, and quite a lot of it. Mother would have to heal that union if she ever wanted to see a penny; she'd make sure to pick up that relationship later on.

* * *

The summer I was 15 was gearing up to be a good one. It was hot and sunny and Katie, Clare and Morgan often came to the lake to swim and sunbathe. Sometimes we'd just sit in the shade in the garden talking, gossiping about boys and moaning about school. I loved those days because Mother was a delight when I had friends round – she'd bring us out cold glasses of lemonade, plates of fresh fruit, ice lollies. When it was Katie's birthday, she even brought out a few icy beers. Katie, with her sweet but strict parents, was elated. 'I love how she treats us like adults,' she said as she sipped her beer. 'You're lucky, your mum's more like a friend than a parent.'

That seemed to be the way Mother wanted to be thought of that summer. Sometimes she pulled up a chair and chatted to us, and told us rude jokes and asked about our love lives. 'You can ask me about sex, if you like,' she said. 'Go on, ask me anything!' I pulled my towel over my face in embarrassment, but my friends laughed. They asked her questions and she answered in crude detail, often referring to her own experiences, which were multiple and diverse. I had no idea she'd had so many sexual partners before my father, but then I remembered what *Grand-mère* said to me years earlier: *'So many men.'*

Mother was contemptuous when she talked about these men, laughing at their respective shortcomings, grinning as she recalled their infatuation with her. 'I don't want to brag,' she said, 'but I was quite the temptress in my day. Men were *obsessed* with me, I don't know what it was.' In spite of my humiliation, in these moments I saw Mother how my friends saw her. I saw her wit, her zeal, her talent for spinning yarns; I saw what an enchanting woman she was, how in control and disciplined she was in showing only one side of her face. If I told my friends about Mother's other side, they would never believe me.

* * *

The day before I left for summer camp my parents called me downstairs. 'We have some exciting news for you,' my father said. He didn't look excited. His arm was draped over Mother's shoulder in a pose I think he thought was casual.

'What is it?' I asked cautiously. I'd learnt to dread exciting news.

'We're moving,' Mother said, a big smile on her face. 'Isn't that exciting?'

I stared at her. There had been no talk of moving, none at all. She seemed happy by the lake, in the summer months at least. Her business was thriving and she spent long days in the shed, keeping up with her orders.

'Why?' I asked.

'Why not?' Mother said, as I knew she would. She was eating a doughnut; there was sugar on her chin. It looked like a dusty white goatee beard, the ones teenage boys try to grow. 'We've been in Germany for nearly five years now, that's longer than we've stayed anywhere. It's time to go somewhere new.'

Frustration shot through me. 'Why do we always have to move? Why can't we just stay until I've finished school?'

'When it's time to go, it's time to go,' Mother said, still smiling. 'Lucky for you, we'll be doing all the hard work while you're having fun at camp. You'll be able to come back from Canada and move right in. It'll be lovely.'

'Where are we even going?'

'We're moving to Monaco.'

'Monaco! Why?' All I knew about Monaco was that it was where rich people lived. We weren't poor, but we weren't exactly rich either. It seemed like a pointless, random move.

'I've been offered an excellent job,' Mother said. 'I'm going to be teaching again. Isn't that wonderful?'

'Teaching where?' I asked, though I think I already knew the answer.

'At the international school, of course. I've got your father a job there too. And you'll be going as well, so we'll all be there together! Isn't that great?'

I looked at her, at her triumphant smile, at my father's arm around her shoulders. For a moment I wondered if she really thought I would be happy about this. Then I realised how stupid I was being. Of course she didn't: it was a reminder to me, a warning, that she was the one in control. It would always be that way, no matter how old I got.

'Why are you only just telling me this?' I said. 'If you've both already got jobs, then you've known for a while, right?'

'Well … a little while,' my father said, speaking for the first time. Mother didn't say anything. She licked her lips, cocked her head, looked at me expectantly. I could see the excitement glinting in her eyes.

'Then why are you only telling me now? You're telling me that this is my last night in Berlin? That when I come back from Canada I'll be flying to Monaco instead?' Mother nodded, eyebrows raised sceptically as if I was making a big deal out of nothing and she was being very patient for hearing me out. 'So why didn't you tell me before, so I could say goodbye to my friends, at least?'

'Goodbye!' Mother scoffed. 'We're only moving to Monaco, Olivia, it's not the end of the world. You'll see your friends again. I thought you'd be thrilled – Monaco is beautiful and hot and glamorous.'

'I like it here,' I said.

'It's boring here,' she shot back. Her tone had that air of finality to it. 'Go and pack up your stuff.' We looked at each other for a moment. Somewhere inside me I could feel indignation and resentment, but it felt dull, hollow. I'd taught myself not to care. If we were moving, we were moving. There was nothing I could do. She always won.

As I packed up my things that evening I found my old diaries. I'd hidden them in various places over the years so Mother would never find them. They were all paperbacks, so I could slip them easily between bulky novels or inside secret zip-up pockets of backpacks. I flicked through them for a while, reading my past turmoil with a curious detachment. Certain words I'd underlined or capitalised: *lying, liar, sick, wish, crazy, die.* On some pages the ink was stained with what I assume were tears; in other places I'd pressed so hard with my pen I'd indented the next 50 pages. Desperation seeped through the diaries, but it was more than that; there was terror there too, and guilt and shame and misery. But it all seemed so long ago.

I remembered the things I'd written about, but they seemed as though they'd happened to a different person. It seemed far away, like thinking of a dream that hasn't quite faded from memory. Was it ever really that bad? Had it all seemed worse because I was so young? I looked at myself in the mirror, at my staring green eyes and my collarbone bob, and I couldn't imagine being so afraid. I flicked further back through the diaries, and as I read, certain memories jumped out at me: Mother smiling at me from across the table; the taste of strawberries, warm from the sun; wilting purple flowers, forgotten in the bin; a black and white butterfly, beating its wings. The memories were vivid and made me feel uneasy, and then other images started springing in my mind but I wasn't sure if these were real or not: Mother squirting washing-up liquid and laughing like a lunatic; Mother's fist wrapped around my hair; my father crying, alone in Martinique; Mother shovelling soil over my puppy's small white body. Something swooped through my stomach and I didn't want to read anymore. It was in the past, it was buried, it should stay that way.

I wanted to throw the diaries out – I didn't want to look at them, didn't want them coming to Monaco with me. I snatched them up from the bed and gathered them in my arms, but as I began marching towards the door, something stopped me; an edgy feeling, an odd but crucial sense that if I did, something that should be remembered would be forgotten. So instead I stacked the diaries up, one by one, and then I wrapped them up in thick brown paper until it felt like a box, not a stack of books. Then I wrapped that up in pretty floral wrapping paper, and I stuck a little note on the top that read 'Happy Birthday, Maman! Love, Livvy', and I hid it in one of my shoeboxes. If Mother ever searched through my possessions, this was my best chance of her not discovering the diaries.

The rest of that night I spent packing. It was only on the plane the next day, away from Mother and my memories, that I finally slept.

* * *

Camp was always the highlight of my year. For three glorious weeks I felt like any other girl my age. Away from Mother's grip, I was an entirely different person. At the end of camp the previous summer we were given little wooden paddles on which the other campers wrote notes and jokes and goodbye messages. All my notes were about how funny I was: how much I'd made someone laugh that summer, how I was the funniest girl in camp, how they'd never forget my joke about the poison ivy. It was a validation to know that people found me funny, that they saw me as Olivia, a silly girl who made them laugh, rather than Olivia, a guilty girl with a dark secret. When I got home and my father read my paddle, he was mystified.

'Funniest girl in camp?' he said, looking from the paddle to me and back again. '*You*?' I smiled thinly but inside there was a flicker of sadness. Even my own father didn't know who I was. But then later, I wondered if that was true. Which one was the act, the front? The camp clown, the joker – or the aloof, distant daughter? I surely couldn't be both at the same time. Perhaps I was more like Mother than I thought, assuming and shedding personas as if shrugging off a coat.

It was strange, flying to Canada from Berlin and then flying home to a different country. When my parents picked me up from Côte d'Azur Airport I was nervous, though I tried to hide it beneath chatter of camp and what I'd been up to. Our new home was in the Les Révoires ward of Monaco, and as we drove along up the steep, rocky streets, I craned to look at this new place, my new home. The houses here were painted soft colours, peach and fawn and sandy apricot, or else they were white stone with terracotta tiled roofs. Palm trees sprang up in the spaces between buildings, and behind them the Mediterranean Sea glittered. Our new home was on the fourth floor of a biscuit-coloured apartment complex.

Though smaller than our house by the lake, it felt eerily similar: it was like our old home had been transported perfectly into a different house in a different country, with the furnishings and decorations set up in the exact same way.

'How do you like it?' Mother asked after I'd been given the Grand Tour. I looked out the window towards the hundreds of white yachts bobbing on the sea, to the hulking mass of the Rock of Monaco beyond.

'It's nice,' I said. It was nice, but there was an emptiness to it. In spite of the beautiful scenery, the excited tourists, the fast cars and glittery hotels, Monaco seemed blank and vacant. I turned, caught a glimpse of my reflection in the mirror. My blank, vacant face looked back at me – perhaps Monaco was where I belonged.

'I think we'll be very happy here,' my father said in a jolly voice. I stared at him, this man who was so familiar to me, whom I loved so much, and he didn't feel like my father anymore. But I wasn't sure when that had happened, I wasn't sure what he had done.

August stretched ahead of me, as empty as I felt. I didn't know anyone here, I didn't have the energy or the confidence to walk around and try to make friends. I decided I would wait until school started, then I would remember who I really was – the camp clown – and I would crack jokes and make people laugh and make friends again. But Mother had other ideas.

'Put on something nice,' she said one evening shortly after we arrived. 'We're going for dinner at Caroline's house. That's Mrs Hunt to you.'

'Who's Mrs Hunt?' I asked.

Mother rolled her eyes.

'She's the headteacher, of course. At the international school. She's kindly invited us over for dinner tonight. Isn't that nice?'

'Yes,' I said dutifully. So we went for dinner at Mrs Hunt's house. She seemed like a kind woman but I wasn't fond of her husband. He had a red, sweaty face, like he drank too much, and restless eyes that lingered on me for too long. There was also a son, Tim, who was 17. Tall and thin, with dark hair that flopped over his eyes, he was shy and looked away whenever we accidentally made eye contact.

That evening I learned that the school I would be attending was a new school – literally a brand new school that had just been built – and I had a suspicion this was why Mother got the art teacher job so easily. My father would be teaching Geography. It must have seemed perfect to Mrs Hunt, this pair of teachers dropping into her lap. How fortuitous.

'I think Tim should be your boyfriend,' Mother said as we walked home that evening. I stopped and goggled at her.

'Why?'

'He's perfect for you,' she said. 'He's very tall, which is a good thing. You're too tall for a girl, you won't find anyone else who likes you who's taller than you.' When I continued to look at her, she shrugged and carried on. 'Plus, he's dyslexic, too. You can bond over that.'

'He seems a bit stupid,' I said, and Mother laughed.

'Then he really is perfect for you.'

* * *

I thought, foolishly, that Mother was just joking about Tim being my boyfriend, but a few days later, I came home from the beach with Father to find Tim and Mrs Hunt sitting on our sofa. Tim flushed when I came in the room and didn't look at me; Mrs Hunt gave me an awkward grin. Both were sipping wine from large blue wine glasses.

'Clive, Olivia!' Mother cooed, standing up and breezing towards us. Just as she'd changed herself in Berlin, she'd already done the same in Monaco. Instead of the rings she'd copied from Enid, Sarah's mother, she now wore dozens of gold bracelets that jingled on her wrists. Her clothes were flowy and bright, in splashy, garish designs. I remember that day she wore a floaty turquoise dress patterned with green ferns and yellow flowers. I think the vibe she was going for was 'quirky, bohemian art teacher'. She poured me a glass of wine and I took it self-consciously. I'd only ever drunk wine at Christmas, I didn't know why she was pouring me one now.

'Did you have a good time at the beach?' Mrs Hunt asked, but before my father or I could reply, Mother interjected.

'Olivia, why don't you show Tim the view from your bedroom?' There was a loud silence, and my face turned as red as Tim's. I turned and stalked to my bedroom without looking at him. I hoped he wouldn't follow me, but I could hear his soft footsteps behind me. I don't remember what we first talked about in my bedroom – the sheer mortification must have been enough to try to forget – but we did talk. I remember bringing up the fact that we were both dyslexic, but Tim wasn't interested in that. He was just a typical 17-year-old boy – he didn't want to talk about school or homework or learning difficulties. He was sweet but dull. The only thing I found interesting about him was that he was colour-blind – I thought that was cool. Most of that first meeting I spent pointing at things from my window and asking Tim what colour they were.

'Erm ... yellow,' he said as I pointed at a red car. I found it fascinating, and I wondered whether he also saw me differently to how I really was. I hoped that in his eyes my porcelain skin looked tanned and glowing, my light brown hair lustrous and dark. I can't have looked that bad in his eyes because he asked to see me again before he left. We arranged to go bowling the next day, and Mother insisted on walking me there. She kept smiling at me and squeezing my arm as we walked.

'This is so exciting!' she said. I didn't mind her being excited, but I didn't like the way she kept looking at me; she looked sly and speculative and it was making me nervous.

My first date with Tim was more boring than exciting. There wasn't any opportunity to talk, not that he seemed bothered, because one of us was always bowling. While I bowled, Tim stood a few metres behind, hands in his pockets, assessing my technique. While he bowled, I sat down and picked fluff balls from my top. Afterwards he walked me home in an awkward almost-silence. To break it, I pointed at things and asked him to tell me what colour they were.

From that point I suppose Tim became my boyfriend, although we didn't do much for the first few weeks apart from wander around town holding hands bashfully and eating ice cream. Mother was very curious about it all.

'Have you kissed him yet?' she demanded one evening in late August. We were sitting around the table. My father was making dinner – linguine with fresh clams and shrimp, caught that very day, he said – and I could smell it, garlic and tomato and that salty ocean smell. Mother poured me a glass of wine, as if that might suddenly make me loose-lipped. It was strange, the way she'd suddenly decided I was old enough to drink wine.

'*Maman* ...' I entreated, looking away. I didn't want to talk to her about what Tim and I got up to, particularly with Father in the next room.

'Have you ever kissed a boy?' she asked. I could see she wasn't going to take no for an answer. She was sitting across from me, elbows on the table, her head propped on her hands. She was giving me what I'd started to think of as her 'innocent' face: eyes wide, so I could see the whites around her irises, and she was blinking, fluttering her eyelashes in a way I supposed she thought was adorable.

'Maman ...' I repeated, but when she kept staring at me I buckled. 'No,' I muttered, looking down at my wine glass. 'I haven't. Okay?'

'Do you know what to do?' she asked. 'Do you want to practise kissing on me?'

She asked the question in such a casual, innocuous way that at first, I thought I'd misheard her. Then I realised I hadn't. Something icy shuddered through me, I was frozen. My gut reaction was one of disgust – Frenching my own mother was the last thing in the world I wanted to do, thanks very much. But that sense of aversion was shielding other feelings: horror, confusion, fear, panic.

'No,' I said, still staring into my glass as if the wine was mesmerising. I hadn't thought about this moment for a very long time, and when I remembered a cold chill went through me. I don't know what to make of it, even now.

Mother was irritated that I didn't want her to be my first proper kiss. She sighed like I was being unreasonable, then asked again. The same feeling of paralysis settled over me, and it was all I could do to say 'No,' in a quiet, clipped voice. When she realised I wouldn't be practising kissing on her, she decided to instead help me by explaining how to kiss in painful, mortifying detail. 'Not too much tongue,' she said as I tried to block her out. 'Remember that. *Not too much tongue!*'

Tim and I did end up kissing soon after that. He could have done with some of Mother's lessons. His kisses were sloppy and driven – it felt like he was rushing through them so we could reach our kissing quota before one of us had to leave. I didn't fancy him very much, but I did relish the new, intoxicating feeling of being wanted. Whenever he walked me home, once we'd come through the entrance of our building, he pushed me up against the wall of the corridor and kissed me as if his life depended on it. It felt like he wanted to keep me in the corridor and kiss me forever; in those moments I wanted him to. But then he let me go, and I walked slowly up the stairs and let myself into our apartment.

Mother questioned me endlessly about what Tim and I got up to. My father took little interest in my relationship, making light conversation with Tim and joking to me that I was 'another man's problem now', but Mother was so eager to hear every detail it disturbed me. I told her as little as I could.

'Prude!' she said, when I shook my head wordlessly at her questions. 'How did I raise such a puritan daughter? You're such a goody-goody, such a cold fish!'

It felt like she was living through me, having her very own teenage romance by making me experience it for her. But it wasn't enough that I had a boyfriend, she wanted more. Her next idea was to put me on the pill. I was a 15-year-old virgin who'd only just had my first kiss – birth control wasn't even on my radar. She even managed to get my father on board by telling him how irregular my periods were, how it wasn't healthy for me, how going on the pill would make me normal. It didn't occur to me then that there were other reasons.

One weekend Tim invited me round to his house when his parents were away, and Mother insisted I stay the night – so I did. Tim was sweet and had assumed we'd be staying in separate rooms, and even though we did share a bed in the end we did nothing more than kiss in it. When I got home and told Mother that no, we hadn't had sex, she exhaled.

'Who are you holding out for?' she said. 'Think you're too good for him? You have too high an opinion of yourself, you little madam!'

I didn't want to have sex with Tim, but I did grow fond of him. Kind and affectionate, he was an escape from Mother, and when I went to his house all I wanted to do was lie on his bed, my head on his chest, feeling his arms around me, his breath warm on my neck. 'You're special,' he sometimes murmured into my ear, and I loved hearing him say that – I couldn't remember being told I was special before.

* * *

School started, and being with Tim made everything easier. He was two years above me, so I wasn't just the new girl this time: I was the new girl with the older boyfriend. But I dreaded my first art class with Mother. I watched her introduce herself in her gentle, silky voice, the way she waved her hands about (she never lost that quirk picked up from Sarah's mother), the way she drifted around the classroom, her perfume trailing behind her. Even though she'd lost her beautiful long hair and her slim figure had disappeared, there was still something about her. She seemed so *genuine* – that was the word you'd use to describe her. When she talked to the other students she looked them right in the eye, nodding when they spoke, as if she respected them, as if she cared. When she got home she rolled her eyes. 'Honestly, Clive, these kids are retards! Olivia's one of the best in the class. And you *know* that's saying something!'

But it was in Mother's art class that I met Lily. I'd noticed her almost instantly; she looked like a porcelain doll, with huge blue eyes, a sweet rosebud mouth and the most beautiful complexion I'd ever seen. While we sketched the fruit bowl Mother had arranged, we started talking. Lily was also English and new to Monaco, and we bonded over that instantly. Spending time with her gave me an insight into what it was like to be a teenager in the UK. I hadn't been back since we'd left for Berlin five years ago, and I felt estranged from my own country. Lily told me what girls my age wore (nothing like the clothes Mother made me wear), what people watched on TV, what music was popular. We sat next to each other in every class, arms touching, heads close together, whispering and giggling.

I thought – or perhaps hoped – that returning to teaching would make Mother happy. It had been years since she'd taught, and I knew how much she loved the influence, the control, the idea that she was moulding and shaping these students so that one day, maybe, if they were very lucky, they could be as talented as her. But while she was always professional in class, when she got home, she was haughty and heated. I'd thought she liked Mrs Hunt, but behind closed doors it was a different story. She was appalled by the art materials in the stockroom, furious that someone of her calibre had taken such a step down.

'It's all feathers and pom-poms and foam shapes and fucking pipe cleaners!' she spat over dinner. 'I didn't sign up to be a fucking arts and crafts teacher, I'm an *artist*,' she stressed as my father and I nodded our heads sympathetically. 'I'm an incredibly successful artist. My work sells out instantly, I've been featured in God knows how many publications, *Vogue* and *Tatler* and *Harper's Bazaar* and *Homes & Gardens*, to name just a few.'

I caught my father's eye. Mother's work had never been featured in *Vogue* or *Tatler* or *Harper's Bazaar*. She was so used to lying, to embellishing the truth to make herself more successful, more important, that she'd simply forgotten who knew the truth and who didn't. Even though I understood by this point she knew she was lying, she still seemed to think she was a genius. Her work was unrivalled, comparable only to the greats. How lucky these students were to be taught by such an accomplished master. How benevolent she was, to deign to teach such amateurs.

And how lucky I was, to have such a maestro for a mother.

PSYCHOPATHY SYMPTOM #13

Grandiose sense of self

Psychopaths are narcissists. They have an overblown view of their own importance and are entitled and egocentric. Rules don't apply to psychopaths; they are special, unique, at the centre of the universe. They have a need for excessive admiration and are convinced they're the best at everything they do. In the eyes of the psychopath, rarely has the world encountered someone so extraordinary.

14
NARCISSISM

*'Psychopaths are entitled and egocentric,
convinced they're the best at everything they do.'*

It only took a few months for Mother to turn on Tim. Though she'd
been the instigator of our young relationship, she soon tired of him, and
once she was tired, I had to be as well. Though I don't know what it was
exactly that made her turn, I have a hunch. I sometimes saw her staring
at Tim and me through narrowed eyes: our entwined hands, our secret
smiles; the gentle intimacy of my head on his shoulder. Was she scared
someone else might take her place and she might no longer be number
one? Was it that Tim gave me strength, that he told me I was special?
Whatever it was, Mother didn't want me getting delusions of grandeur,
and she began pulling me aside whenever he left our apartment.

'Did you see how ungrateful Tim was tonight?' she hissed, shaking
her head in disbelief. 'He didn't even thank me for dinner. And did
you see the way he guzzled down that wine? He's going to turn into an
alcoholic like his father, mark my words. Be careful there, my love. Better
to get out now, before it's too late.'

I tried not to listen but her words had a way of seeping under my
skin. She got to me, no matter what I did. I didn't know why but I felt
a strange pull of loyalty to her. Tim *should* have thanked her for dinner.
And maybe he *did* drink too much wine this evening. Maybe he *would*
turn out like his father. Like father, like son, everyone knew that. I hated

that her opinion had such an impact on my own, but I wanted to be on the same side as her. If I wasn't with her, I was against her, and I didn't want to be against her so Tim had to go.

I became cold and distant; I was very good at it. I held my breath when he asked me questions, I looked away when he gazed at me. When he put his arms around me I was stiff and unresponsive. When he squeezed my hand, I kept it floppy. But it wasn't enough: not for Tim, not for Mother. My parents had bought me my first mobile phone that term, and one day in November, Mother urged me to put it to use.

'Just send him a text. For God's sake, Olivia, it's not hard!'

'I don't know what to say,' I said. I was sitting in the armchair in our living room. Mother was across from me, lying on the sofa in a patch of sunlight, her legs resting on the arm.

'I'll do it,' she said impatiently, holding her hand out for my phone. 'Come on,' she said when I didn't move, 'give me your phone.'

And I did so. I watched her as she typed, a smile on her face. It wasn't the message itself that upset me – 'Sorry Tim, it's not working out, let's just be friends' – but the way Mother handled the whole affair. After she sent the message, Tim called me ... again and again and again. Mother cancelled the call each time, but then she placed my phone on the table in front of her and watched it expectantly, the smile spreading across her face. Then Tim started texting, as she knew he would, and she replied as if she was me.

Tim was confused. What had gone wrong? Had he done something? Things were fine yesterday, weren't they? What had changed? Please, please, wouldn't I reconsider?

The more he begged, the wider Mother's smile got. I watched her thrive on the drama, leeching off his misery, and I felt sick. All the while she texted, pretending to be me, her face was pink and gleeful, her eyes glistening. I sat in my chair and watched, passive and flat. It felt like a bad dream, watching Mother impersonate me, seeing the way she mimicked my face as she typed in my voice: my wrinkled forehead, my worried eyes, my nervous mouth. But as I watched her, it also felt like an awakening, like everything else had been a dream and this was the reality; all was as it was supposed to be.

After a while Mrs Hunt phoned Mother. Tim was distraught, she said. He was in tears in his bedroom, heartbroken. Wouldn't Olivia at least speak to him?

Mother was firm but apologetic. It was better to end things now than later, she said. Better to get out now before we fell in love – 'Tim would come round soon enough, you'll see.'

I listened to her phone conversation from the other room, idly, as if her words didn't concern me. I was a spectator, sitting in my seat and watching Mother live for me; a bystander in my own life, a ghost.

* * *

After Tim and I broke up I was no longer the girl with the older boyfriend. I was just Olivia, the new girl, so I worked even harder at being funny, at making people laugh. I didn't care about being popular, but I desperately wanted to feel like I belonged, and in Monaco, I finally did. Everyone was from a different country, everyone had spent their childhood moving from place to place, just as I had. With all the money here, teenagers did as they pleased. Their parents were rich and preoccupied, and the kids had a freedom I could only dream of. I wanted to surround myself with people like that: strong-willed, independent teenagers who did what they wanted, when they wanted.

I made a good group of friends. We were a sextet: three girls and three boys – Lily, Natalia and me, Harry, Fred and Sid. When I was out with my friends I became like them, carefree and boisterous, but when I went home it was like stepping back into my shell – there was no other way to be.

It was horrible having Mother teach at my school. In the week I had no safe place, nowhere I could go to escape her watchful glare. Early on, she found out who my friends were and made sure she got them on side. She was lovely to them during class, praising their work, telling them what talent they had, that she was astonished with their progress. She laughed with delight when she evaluated their canvases, touching the dried paint gently like she was admiring their strokes, saying, 'Well done, Harry ... *well done*,' with a soft smile and earnest raised brows. And they believed her; they ate it all up.

Sometimes she tried to turn my friends against me, although she didn't have much success with that. After class one day, Natalia asked what had happened with my mother. 'What did you do?' she whispered excitedly. 'I won't tell, I promise.' When I asked what she meant, she told me that Mother had taken her aside in the art storeroom. 'I'm sorry if you feel any tension in class today,' she had said. 'But Olivia did something terrible last night – something truly terrible, I won't bore you with the details – and we aren't currently on speaking terms.' I tried to laugh it off, but I was ashamed; of Mother, but also of myself.

At home I faced a constant onslaught of disapproval. Mother was disgusted I hadn't inherited her artistic talents and made sure to tell me how inferior I was every day. Under the guise of helping, she began to dictate all my projects, and my artwork became Mother's work – her ideas, her vision. She wanted me to create something she wanted, something she deemed worthy of art. Every evening she came into my room, snatched up my art book without a word and sat down at the kitchen table to pick it all apart. I think it was her favourite part of the day. She bought special coloured Post-it notes to stick in my book, so when I leafed through the pages her comments jumped out: '*What is this?*'; '*How is this original?*'; '*HOW DOES THIS RELATE TO YOUR ART OBJECTIVE?*'; '*What the FUCK is this?*' In the mornings she made sure to remove all the Post-its before I went to school – she couldn't have any of the other students seeing.

Mother had never given me a hard time about being dyslexic before, it was actually one of the few things I remember her being patient with. But in Monaco all that changed. She began devising new ways to punish me, and the most tedious was making me write lines: she wrote out the first line in her own handwriting, making her curly script even more elaborate so it was harder for me. I had to copy out the lines 300 times, or when she was really angry, 500.

'I will not disrespect my Maman at work or in front of her colleagues by ignoring her in the corridor at school.' Or *'I will not come home with an attitude when I have to do the housework Maman has set me.'*

The lines had to be neat with no mistakes. They took me hours and hours to copy out. I wrote until the early hours, terrified I wouldn't be finished by the time Mother woke up. On one occasion when I hadn't finished in time, she said not to worry about the missing lines; she'd let me off, because that's what a good mother she was. Wasn't she the best fucking mother in the world?

But times had evolved, and there were new ways to punish me in 2006. This was the dawning of social media, the time when everyone came home from school and jumped on MSN to chat and flirt and say things they wouldn't dare to in class. If Mother was punishing me, she only had to take away my connection to the outside world to get at me. If I did the smallest thing that displeased her, if she sensed I was becoming too sure of myself, too independent, she simply took my phone away. Then it was my computer. She always, always waited until I was on it, chatting to one of my friends on MSN, then barged into my room, ripped the plug out of the wall and carried the whole computer out the door. She always smiled as she did so, a big wide smile to bare those big shiny teeth.

But it wasn't just electronic devices she started taking away from me, it was any escape, any means of eluding reality. She began taking the book I was reading right out of my hands, but I soon learned to outsmart her. I started keeping another book, one I wasn't reading, under my pillow; when I heard her footsteps coming towards my door, I quickly swapped the books over. Mother snatched up the book, always with that triumphant smirk, and sailed out the room holding it aloft, as if it were a trophy. After she'd gone, I read my real book under the covers, glowing at the deceit. I treasured these moments. How stupid Mother was, not to realise I'd outfoxed her. How rare it was, not to feel like a disappointment, a disaster, a stupid, fat cow.

I tried hard in school that year, terrified of what Mother might do if my grades weren't good enough, but I also craved recognition – I wanted her to be proud so much that it sickened me. If a teacher praised me it meant nothing if they didn't pass it on to Mother in the staffroom later. A few times she surprised me, at home, usually over dinner, with an acknowledgement: 'I heard your essay on *To Kill A Mockingbird* was good.'

That was it. In those moments I became aware of the absurdity of it all. All those hours staying up late into the night, blinking back tears of frustration, refusing to be held back by my dyslexia – for what? All to please Mother, to try to make her proud. I dreamed of her throwing her arms around me, telling me what a clever girl I was, how proud of me she was. All I ever got, if I was really lucky, was a throwaway sentence.

* * *

That year, after I turned 16, Mother arranged another love interest for me. The thing about my mother teaching at school was that she knew everyone. I hadn't been involved with any boys since Tim, but she would come and stand behind me when I was on MSN and tell me not to talk to certain people.

'Why are you talking to that deadbeat? End the chat, raise your standards!'

But Lucas joined the school in the summer term. He was half-French, half-Italian, and his mother decided to move him to a new school in

Monaco after a bitter divorce from his father. Lucas was very good-looking, with curly chestnut hair, a square jaw and a pouty, sullen mouth. Mother's eyes lit up as soon as he walked into her class, and once she met his mother at parents' evening, she decided that he would be my new boyfriend. She invited his mother round for drinks under the guise of sisterhood.

'But of course you must come over for an aperitif on Friday, Cecilia,' Mother said, her hand on Cecilia's arm. 'Us women need to stick together! And bring Lucas along, it'll be nice for Olivia to get to know him.'

But Lucas was aloof, and when Cecilia turned up at our apartment she was alone. I saw a flash of anger pass over Mother's face; it rippled like a wave, from her contracted eyebrows to her flared nostrils to her pinched mouth, then it was gone. In another second she was smiling her lovely welcoming smile and saying, 'Come in, come in!' and plumping up cushions for Lucas's mother to sit on. She probed the unsuspecting Cecilia for information that night, and later, came into my room to share what she'd learned.

'Lucas likes blondes,' she said. 'I think it's time you changed up your hair, don't you?'

When I woke up the next day, Mother had already been to the shops. She'd bought bleach and plastic gloves and she was excited. I was confused. For years I'd accepted that my mother didn't want me experimenting with my hair. The short, tufty cut she'd inflicted four years ago had long grown out, and since then I'd worn my light brown hair in a low, neat ponytail. On occasions, when I was with friends and Mother wasn't around, I wore my hair loose. It made me feel like a different person, more like the funny girl I tried to be with my friends. But I was always careful to scrape it back before I got home.

'I thought you didn't want me doing things to my hair,' I said. Mother was humming to herself, laying sheets of newspaper on our kitchen floor, stirring the bleach up in a bowl. She glanced up at me, and for a moment she looked confused.

'That was a long time ago,' she said. 'You're 16 now, things are different.'

But I was still scared. She wore her own hair short now, pretending that was how she wanted it, but I knew she would have done anything to get her old hair back. I didn't want her to dye my hair and then blame me for it.

'Are you sure?' I asked. 'Are you sure you're okay with it?'

Mother sighed and stopped stirring. 'Yes, I'm sure.' Then she leaned forward and gently placed her hand on my cheek. 'You'll make a beautiful blonde,' she said, and a flicker of warmth shot through me. 'And besides, how else will Lucas like you?'

When she had finished with me my hair was a light, yellow-tinged blonde. I ran my fingers through the bright strands and stared at myself in the mirror: I didn't look like me. I wasn't sure if I liked it, but Mother was thrilled.

'It looks fantastic!' she said. 'Don't you think?'

'I suppose so,' I conceded. 'Maybe I just need some time to get used to it.'

'Well, Lucas will like it, and that's all that matters,' she said.

Usually I was allowed to see my friends on the weekend, unless I was being punished. Mother only let me out for a few hours, and I had to be home by nine. After what happened by the lake, I never missed a curfew again. But because I had to ensnare Lucas, she bent the rules. One of the good things about being in Monaco, with so many rich and absent parents, was that one of my friends almost always had a free house. We'd gather in someone's living room with cans of beer and bottles of cheap wine and talk and laugh and flirt. I'd never been allowed to stay out late enough to attend one of these gatherings, but now Mother's plan was in motion the rules had changed, just as they had with my hair.

It might have been my new blonde hair that caught Lucas's eye that night or that I kept looking at him. Whatever it was, we spent much of that evening talking, and by the end of the night, I knew I really liked him. He had a gentle way about him, like he was a young boy in a much older boy's body, and I liked that; he seemed sensitive, innocent.

When I came home just before midnight Mother was waiting for me. Not to see whether I got back home safely, of course, but to see if her plan worked.

'Well?' she demanded as soon as I stepped through the door. She was sitting on the edge of her seat, literally, looking at me as if I was about to tell her the most incredible secret. I swallowed. I knew she was going to be disappointed.

'Lucas talked to me,' I said, trying to make my voice bright. 'For most of the evening. I think he likes me.'

'Is that it?' she said, visibly deflated, her shoulders sagging. 'What did you do wrong? Why didn't he kiss you? Didn't he ask to see you again?'

Though I tried to calm her, to assure her that Lucas really did seem interested, and maybe he was just shy, she didn't speak to me for the rest of the weekend. I do remember wondering why Mother wanted Lucas to be my boyfriend so much. Did she want him for herself? Was it another game of control, or was I being unfair? Maybe she did have my best interests at heart. She'd already branded several boys from school 'Not good enough' so perhaps it was that Lucas was the only one she deemed worthy of me? I hoped, rather than believed, this was the case. But in all honesty, I didn't really give it much thought: Mother wanted me to go out with Lucas, so I had to go out with him.

More weekends went by, more weekends when Lucas didn't ask me to be his girlfriend and Mother didn't hide her disgust. But he and I had become close. One evening before school broke up for summer, we went for a walk around the city – we were meant to be buying wine to take back to someone's house but became distracted. We talked, walking close to each other, our hands knocking together. As we strolled, Lucas began opening up to me. He told me about his abusive father, about what it was like growing up in such a household; how bad for his mother he felt, how sad he still felt himself, and as he talked, a gentle aching started in my chest.

I recognised so much of what Lucas said. I shared the same guilt, those same feelings of anguish, solitude, regret. I too felt clumsy and weak, I too wanted to be loved.

I wanted to tell him about Mother more than I'd wanted to tell anyone. It would have given us a bond, a kinship. But I didn't. Instead, when Lucas finished speaking, I looked him right in the eyes and I said, 'I'm sorry, I know how you feel.'

I hoped he would somehow grasp what I was saying, that he knew he wasn't alone. I hoped he could understand that I had suffered as he had, but unlike the cause of his pain, mine was still present in my life. But I couldn't speak about it, I just couldn't.

Perhaps Lucas did understand. He stared at me for a long time, then looked down, nodded curtly, and carried on walking. I hurried after him, wondering if I had done something wrong – his movements had become stiff, jerky. I thought he was upset so I asked him what was wrong, and then shyly, without looking at me, he reached inside his jacket and pulled out a single red rose.

'Will you be my girlfriend?' he said. I wanted to burst into tears. It was so sweet, so awkward, so painfully romantic. I don't remember saying yes, but I must have, because the next thing I remember was kissing him. The summer night was darkening, and as we ambled under the starlight, hands entwined, I never wanted to stop walking. In that moment I always wanted to hold Lucas's hand, to look at his profile from the corner of my eyes and marvel at how handsome he was, this lovely boy who had given me a rose, this sweet, gentle boy who liked me for who I was.

But then also, as we walked along hand in hand, another part of me wanted to stop. To turn, shake my hand free, and run home to Mother to tell her my news. To have her know I'd succeeded, I'd done what she wanted. Would she be happy with me, then? Would she be proud? Would she break into one of those big smiles and throw her arms around me and say, *Well done, my little Olive. Well done, I'm proud of you.*

Are you happy with me, Maman? Did I do you proud?

* * *

That summer Lucas and I spent as much time together as we could. It was never as much as we wanted, because in Lucas, Mother found the perfect new punishment. Whenever I disappointed her, whenever she thought I was becoming too strong, that was it: no Lucas. But then sometimes, when I was at home drawing in my art book, trying to keep up with the extra summer work she always set me, she looked at me. She saw my miserable face and my half-hearted sketching, and she sighed.

'Go on then,' she said, shaking her head. 'Go and see Lucas. Go on, off you go.'

'Really, Maman?'

'Yes, really. Go on, before I change my mind!'

I jumped up and flung my arms around her neck and kissed her soft cheek. 'Thank you! Thank you, Maman!' She put her hand over mine, just for a second. Her touch was light and made my skin tingle, like a butterfly gently moving on my hand. As I felt her warm skin on mine I remembered my black and white butterfly, how we held hands as we watched it fly away, how she'd stolen it for me and looked after it, for me. In these moments I knew she only wanted what was best for me. In these moments I still loved her so much it took my breath away.

After one month, Lucas told me he loved me, and I said it back. Did I love him? I think I did. I felt safe with him, I trusted him more than I'd trusted anyone before, except maybe my father when I was young. Lucas always put his arm around my shoulder when we walked and I leaned into him. It became my new safe place, there in the nook of his arm; it was where Mother couldn't reach, where nothing could hurt.

In the evenings we went to Cactus bar, where my friend Natalia's older sister Nadine worked. We'd go as a group, Lucas and Lily and Natalia and me and Harry and Sid, and Nadine served us drinks with a wink. One evening, we drank wine on the deck outside the bar, and Lucas and I held hands over the sticky table. It was a beautiful, balmy evening, his hand was warm in my own. Opposite us, the blue sea glittered.

'Want one?' Natalia held out a packet of cigarettes. I don't remember the brand name but I do remember the emerald green box, the way the white paper stuck up around the cigarettes.

'No, thanks,' Lucas said, shaking his head.

I looked at the proffered pack, thinking.

'Livvy? Do you want one?' Natalia asked. I'd never smoked before, never wanted to try it. Mother hated smoking. I knew it was bad, of course, but she hated it with an almost irrational passion, like smoking was the cause of all her problems. Whenever we walked past someone smoking on the street, she coughed theatrically, glared at the smoker and told me in a loud voice, 'Smoking gives you CANCER, it kills you. *I* had cancer, I almost died. Promise me you'll never smoke, Olivia.' I knew Mother's cancer was leukaemia, it had nothing to do with smoking. But smoking was still a disgusting, smelly habit and I had no reason to want to do it.

'I know, Maman,' I would say. 'I'll never smoke, I promise.'

But now cigarettes were being offered up to me. It was all so easy. Something about the cigarettes, the way the snow-white cylinders peeped out of the packet, was alluring to me. Mother hated smoking, and I had promised never to smoke. A silent rebellion!

I reached across the table and took a cigarette. Lucas sniffed in disapproval but I pretended not to hear. I lit it with the lighter Natalia offered and inhaled, trying not to cough as the smoke filled my lungs. I liked the way the cigarette looked in my hands. My stubby child's hands had lengthened and I now had Mother's hands, the same soft palms, the same long, thin fingers. But she had beautiful nails, my own were ragged and bitten. As I held the cigarette between my fingers, my hands looked elegant and delicate, like artist's hands. I liked the way I moved while holding a cigarette, the way my hand was loose, relaxed, the way my wrist faced up to the sky. I could almost see myself as I smoked, and if I was a stranger looking in, I would think I were someone very different to who I really was. I looked serene, sitting back in my chair, legs crossed at the ankle; I was sophisticated, tilting my neck back and blowing streams of smoke towards the sky. And all the while that I was being someone else, someone cool and carefree and mature, I was doing something Mother hated. I was going back on my word, I was cheating. If she knew, she would be angrier than I could imagine. But she wouldn't know. In Monaco, in 2006, everyone smoked. When Mother smelt it on my clothes and hair she just tutted.

'I can't believe people are still smoking,' she'd say. 'How awful to go out for a drink and come back smelling like an ashtray.'

'I know, it's disgusting,' I sighed, shaking my head. Inside, I shivered at my own deviousness. Mother hadn't even entertained the idea that it was me who was smoking – the idea of me wilfully disobeying her was unthinkable.

Every time I lit up a cigarette I felt a flicker of delight. I knew Lucas hated it; whenever he kissed me after I'd been smoking, he pulled away and said, 'Ugh! You taste like cigarettes.' He always said it in a funny voice, imitating Forrest Gump, so I knew he wasn't that cross about it. But I knew he still hated it – I just didn't care. It was more important to feel like I'd beaten Mother than to make my boyfriend happy.

* * *

In July I went back to camp with my old friend Sarah, but this time it was different. Now I was 16, I could take part in the Counsellor-In-Training course to become a camp counsellor. I'd wanted to become a counsellor ever since I'd first visited Canada, aged 12, and the CIT course was four whole weeks of freedom. Even though I was sad to be leaving Lucas for a month, I was so excited to go. But I was foolish: I was too excited, and I let it show on my face. When Mother looked over at me and saw me smiling, she was angry.

'Wipe that grin off your face, you look deranged!' she said, and so I made my face look glum for her. If she could have stopped me from going, she would have, but Enid, Sarah's mother, had already bought the flights – a belated present for my 16th birthday, she said. She and Mother spoke on the phone the month before, and I listened from the next room. There was something about Enid that made Mother feel inferior, and that was alien to her. She told lie after lie about her success in Monaco while I listened with a faraway interest: she'd been promoted to deputy head; the school was so impressed, they'd already given her three pay rises; she was appearing on a French TV show about successful female artists. She laughed throatily as she spoke, the same laugh she'd stolen from Enid, and I wondered if Enid could hear it – if she would recognise her own laugh echoing back from the other end of the line.

It was too late for Mother to stop me from going, so instead she tried to make me feel guilty. 'While you're busy wishing your time away here, have you given one thought to how I'm going to cope without you? You don't understand how much I'm going to miss you, and you know I've been feeling sick again recently. I'm worried it's my illness coming back. Not that *you* care, all *you* want to do is to rush off to Canada.'

'You know that's not true, Maman,' I lied.

'*Grand-mère* and *Grand-père* are coming to visit, they'll be devastated not to see you.'

'I'll see them next time,' I said gently. 'You know I will, Maman. I can visit them as soon as I'm back, in August.'

'That's not the point,' she snapped. She was looking at me like she despised me. 'You only think of yourself, you always put yourself first. What about me?'

I tried to calm her, to tell her I was thinking of her and would miss her, but she didn't listen. She sighed melodramatically, or else she walked out of the room while I was still speaking, shutting the door pointedly behind her.

My father drove me to the airport early in the morning. Before I left, I wanted to say goodbye to Mother, but as I was about to knock on her door, Father caught my arm.

'She doesn't want to say goodbye to you,' he said. 'She's too distraught that you're leaving her.' I opened my mouth but he cut me off with a shake of his head. 'No. She needs her rest, she's worried she's becoming sick again.'

Was it my imagination or was there accusation in his voice? But I wouldn't let Mother ruin this for me. Once I arrived at camp, it was like coming home. I loved everything about it – I loved Sarah, I loved the other kids, I loved the rituals, the singing around the fire and washing in the lake. The fresh smell of the biodegradable soap, that light crisp scent of green apple, my favourite smell in the world – the smell of freedom and happiness and safety. I loved the training, the hiking and canoeing and swimming we did every day. I even loved it when we had to carry our canoes on our shoulders to the lake, grunting under their weight, stumbling over rocks and tree roots, slapping at the mosquitoes buzzing around us. In the evenings I was filthy and bruised, burnt and bitten, but I wore my blemishes like badges, my perma-dirt like armour . I'd never felt more wonderfully part of anything in my life.

I loved the way the other kids laughed at me, the way they gently shoved me if I did something silly and said, 'God, Livvy, you're nuts!

You're crazy!' I liked being nuts, I liked being crazy. Not crazy like Mother, but good-crazy. Funny-crazy. Most of all, I loved how none of the kids except Sarah even knew who Mother was. To them, I was just another camper like them, silly and breezy and wild.

I'd hoped at camp I could pretend Mother didn't exist – that I could turn off the part of my brain that belonged to her and only switch it back on when I touched down in France. But I couldn't, because that summer I had a mobile phone.

On the first day I received a furious message from her – how shocked and hurt she was I hadn't bothered to say goodbye before I left – and that to make up for my insolence, I had to call her every day. Whenever we spoke on the phone I sloped off into the forest where no one was around; I didn't want anyone to see this version of me, to hear the pathetic apologies that dripped from my mouth. As soon as I heard her voice I could feel myself diminishing, shrinking from a lively camper to a feeble, snivelling wreck.

We spoke every day, but Mother's text messages still came in thick and fast. How disappointed in me she was, that I cared so little for my family. How kind she had been, to allow me to go away for so long. How *Grand-mère* had wept when she realised I'd chosen to go to camp *again* rather than see her. How her liver was troubling her, and this time it really looked like the leukaemia was coming back. How the fear and the worry was hurting her heart, how it pounded all day long.

Every night when I got into bed I switched my phone on and her messages came through in a flurry. I read them and then lay there, eyes wide open, staring up at the wooden ceiling, waiting for my stomach to stop twisting. She also emailed me. There was only one computer at camp, a big, slow machine in a far corner of the rec hall. There was always someone on it, and I spent hours waiting for it to be free so I could jump on, read the 15 emails she'd sent over the past week and rush off my apology-riddled replies. I was sorry I couldn't contact her more, but

I could hardly ever get on the computer and most of the day we were out in the wilderness; I was sorry for making her worry, and I really did want to hear all her news; I was sorry for making *Grand-mère* so upset, I felt truly dreadful, really so terrible.

It was one night that summer, as I sat in front of the computer reading Mother's latest diatribe while everyone else slept, that I realised I would never be rid of her. She would always follow me, always hold the power to make me miserable and ashamed, even now, when I was halfway across the world. It was like she was reaching out with those long fingers and choking me from across the ocean. She was with me at camp as surely as if she'd gone there herself. She sat next me as I sang around the fire, swam behind me as I paddled on the lake. She marched alongside me as I trudged up mountains, she lay beside me in my narrow camp bed. I could almost feel her presence next to me, heavy and corpse-like, her head on my pillow, her hands round my neck.

15

DUPLICITY

'Psychopaths use flattery, guilt or sympathy to get what they want.'

The new year at school started, and this time it was serious business: I was starting my International Baccalaureate – the IB, as everyone called it. It was hard work, much harder than anything else I'd done at school, and so to 'help' me, Mother stepped up her criticism of my art. My work just wasn't good enough, it wasn't right. It had no meaning, it lacked depth. Everything in IB Art had to have a purpose, a story, a message – something I was too shallow to understand.

I threw myself into my work but I struggled that year. Mother had been punishing me ever since I came back from Canada, but in a subtle, long-winded way: she stopped letting me out on the weekends to see Lucas. She said it was because I needed to concentrate on the IB. Lucas sulked when I told him Mother wouldn't allow me out; he said I should 'stop acting out' at home. Mother was such a delight in school that he couldn't believe she would be so draconian without proper cause. I hated letting her see that she was hurting me, but once, after a whispered and frustrating conversation with Lucas, I begged her to let me see him.

'We'll see,' she said with an infuriating smirk on her face. 'I'll think about it.' Then she looked at me more seriously. 'Do you love him?'

I thought for a moment, not knowing what she wanted to hear. I was terrified of saying the wrong thing and making it worse. 'I think so,' I said eventually. 'I think so, yes.'

'Good, that's good,' she said softly. 'That's gooood!' She stretched out the vowels and her words seemed to float and hum around the room. 'That's *good*!'

The next weekend was Lily's 17th birthday. Mother let me go and I was excited – a whole evening with Lucas! I was going to stick to him like a limpet. But that night Lucas didn't want to be stuck to. There was something different about him. It felt like there was a cold anger inside him; he tried to hide it, but it manifested in the most unsettling ways: the impatience of his touch, the tightness of his face. I asked him what was wrong but he said 'Nothing, nothing,' and his voice was tight too. I tried to ignore it, to push the unpleasant thoughts from my mind. I drank sparkling wine and I danced and chatted, but I was always aware of Lucas standing stiffly in the corner, his mouth clenched, arms hanging heavily by his side.

At the end of the night he walked me home, and when I reached for his hand he jerked it away. 'Lucas, what's wrong?' I asked. 'And don't say nothing, I know it's not nothing!'

He looked away from me. 'It's nothing,' he said.

'Tell me what's wrong!' I demanded, and suddenly I was furious at him, for his stupid obtuseness, his nasty, cold silences. 'For God's sake, tell me!'

But Lucas didn't say anything. He groaned instead, an awful, guttural sound that seemed to come from deep inside him, and then, without looking at me, without saying anything, he started to run. He ran along the road, away from me, head jerking, his fists balled. After a short distance he stopped, and I was sure he was going to come back; he was going to run back to me and put his arms around me and tell me what was wrong. Instead, he punched a tree. I heard his yell of pain, I saw his face – fury and frustration and this strange, savage expression – and suddenly I was scared. A cold panic settled over me. I didn't know who this person was: my Lucas was gentle and kind, who was this aggressive, secretive stranger? I didn't want to look at him, standing there alone by the tree. I wanted to put space between us. I turned on my heel and walked home tearfully.

When I got back, Mother looked at me, noticing my red-rimmed eyes, my pink, blotchy face. She didn't ask what was wrong.

* * *

Lucas and I didn't speak or exchange messages for the rest of the weekend. On Monday at school, I tried to keep my distance. Confused, I didn't know what to think. But after school Lucas shuffled up to me in the corridor: he said he wanted to talk.

'What about?' I asked.

There were inky rings under his eyes and his face was pale.

'You know what about,' he said. He took my hand in his, but I kept it slack. 'I'm sorry for how I acted the other night, I'm sorry I didn't talk to you. And I'm sorry I ran off and didn't walk you home.' He took a deep breath. 'Your mother …' Then he stopped and looked away. I could see his jaw working as he chewed the inside of his mouth.

'What about my mother?' I asked.

He swallowed, shook his head.

'I said I wouldn't say.'

'Why mention it then?' I snapped. I felt foolish, uneasy.

'I'm sorry,' he said again. He scratched his neck; he looked miserable.

'Did my mother do something to you?' I asked.

'No,' he said in a low voice. 'She didn't do anything to me.'

'Then what?' I said. 'What are you trying to tell me?'

Lucas licked his lips and looked at the floor. 'She said something to me,' he said eventually, still not meeting my eye.

'What did she say?' My heart was beginning to throb, my chest felt tight.

'Something horrible,' he said. 'Something I'll never repeat.'

A dizzy feeling started to sweep over me, and for a moment I thought I might faint. I felt heavy, but at the same time hollow, empty. All I wanted to do was get away, get out of this dark corridor, get away from Lucas's agonised face.

'I have to go,' I muttered, but he grabbed my arm before I could turn.

'Olivia, please. I'm sorry. Please don't let this ruin us.'

'I need time,' I gasped, and I tore myself away from his staring eyes. There was a bleakness to him now and his pain was tiresome for me: it was too raw, too desperate, too hopeless. It was too similar to my own.

That night I lay in bed, Lucas's squirming face floating before me. I tried to think of our happy memories – his shy face when he'd given me the rose, his sweet, gentle kiss – but it felt like a wall had gone up between us, and the old Lucas was hidden behind it. Whenever I pictured him in my mind, he looked tormented. I saw his tense, troubled face, I saw him ball up his fist. I saw him punch the tree, I saw him run away from me. In the back of my mind, faintly, like an echo, I could hear Mother's voice. 'Good, that's *good*!' she said in my mind, like she'd said to me days before. 'That's goooood!'

* * *

I finished with Lucas at the end of the week. He cried openly at school, it was horrible to see. I still cared about him, but something shifted after Lily's birthday. I didn't see him the same way anymore: he was spoiled, Mother had spoiled him.

Years later, friends asked me if I ever found out what Mother had said to Lucas. No, I replied, I hadn't. But didn't I want to know? Hadn't

I tried to find out? How could it not eat me up, not knowing what she'd said to make him act that way? But it didn't matter to me what she said, what good would it have done? What would I have learned? That Mother was manipulative and deceitful? That she was a liar, that she was cruel? That she gave things to me only to take them away? I knew all those things anyway.

It hurt, breaking up with Lucas, but I didn't cry. I did this, it was my choice. He begged me to take him back, and I was as kind as I could be. I didn't like seeing him like this, with wet eyes and a pink face and a wobbling toddler's mouth, it made my heart ache. But beneath that pain there were also other feelings, ones I knew I felt but didn't want to acknowledge. Standing in front of Lucas while he cried like a child made me feel powerful, mighty, unforgiving. In his eyes I might be cold and unfeeling, but I knew really, I was poised and resolute. I was undaunted, unrelenting, I was unshakable.

After I broke up with Lucas, Mother relaxed her hold on me, just a touch. I was allowed to see my friends on the weekend, but of course only on her terms – if she was happy with my art work, if I hadn't been moody on Tuesday afternoon. Without Lucas by my side I started spending more time with my male friends, and a new boy called Eddie, who was smiley and charming, joined our little gang. He had a little gap between his front teeth that I thought was adorable.

One night, when we were having drinks at Sid's house, I decided that I was going to sleep with Eddie. I didn't fancy him, but I trusted him and that was enough – I just wanted to lose my virginity, I didn't want to feel like a little girl anymore.

So that night we had sex. It didn't last long but it wasn't awkward and I felt comfortable with him. As we lay in bed, things Mother had said about my skin, my stomach, my breasts crept into my head. No one had seen me properly naked before, not even Lucas, but under Eddie's friendly gaze, I felt warm.

Afterwards I told Eddie that I just wanted to be friends, that this was just a one-time thing and I didn't want it to ruin our friendship. He was shocked – 'Are you sure?' he kept saying, 'Are you sure?' – but I knew what I wanted. Or I knew what I didn't want, and I didn't want Eddie, with his sweet simplicity, his gappy grin, his soft skin that smelled like cocoa butter.

What did I want? For a while I thought what I wanted was Fred, and that spring I turned my attention to him. Fred was a year older, tall and handsome in a dangerous sort of way, with wolfish grey eyes and dark, heavy eyebrows that made him look like he was frowning. He was very clearly emotionally unavailable but I think that was what attracted me, and we started going out just after my 17th birthday. We bonded on a strange level early on, when he told me his mother had died from cancer. I told him mine had survived cancer.

'You're lucky,' he said.

'Trade places with you in a heartbeat,' I replied, and he looked shocked but then laughed. I'd taken to making flippant comments about Mother to my friends – never divulging anything real or important, but disrespecting her in a glib, silly way that pleased me. It was a small way to vent, to tell people that she wasn't what she seemed.

The problem with Fred was that he was in love with another girl from school, Fran. I knew it, he knew it, everyone knew it. I also knew he was just using me for sex, but I didn't care. Lily didn't understand: 'How can you let yourself be used this way?' she'd say. 'Don't you have more respect for yourself?'

But I didn't respect myself. All my life I'd heard that I was an awful girl, a deceitful pig who caused pain to everyone she knew. No man would ever love me because I was too tall, too fat, too thin, too demanding, too weak. When I looked in the mirror, I hated myself. Even though I had grown out of my awkward stage now and boys seemed to find me attractive, I could only see what Mother saw, the things she told me I was. When I looked in the mirror, I didn't see big green eyes or long legs or full lips, I saw the person underneath – the stupid, fat cow who was shallow and spoilt, lazy and unlovable.

But Fred didn't care about me, so he didn't care about the person underneath. In the ten minutes we were having sex he wanted me, and that was real, it wasn't fake. I felt detached from everything; I felt absent from my own life. I wanted to feel something, and I could feel sex. It was a connection to life, to another person, even if to Fred it meant nothing. Why should it matter that he didn't care about me? When we had sex nothing else mattered but the fact that Fred wanted me, and we were alive, we were connected.

* * *

The work for my IB was so time-consuming that Mother only let me out for a few hours most weekends, so I would pretend I was going to Lily's when really, I was going to Fred's. After we had sex, we watched TV together on his sofa, not touching, not talking. Then, when my curfew was approaching, I'd gather up my things and walk home slowly, back to Mother and my passive father, back to extra homework and housework and barbed comments about my appearance.

In the final term I had four wisdom teeth removed, and then I contracted blood poisoning. I was off school for a week, and as I lay in bed, swollen with pain, Fred texted me to say things weren't working out. I'd known it was coming, but it hurt far more than I anticipated, and I lay in bed weeping from rejection, and then from the agonising pain in my mouth. Mother heard me crying and came into my bedroom.

'What's the matter?' she asked. 'Do you need some more painkillers?' She'd been quite sympathetic since I'd been off school, bringing me ice packs and snacks, fluffing my pillows up and making sure I drank enough water. Sometimes she even placed a cool hand on my forehead and said, 'Hmm, you're too hot. Let me get you a cold flannel.' I closed my eyes under her touch and for that short burst of time, it was like she really cared.

'Fred broke up with me!' I wept, exhausted and drained. Every part of me seemed to hurt. Mother sat on the end of my bed and I thought, for a moment, that she was going to be kind. It wasn't an irrational idea. She was, sometimes, when I least expected it.

'Well, what did you expect?' she said, leaning back and appraising me. 'If you don't respect yourself, how can you expect anyone else to?'

'Please don't,' I sobbed. 'Please don't say things like that now.'

'You were easy for Fred. That's all you were, easy. Easy Olivia!' I put my hands over my ears to block her out, but she pulled them away. 'Your father and I have the most perfect marriage. And why's that? Because we have so much love and respect for each other. How are you ever going to find someone to love and respect you the way you are? Look at yourself!' She nodded at my mirror. 'Go on, look at yourself.'

I looked in the mirror, still crying. My eyes were red, my jaw puffy. Fat tears streamed down my cheeks, sluggish and pathetic, and I tore my eyes away, not wanting to see myself. My bloated face was white as bone, and as hard too; if I smiled it would crack and shatter into a million tiny pieces.

* * *

I got through that first year of my IB by thinking of the summer ahead. Now I was a camp counsellor, I'd be going to Canada for two whole months and the summer stretched ahead of me, beautiful and free. Mother used the same excuses as the previous year in her quest to stop me going – she was sick, she'd miss me too much, *Grand-mère* was dying – but this time she also used schoolwork. I had only one more year of school left, one more year to get the grades needed to get into a good university, why would I spend two months running around after other people's kids when I could be putting that time to better use? I'd be better off staying at home and studying. But this time, to my astonishment, my father refused to back her up.

'If Olivia's going to university in another year, she needs to become more independent,' he said. 'And besides, what on earth's the point of her going to camp all these years and training to be a counsellor if she's not going to put it into practice?'

He asked the question like he was genuinely confused, like he didn't understand why she was reluctant for me to go. I was grateful to him for sticking up for me, but I remember looking at him as he was speaking and thinking, *Do you really not know, do you really think this is about school? Can you not see that this is about control?*

I was 17 now and the control Mother had over me was slipping. When we were together it was the same as it had always been – I craved her approval, I allowed her to dominate me, too afraid to resist. What was changing was situational. I wasn't a little girl anymore. If she wanted me to go to a good university – and she did seem to genuinely want that – she knew I couldn't do that under her roof in Monaco. She would have to let go of me, to unfurl her claws from where they'd dug into me for so long. The thought terrified her, so naturally, she had to step things up.

* * *

Camp was as magical as I'd hoped. I was put in charge of the youngest children, the seven- and eight-year-olds, and I loved it. They trailed after me like ducklings, and it was gratifying in a way I'd never known, to feel needed and loved like this. These kids wanted nothing from me but attention and hugs, praise and acknowledgement. They looked up to me. In their eyes, I was useful, I had value.

On the walls of the wooden cabins where we slept were little plaques, and on each plaque were the names of the counsellors for that year. I remember running my fingers over my own name and swelling with pride. When I looked at my name inscribed in the plaque it was like I belonged there, etched into the wood, a tangible part of camp forever. I felt permanent, substantial; like I mattered.

At first Mother just played her old tricks. Every night I switched on my phone and the messages surged in: I was selfish, I wasn't keeping in touch enough, I didn't care about their summer, I hadn't asked about *Grand-mère*. The emails were the same, only longer. For the first few weeks, I emailed whenever I could get on the computer. They were long, gushy emails filled with 'I'm so sorry, Maman,' and 'I understand why you're so hurt,' and 'I really am interested in your summer, please tell me your news.' But it wasn't enough. I began dreading the evenings, when I switched my phone on and her poison came seeping into camp life. Every night my mind was filled with Mother's toxic words, and I couldn't sleep. Her scornful face danced in front of my eyes as soon as I shut them.

'Why don't you just keep your phone off?' Sarah asked me one day. I was yawning, rubbing my bleary eyes and swaying with tiredness. 'If she's being needy and stressing you out with all her messages, why don't you just leave it off?'

To Sarah it was that easy. She didn't know what Mother was like, she didn't know what the ramifications of that action would be – but I did. Then suddenly, on the other side of the ocean, I decided that actually, I didn't care. I sent one final message saying we were going on a camping trip and I wouldn't have any reception, then I turned my phone off and buried it at the bottom of my bag. I stopped going on the computer and checking my email, and I tried to distract myself from thinking of Mother and what she had in store when I got home.

I flirted with the male counsellors, knowing that in their eyes I seemed somewhat exotic – I had an English accent, I'd had older boyfriends. That summer I slept with two counsellors; both of them lost their virginity to me. I felt helpful, being their first. They were teenage boys, they just wanted to have sex, and here I was, ready and willing and with a bit of experience on my side. I was useful to them, I was valuable. I knew neither of the boys was interested in me seriously, but it didn't bother me, I didn't care.

* * *

In the second month of camp I realised the lengths Mother would go to in order to hurt me. Every two weeks a new group of campers arrived, and at the end of each two-week session we had a campfire ceremony. We sat cross-legged around the fire, gazing at the flickering, shadowy faces of the campers opposite us, sharing stories and jokes about the past two weeks. I could smell wood smoke and pine trees, cooked food and sun cream; I could hear the lilting chirp of cicadas. I remember looking out at the dark glistening of the lake and feeling entirely content. At the end, when everyone was getting up and stretching and brushing grass from the backs of their legs, I saw Tedd, the camp director, striding towards me.

'Can I have a quick word, Olivia?' he said in a light voice, and in that moment I knew.

'Sure,' I said, keeping my voice just as casual. I followed him as he walked away from the other campers, away from the fire, towards the gloom of the forest.

'Erm,' Tedd began. It was dark but I could still see how awkward he looked. 'I believe your mother – a Josephine Lacroix? – has been emailing me?' His voice was pitched up, like he was asking a question, but I knew these were facts: of course Mother had been emailing him. 'Do you ... Do you know anything about this?'

'No,' I said. Horror was beginning to slink over me. I could feel my face getting hot and I was suddenly glad it was dark. 'What's she been saying?'

'She, er ... Well, to tell you the truth, she hasn't been saying anything very nice at all.'

'Can you tell me, please?' My voice was clipped, business-like. I wanted Tedd to see me as an adult, a peer. Not a naughty child, a horrid spoilt girl.

'Well, she ... she's been saying that you did some terrible things back home – no need to go into details – and you shouldn't be looking after children.'

'I'd like to hear the details, please,' I said. Tedd looked at me for a moment. He was twisting his fingers together, moving his weight from one foot to another.

'She mentioned some upsetting incidents where you'd been in trouble with the police back home,' he said in a small voice, and I knew he was still keeping things from me. 'She said that due to these incidents, you shouldn't be alone with children. You certainly shouldn't be in a position of responsibility with them.' Then he coughed. He looked mortified, and I could so easily imagine the disturbing incidents Mother had regaled him with.

'I've never been in trouble with the police,' I said, trying to keep calm but my voice sounded weak and childish. 'Please feel free to run a full background check on me. I assume you already did that when I became a counsellor?'

'Olivia, I don't believe her,' Tedd added hurriedly. 'The things she was saying were, frankly, unbelievable. But I wanted to know *why* she was saying them.' He looked at me; he was trying to understand. I felt sorry for him. 'Do you know why?'

'My mother ...' I started, then trailed off. What should I say? How could I possibly explain? I exhaled slowly. 'My mother is insane,' I said. It was the easiest explanation.

Tedd stared at me.

'Like ... really insane?' he asked.

I nodded.

'Yes.'

I wasn't sure what else to say, but I didn't like the way he was looking at me, a mixture of pity and alarm on his face. 'She's mad, you need to ignore her.'

'I thought I should maybe reply to her?' he said. 'Maybe it might help if I tell her how wonderful you are with the kids, how much we love having you at camp.'

'*Please don't*,' I said, and this time I knew my voice was panicked. 'She'll only get angry. It's not worth it, really. You just need to ignore her, that's the only thing to do.'

'Well, if you're sure ...' he said doubtfully.

'I am.' I looked at him. 'You should probably block her email address. And you should also probably tell the other leaders that they should expect some emails from her, and they should ignore them too.'

'Really?'

'Really.'

I knew that once Mother stopped getting a response from Tedd, she would try someone else, and of course she did. Every member of staff got emails from Mother that summer. She pretended to be a concerned parent, a mother who loved her troubled daughter but also knew what she was capable of. When she was ignored, time and again, her emails got angrier and more desperate. If something was to happen to any of the children at camp, don't say she didn't warn them! They'd go to prison, along with Olivia – her perverted daughter – and the other parents would never forgive them.

I tried to enjoy my last month at camp but it was tainted now. She'd ruined it, just as she'd ruined Lucas. I was glad to have the support of the staff, to know they didn't believe what Mother was saying, but I knew they saw me differently now. My mother was crazy, and so by connection some of that must rub off on me. I was a girl they should pity, console – but also one they should tread carefully around.

This was the first time I became aware of Mother's tenacity in stalking.

I wish it had been the last.

16
CONTROL

*'To the pychopath, people are seen as objects
to be used for their own fulfilment.'*

When I landed, my father was waiting for me at the airport, and because Mother wasn't there, I knew my punishment had already begun – the toying with me, that old waiting game of knowing something was coming, but not knowing what or when.

'We've got some news for you,' Father said as he drove home. 'Your mother will tell you everything when we get back.'

'We're moving,' I said. It wasn't a question. He said nothing, glanced at me, smiled. As we drove home, I thought what that meant: another move, another school, the disruption of moving halfway through my IB. I thought about Lily and Eddie and the friends I'd made, about our plans for the rest of the summer. I wondered whether Mother had arranged it again so we'd leave at once and I wouldn't have a chance to say goodbye.

When we got home she was sitting at the kitchen table. My first thought was how healthy she looked: her eyes were bright, her face rosy. She gave me a smile as I walked in, the big smile that showed all her teeth, but I could see fury flashing behind that chilly grin. I knew then that she wasn't going to mention the emails or me turning my phone off, or all the terrible things she'd said: we were going to pretend it hadn't happened.

'Darling, I've missed you,' she said, holding out her arms. 'Come and give me a hug.' I pushed my suitcase against the wall and walked over to her stiffly. She snaked her arms around my shoulders, rubbing my back, stroking my hair. Her fingers pressed against my spine and I thought of her typing, tapping those same fingers against the keyboard as she composed email after email, all the abhorrent lies she'd invented. 'I've got some exciting news for you,' she said. 'Sit down.' I sat opposite her. I should have felt nervous but I felt flat – I suppose I would have been nervous, if I had the energy. 'Guess who I've been in contact with.'

'Who?' I asked.

'Your grandmother!' Mother said brightly, and then she sat back in her chair, arms folded, with a self-satisfied, you-didn't-expect-that-did-you? expression on her face.

I hadn't expected it. I looked between her and my father, wondering if this was one of her jokes. 'Granny?' I said. 'Why?' As soon as the word left my mouth, I realised why: money. Mother wasn't going to risk missing out on Granny's will after the disappointment of my grandfather's death.

'Because she's family,' Mother said, as if she hadn't spent the past six years scoffing at the idea. 'And life's short,' she added with an elegant shrug. 'It's time to reconnect.'

'That's great,' I said carefully. I looked at her. I knew there was more.

'After I spoke to your grandmother, your father and I had a long chat,' Mother continued. 'We've been away from England for a long time now, and we discussed whether that's still in your best interests.' She looked at me fixedly; now I was nervous. 'After much consideration ...' She paused, licked her lips. 'We've decided that you'll move back to England to finish school. You'll have a better chance of getting into a good university with some A-levels under your belt. You'll live with your grandmother.'

'Aren't ... aren't you going to come too?' I asked, holding my breath.

'No,' she said simply. 'I'm not ready to leave Monaco.' She leaned forward, rested her head on the back on her hand. 'Now, darling, I'm sorry to say that you'll have to redo this past school year. I've spoken to several colleges and you need to have two years of A-level study. There's no way around it, I'm afraid. Your IB is worthless in England.'

And there it was – what this was really about. She'd upped her game; she was punishing me for the whole year. My friends would move on and progress, but I would regress. I'd lose ground, I'd recede. She would stretch out my misery for 365 days and I'd retreat, younger, weaker. I'd have to do it all over again.

She raised an eyebrow at me, waiting for my reaction. What did she want? She wanted me to plead, to beg and cry that I couldn't *possibly* redo another year of school: it was too frustrating, I'd feel stupid, I'd be older than the other kids. I sighed loudly and rubbed the front of my head like it hurt. I needed her to think she'd got to me, but I couldn't believe what I was hearing. If this was my punishment, it was more bittersweet than I could imagine. Bitter because once again she was dragging me away from my friends, my school, the place that had been home for the two years; bitter because yes, it would be infuriating to have to sit through another two years of school before I could go to university, before I would have real independence.

But sweet, oh so sweet, because I would be free.

* * *

The next week was a flurry of planning. My father and I pored over prospectuses for colleges. Which ones were close enough to Granny's new home? Which ones did courses that interested me? 'You should study something you're *good* at,' Mother said, watching Father and me leaf through pamphlets. 'The trouble is, I'm not sure what that is,' she added, pretending to look puzzled.

I wanted to study something new, to learn something Mother knew nothing of. So I decided on a course in Interactive Media – it was in Chichester, close enough to Granny's new home, and the course counted as three A-levels. After I applied to the college I spoke to Granny on the phone. I hadn't spoken to her since I was 11 years old, but as soon as I heard her voice, everything came flooding back: baking in the kitchen with her big ceramic bowls, the smell of paint and cracked leather in the old cottage, the overwhelming sense of safety. In a few weeks I'd be with her; I'd be back in Sussex with Granny, just like old times. I was glad she'd moved to a new house, I didn't want to go back to the cottage. I knew I'd loved it there but thinking about it made me uneasy. I supposed something must have happened there a very long time ago, but I didn't want to look back. I might be repeating a year but I would still move forward, eyes to the front.

'This is for you, Olivia,' Mother said several times that week. 'I'm doing this for you, for your future.' She hadn't grasped that her punishment had backfired; she'd thought I would be furious, that she'd have to reassure me, through curved lips and glittering eyes, that she was only doing this for my own good. That one day I'd thank her for it, even if now it looked like she was trying to hurt me.

'I know,' I sighed. 'Thank you, Maman.'

There was a sense of anticipation that summer, of doors opening and things speeding up and life rushing towards me, but, towards a conclusion, an ending; an outcome, impending, unavoidable.

* * *

Mother didn't come to England with me. She was too busy, she said, but I knew it was because she couldn't bear to see Granny. Talking to her on the phone was one thing, but seeing her in the flesh was another; for years just the mention of her would make Mother's face twist. It unnerved me, watching her speak to Granny on the phone. She laughed delightedly, she made her voice all bright and warm – you could *hear* the smile – but always her face was impassive. It was like her voice and face belonged to two separate people. 'Oh, how lovely!' she cooed, 'What a treat! Jean, that sounds hysterical!' Mother sounded sincere and excited, her voice low with laughter, but when I glanced over her face was slack, her eyes contemptuous.

My father helped me move in. As he moved boxes from the car into the house and constructed IKEA furniture, he was awkward. He hadn't seen Granny since my grandfather died, when he left before the funeral, and the weight of the past six years hung between them. I felt bad for him, but also, I thought he deserved it, to feel ashamed of himself.

Granny gave him a big hug when he left. 'My Clive,' she said quietly, a hand clutched to the back of his neck like he was a child. Together, we watched my father leave. He walked around to the front of the house, unlocked the car, sat inside and strapped himself in. We watched him switch on the headlamps and look over his shoulder, and I remembered quite suddenly watching him drive away in Martinique when Mother went on the run. I remembered my fear and anxiety, my terror at the idea my father was leaving me. This time I watched him drive away with a steady coolness.

'Well,' Granny said, turning to me with a smile. 'It's just you and me, now.'

* * *

I loved living with Granny. It was easy and simple and safe. Every Sunday we baked a cake, Victoria sponge or a fruit cake, or maybe a crumble, and we'd have some with a cup of tea every afternoon. We chatted and chewed companionably, and Granny liked to point out, with a bit of a smirk, that this definitely wasn't in accordance with the diet Mother thought I was on. She'd written up a weekly diet plan for me to give to Granny; Granny read it silently, rolled her eyes and tore it in half. 'Preposterous!' she said to me, shaking her head. 'Preposterous! If you get any thinner, you'll fade away.'

In the evenings we played Scrabble and talked and watched TV. Granny liked old-school murder mysteries, things like *Inspector Morse* and all the old Agatha Christie shows, and we watched them cuddled up, blankets over knees, biscuits in hand. In my room there was a double bed and a side table and a lamp and a desk and a wardrobe. It was small, but I loved it: no Mother to come barging in to rip the book from my hands, no Mother to push me inside and lock the door.

I loved college, too. I loved learning about something that was new to me, and I found my course even more interesting than I'd hoped. We created videos and learned about web design and creative marketing, and I remember thinking at the time, this is something I will actually use, this is what my job will be.

In my first week at college I met two girls, Faya and Isabel, and they slowly introduced me to teenage life in England. I learned that I needed a fake ID, something I'd had no use for in Monaco; that Wetherspoons was the cheapest place to 'pre-drink' and six bottles of WKD Blue was probably enough. Granny didn't mind me going out with my friends. She didn't make me feel bad if I wanted to spend the evening with Faya and Isabel.

'Go, go!' she always said. 'Be safe, have fun.'

* * *

Of course, Mother had set ground rules: I must come home for every holiday and long weekend and I must ring home every day at 6pm, no exceptions. It was far too frequent to have anything interesting to tell her and she knew it. She just wanted to curb me, to add an extra chore to my day, something I had to get out the way before I could relax. Every day before I rang her I thought about what I could talk about, what things I could say that she'd be interested in. But she wasn't interested in anything I had to say. Everything was about her: how much weight she'd lost, the insightful new art project she was working on, how her lessons had changed a student's life. When I told her about my course and how well I was doing, she took the credit. I didn't get the highest grade that term because I'd studied hard and slaved over every piece of work, I got it because of her, because she was the one who had decided I should go to college in England, she was the one who pulled me out from the IB. She was the one who should be thanked and acknowledged.

I agreed with her when she pointed this out, and I said, 'Thank you, Maman, you were right,' and I made excited 'Ooh!' sounds at her news, but it wasn't always enough. Mother wanted to continue our old cycle from afar, and about once a month she began picking big fights: I'd been late to call, I hadn't emailed enough, I wasn't responsive enough on the phone yesterday. I was a disappointment, a disgrace; I wasn't worth living for. Even though we were in different countries it was still awful, fighting with her. She got to me like no one else, and I held the phone away from my ear as she scratched away at me.

Once, that first autumn in England, I sat in the living room holding the phone away from me as silent tears slipped down my face. Granny was upstairs, I thought it was safe to cry. I hid my fights with Mother from her as much as I could. I knew their relationship was rocky and I didn't want to cause another rift. And I still felt a loyalty to Mother, a sense that whatever happened was between us: it was private, our secret. But that day Granny pulled the phone from my hand and held it to her own ear. She opened the French doors and walked outside into the garden; I stayed on the sofa, watching through the glass as she talked to Mother. After a few minutes she came back in and gave me a rueful smile.

'Dry your tears, lovie,' she said. 'Don't worry, she won't be ringing back tonight.'

'What did you say?' I asked breathlessly.

'I told her that I wouldn't allow her to verbally abuse you on *my* phone in *my* house,' Granny said, a grin spreading over her face. 'Then I put the phone down on her.' Horror and delight began to creep over me. I couldn't believe she dared to speak to Mother like that. I placed my hands onto my hot cheeks and stared at her in wonder. She looked back at me but now her smile was gone. 'It's not okay that she does this, Livvy,' she said. 'You do know that?'

'I know,' I mumbled, looking down.

'*Do* you?' Granny asked. She looked sad. 'Do you know that this isn't normal?'

I thought for a moment about what 'this' meant. If Granny meant the phone call we'd just had, then yes, it was normal. At least it was normal for Mother and me. But I knew she hadn't meant that. 'Yeah,' I said quietly. 'I know.'

'It's not right that she does this to you, it's not your fault. You know that also, don't you?'

I looked at Granny, at the quiet grief on her face, at her kind blue eyes. I didn't want her to be sad. 'I know that, Granny.'

And I did know: I knew that other mothers weren't like my own, that Mother could be startlingly cruel and I didn't deserve to be ridiculed and berated. So that meant I knew it wasn't my fault.

Or that is what I thought I knew.

But Granny's success was short-lived. When I spoke to Mother the next day she explained to me that Granny shouldn't be meddling in our relationship. Granny didn't understand, that's all it was – she didn't understand the special relationship I had with my Maman. She didn't know about our special bond, how Maman would scream at me and I would cry and apologise and then we'd make up and be closer than ever. She made me pass the phone to Granny while she explained this herself and told her that she must never, ever hang up on her again or come between her and her daughter like that. As I gave the phone to Granny I felt treacherous, like I'd betrayed her. She listened silently, disbelief flitting across her face now and then, but she bit her tongue. She knew how upset I got – she saw me twisting my fingers and biting my lip – and so for me, she kept the peace.

'I understand,' she said crisply before she ended the conversation. I remember thinking then that she did understand – she understood but she didn't *know*. She didn't know how awful it was to feel so small, to crave Mother's love so desperately that you keep going back for it, time and again, hoping this time it would be different, this time she would have changed. To hold out your hands for her warmth, but for her to turn an icy cheek.

* * *

My first year of college flew by, and I did well in my course. I was selected as a young, gifted and talented student and was entered into a creative workshop competition with ITV. Every week, the candidates were whittled down and at the very end I was the only one left. I won a two-week placement with a TV production company: I was to be a junior researcher, creating TV concepts to sell to other channels. I was excited to tell Mother; she told me how well I'd done and I beamed. She took credit for it, of course – it was because of her that this had happened – and tried to tell me what TV concepts I should be creating. I thanked her graciously and told her what excellent ideas they were, then hung up and thought of my own. I was in my element, it was like I'd found myself.

Faya and Isabel and I became very close. Faya passed her driving test and bought a car, and we'd go for wild drives around Chichester, blaring music and dancing in our seats, shrieking and bunny-hopping across the street as she struggled with the clutch. I made friends with boys – some I slept with, some I dated. And I got £250 spending money a month. With no rent to pay it was more than I needed, but when I told Mother, she brushed it off.

'Oh darling, take the money! Buy yourself some nice clothes. Not that tatt from H&M or Topshop – nice stuff. Treat yourself to something lovely and think of me when you wear it!' Then she laughed, the tinkling laugh that raised the hairs on the back of my neck. But I was still grateful. For the first time in my life I was able to buy my own clothes, to have my own style – even if looking back, some of it was pretty questionable. So I bought tight jeans and high-necked shirts to hide the blotchy rash that crept up my neck when I thought of Mother, and I dyed my hair a lighter blonde and wore it tousled and loose.

That summer I went back to Monaco. After the previous year's disaster I asked Mother, tentatively, whether I'd be going back to camp, but she told me I'd grown out of it. Privately, I agreed. I'd been a junior researcher that year, I was moving forwards. My father took me out for driving lessons. I was a good driver, he said, cautious and steady. We drove along the coast of France with the sun on our faces, and when I was behind the wheel and the road was empty, I felt freedom so absolute it almost scared me. I stared ahead at the cobalt blue sea and it felt like I could drive off the road right into it; I'd skim like a stone across the surface, weightless, unsinkable.

Mother took me for drives too. She drove along the winding roads and bitched about Granny, telling me how rude she was on the phone, how she made it awkward for her to call. I nodded along, silent with shame. I knew I was betraying Granny but I needed Mother to know she still had me, I was still hers.

Mother stopped the car in a village outside Nice. She pointed at a little green Mini parked in a garage and told me that if I was a very good girl, she was going to buy it for me for my birthday the following year.

'I love Minis, and so do you,' she told me. And I did love the car: it was old but in excellent condition, with a wooden interior and white racing stripes on the bonnet and an electric sunroof. I couldn't wait to drive it. That summer she also took me out for mother-and-daughter bonding. She took issue with my boring and unoriginal high street clothes – why on earth did I want to look like everyone else? Linking her arm through mine, she steered me through the finest shops in Monaco. I went wherever she led, devoid of will of my own, heedless of where I was headed. She bought me slippery leather jackets and stiff strappy shoes and floaty floral dresses.

Now I looked like her.

* * *

For my second year at college Mother decided I should move into the halls of residence. More upheaval for me, that was the main reason, but she also wanted to disappoint Granny. She was too interfering, Mother said, and besides, it couldn't be good for me to spend so much time with a pensioner – I should be with people my own age. Being an international student, it was easy to secure accommodation in halls, and that September, I moved into a room right across the corridor from Faya. I was sad to leave Granny, but at 18 the promise of unlimited freedom was impossible to turn down. I promised I would visit every weekend.

Life in halls soon developed into a routine and I loved every moment. In the week I walked across the rugby field to my classes, and I wrote pages of notes and colour-coded them and arranged them neatly in folders. When it was hot, Faya and I lay on the grass on the rugby field, staring up the sky and squinting at the sun; when it was cold, we wrapped ourselves in duvets and spent the day watching *Friends* and *Sex and the City* and drinking hot chocolate. Every Friday, we walked to the shop and bought cigarettes and two bottles of £5 Jack's Hard Cider. We smoked and drank and danced around as we got dressed up, as we lined our eyes with black and our mouths with red. We went to Wetherspoons for WKD Blues, then went to the club, where we drank tequila shots and danced until our feet were sore.

But now we lived together I couldn't hide Mother from Faya for long. At first, she thought it was a one-off, that Mother was just having a bad day; she'd met her that summer and loved her. 'She's so funny!' she'd exclaimed, 'She's so smart!' But then she saw it for herself: the endless phone calls, the control, the screaming down the phone until I cried for her forgiveness. The reasons for Mother's pain were endless, but always I was the root of it. There was no end to her suffering by my hand – I hadn't wished her a happy anniversary for her bone marrow transplant, I wasn't good enough company when I last visited, I didn't care how much my Maman missed me. How hard it was for her, to let her only child go; how hurt she was that I didn't care; how kind she'd been, to let me study in England. Mother couldn't absolve me unless I atoned, and once we'd both agreed what an amazing mother she was, she showered me with praise.

Faya read Mother's emails and texts, open-mouthed and incredulous. She didn't understand. Just like Granny, she didn't get that this was just the way it was: fighting and fury, then weeping and grovelling, and finally, understanding and forgiveness.

This was our pattern, and it was unbreakable.

* * *

I started smoking more and more. I always smoked at least one cigarette when I was speaking to Mother. It helped me get through the call, but there was also a stealthy delight in smoking almost in her face. I was smoking so much that buying packs became too expensive, so I switched to rolling my own. There was a quiet satisfaction in laying out the paper and spreading out the tobacco, then rolling it up neatly, licking the gum and tucking it all in. It was like picking my arm, only less painful.

The more I smoked, the less I ate, and I grew thinner and thinner. It wasn't intentional at first – I just didn't have much interest in eating. My mealtimes had always been filled with conflict and spiky comments about my weight; I didn't have a positive association with food. But then as the weight fell off and people started exclaiming and telling me how thin I was, I realised this was something I could control: it wasn't Mother controlling it, it was me. At 18 I stood at 5'10" and weighed 57 kilos. When I look back at photos from this time it's startling how thin I was, but when I went home for Christmas and Mother saw my new figure, she was thrilled. 'At last!' she said, clapping her hands together as she admired my stick legs. 'You've finally done it. Finally!'

That spring we discussed universities. I'd already decided I wanted to go to Brighton University. It had a good media course and I had happy memories of Brighton: I remember very clearly sitting on the hot pebble beach when I was seven, and my father picking up unusual pebbles and showing them to me. He'd say, 'What does this remind you of?' and I'd look at the stone, stroke its smooth edges and say 'A bunny rabbit!' or 'A love heart!' Whatever I said, he smiled at me and said, 'Exactly that! Well done!'

Father accepted that Brighton was my first choice, but Mother took more convincing. She contacted the university and told them that she lived abroad and wasn't able to make the open day – could they possibly find time to meet her when she came down? She arranged private meetings with all my prospective professors, where she was her usual impressive self, chatting and laughing and turning her big eyes seriously to them when they talked. I could see that they bought it, that they thought she was lovely: what a nice mother she was, coming all the way from Monaco to make sure her daughter was looked after. I tried to stay positive –

things had been better since I'd come to England – but I couldn't shake the feeling that this was preparation for the next three years. She wanted to be on first-name terms with my professors, she wanted to email them and call them, she wanted to ask them to 'watch out for me' or at the least 'keep her in the loop'. Most of all, she needed to make it clear that she was the best fucking mother in the world.

I hated her being so involved. I could see my freedom now – it was shimmering away on the horizon, it was *there* – and she was trying to take it from me. Though I stewed with resentment, I never showed it: if Mother could have a mask then so could I, and I'd spent the past two years constructing it. I never let it slip. When I was with her I fixed my face with a grin, wide and toothy as her own, and I lifted my eyebrows, just a touch, so I looked baffled and hesitant. On the phone to her I pitched my voice higher and talked haltingly: I needed to sound young, uncertain. I needed to sound like I was under control.

* * *

That May, I passed my driving test. I was over the moon. My parents had bought the green Mini and the plan was for me to drive it over to England that summer. I saw myself sitting in the car by myself, driving along the winding roads of France until I reached England, then driving my friends, free as a bird. I couldn't wait to call my parents to tell them.

'Wonderful news!' my father said. 'People of England, beware! There's a new girl racer on the roads!'

'I can't wait to drive it to England!' I said. 'My first road trip!'

'Well done,' Mother said. 'But I'm not sure you should drive it in England. It's a French car, after all, and the wheels are on the wrong side, it's too dangerous.'

'But the plan was always for me to drive the car over to England,' I said. 'And I'll be really careful.'

'It's too dangerous,' she repeated. Her voice was sharp now so I left it. Maybe once Mother saw what a cautious driver I was, she'd be happy for me to drive to England.

It was sunny that day, hot too, the first proper day of summer. Faya and Isabel and I brought out blankets and spread them out on the grass by the rugby field. It was late afternoon, I remember the lovely golden light. Faya was playing music, Isabel was chatting about all the places we could drive once I got my car. Then my phone rang: it was Mother and she was livid. 'I can't believe how selfish you're being!' she raged. 'You haven't given me a single thought!'

'I'm sorry,' I said automatically. I didn't know what she was talking about.

'You couldn't give two shits about me!' she went on. 'All you care about is driving your damn car to England so you can drive your stupid, fucking friends around – friends I don't even know! You're an ungrateful brat. *I* bought you that car, you should want to drive it with *me*!'

'Maman, I'm sorry,' I said gently. 'I'm really excited about driving you around.'

'We were so excited for you to pass your test,' she continued, 'but all you want to do is drive away from us. I've never been so hurt and upset!' There was a pause while she waited for me to apologise again. My mouth was open but the words wouldn't come out – it all sounded so ridiculous. I looked out across the rugby pitch at the other students. They were lying on the grass like us, relaxed and carefree, or sitting in little groups and chatting. Everyone was happy, everyone was calm. It was the beginning of summer, I'd just passed my driving test. I didn't want to do this anymore.

'I'm not dealing with you like this,' I said. 'This was my day to be happy and proud of myself, and you've ruined it by making it all about you.' My voice sounded clear, strong. 'You always make everything about you – it's all about your suffering, your pain. I'm tired of it.' Then I hung up. I looked at the phone in my hand. I couldn't believe what I'd done. I couldn't believe I had hung up on her, like she had done to me so many times – screeching and shouting, then silence as her screams rang in my ear. It was her turn to be hung up on. I lit a cigarette and waited for her to ring back. When she did, her voice was shaky with anger; it leaked from my phone and out into the green fields around me.

'You selfish bitch! We've saved for years so you can go to university, and this is how you repay us? Well, guess what? I'm going to give your university fund to some poor African child, they deserve it more than you do!'

'That's a lovely idea,' I said calmly. 'They do deserve it more than me.' On the other end of the line, I could almost hear her blood boil.

'You stupid girl,' she said, her voice quiet now. 'You have no idea what you've just done.' I said nothing. 'This is it, do you know that? I'm done with you, I'm finished. You're not my daughter, I disown you.' I looked straight ahead, I didn't say anything. 'You think you can talk to me like this? Let's see how well you cope by yourself. You are on your own, got that? *You are on your own!*'

And with that, she hung up. I turned my phone off and dropped it in my bag. Alex and Isabel, used to Mother's behaviour by this point, cheered and hugged me like I'd just achieved the inachievable. It was like a weight was lifted: no more daily phone calls to Mother, no more sitting silently while she screamed in my ear, no more high voices and fake smiles. I'd finally stood up to her.

I felt strong and proud, and as I sat on my blanket between Isabel and Faya, I felt like one of them: like any normal 19-year-old, with nothing to worry about, but enjoying the summer ahead. I didn't need Mother anymore, I would be independent. At 19, I was an adult. I was going to university in a few months. It was a new start, a new life. Mother would try to make it hard for me, but I would make it, I would be okay. I lay back on my blanket and closed my eyes. The late afternoon sun was warm on my face, and a soft breeze moved over me like silk.

On the outside I felt warm and soft and sweet, like a peach in the sun, but inside a strange bleakness shivered through me. It felt like a penetrating coldness, running like blood through my body, flowing up past my stomach and spreading through my bones.

PSYCHOPATHY SYMPTOM #14

Shallow emotional response

Psychopaths are generally afflicted with an emotional deficiency. While they do feel emotions, these are stunted, and limited in their range and depth. Being able to flit between intense anger and cool, calm composure can give the impression that psychopaths are merely acting a role in their day-to-day lives. Feelings of fear or pain do not provoke an emotional response as they do in normal people, and psychopaths are incapable of forming genuine emotional connections.

17

MASQUERADE

'Psychopaths are incapable of forming genuine emotional connections.'

Now I was motherless, I was also fatherless. My father came as part of the Mother package – he was a loan, he belonged to her. If she decided to cut me off, he would be part of that. Now I needed to find a job: I would need my own money. I walked around town, visiting nearly every pub and bar in Chichester, handing my CV to the manager and fixing a bright smile on my face. I'd never been allowed to have a job before. Mother pretended it was because she wanted me to focus on school when really she didn't want me to have money of my own. Any money I received was a gift from her and I must be grateful for it. But the money was never mine: it was a loan, just like my father. They both belonged to Mother.

She might have disowned me but Mother couldn't lay quietly. The emails started a week later and I read them dispassionately. I'd heard everything before: I was the greatest disappointment of her life, I wasn't worth living for, she wished she'd never had me. I blocked her email address. She swapped to text messages and voicemails. I blocked her phone number. Once she called from my father's phone, and foolishly, I picked up.

'Good luck finding a new home,' she crowed, the first words she'd spoken to me in weeks. 'I've cancelled the payment for your halls. You'll have to pay the next few months yourself or you'll end up on the street!' I could almost see her on the other end of the line, that smile on her face, that jubilant gleam in her eye.

'That's fine,' I said smoothly. 'I'm getting a bar job, I won't need your money ever again. Goodbye.' And I hung up.

By now it was nearly June. I'd already filled out papers and applied for the maximum loan for university, but I still needed somewhere to live until September. I could have asked Granny, I knew that, but pride stopped me. Whenever we met up for lunch I put on a brave face and assured her that *of course* everything was good, *of course* Mother was behaving. Everything was fine now. Asking to move back in was admitting failure, and if I failed, Mother won. It couldn't happen.

After a time I heard one of my job applications had been successful, and the manager of the bar called me in for an interview. It was informal and I thought it went well, but I didn't hear anything after. I called up a week later: unfortunately, I was told, an adverse reference had come through and the bar were withdrawing the position. Nonplussed, I couldn't imagine who had given me a bad reference. Then a week later, it became clear.

My friend David called me. He worked at a bar in town, and I'd given him several copies of my CV and begged him to help me out. 'I'm not sure I should be telling you this,' he began hesitantly, 'it's supposed to be confidential.'

'I won't say anything,' I said immediately. 'What is it?'

'Well, I asked my boss what he thought of your CV. We have two openings right now so I thought he might consider you for one of them.'

'And?'

'And I showed him your CV, and he took one look and said, "No, not that girl." So I asked him why. He said your mother had rung him and told them to expect an application from you and to ignore it. Apparently, she said that you had a criminal record and have been fired from all your past bar jobs for stealing. I told him that you'd never had a bar job before, but he wasn't interested.' There was a silence. Heat was beginning to roll up my body, waves of shame and humiliation and burning, indignant anger. 'Olivia? Are you still there?'

'I'm here,' I managed to say. 'Thanks for letting me know.'

My head was reeling. As soon as I got off the phone I called another friend, who worked at a Chichester bar. Had my mother phoned them too? An hour later, my friend called back: yes, she had phoned a week ago to warn the manager about me. I couldn't believe it. I was furious with myself for being so stupid, for revealing my plans to her. In my desire to get one up, I'd exposed myself. I'd as good as invited her to spoil it. She couldn't have me earning my own money when it was the only control over me she had left, could she? One comment that I was looking for bar work and she'd contacted every bar in the city. It must have taken her days.

But I was my mother's daughter, I would go one better. I spent the next day traipsing into every bar, pub and cafe that I'd given my CV to and demanding to speak to the manager. If they weren't in, I left a message, then followed it up with an email. I was honest: I said that my mother was disturbed and didn't want me being independent. I told them that they could verify everything I was saying with the police, my college, my prospective university and my grandmother, and I provided contact numbers for each.

It paid off, and I got a job at a bar on the high street. It was a nice bar, with cosy booths you could slip into and friendly, relaxed customers. The staff welcomed me with open arms; they'd heard all about the new girl, the girl with the crazy mother who tried to sabotage her job prospects – they seemed to find it funny.

With college winding down, I took as many shifts as possible. I learned what a shandy top was and how to pour a proper Guinness – after a few weeks I was even drawing clovers in the foam. The staff became my friends and we had fun during our shifts, choking on shots of chilli sambuca when it was quiet and covering each other's backs when busy. The money wasn't great and I left stinking of beer, but I didn't care: this job was my freedom.

But it wasn't enough. I wasn't earning enough to cover the last couple of months in halls. I hadn't told Granny – I didn't want her worrying, and I definitely didn't want her money. I was going to sort this out myself. I told college I was moving out of halls early due to unforeseen circumstances and I settled up the few weeks of missed payments. Now I just needed to find somewhere to live.

It was my friend Silvia from the bar who introduced me to Sean. I told her I was looking for some cheap accommodation for the summer, and she had just the thing.

'Well, this is perfect,' she said as we pulled pints. 'I'm moving out next week, you can take my place.'

'Take your place where?' I asked.

'I share a flat with this guy, Sean. It's only a studio so we both sleep in the living room. It's not luxurious, but it's cheap as chips.'

'I'm not sure I want to live with a guy I don't know,' I said cautiously. 'Especially if we'd be sharing a room.'

'Oh, it's fine,' she said with a wave of her hand. 'He's so nice, really. He's never made me feel uncomfortable or weird or anything. He's not a creep or a perv! He's just a really nice guy. Do you want me to ask him for you so you guys can meet up and see what you think of each other?'

'Yes, please,' I said. I wasn't happy about moving into a studio with a strange man, but I knew I wasn't earning enough to be picky.

A few days later, towards the end of my shift, a young man approached the bar. He caught my eye as soon as he entered the room: he was tall, dark and handsome, and he walked with confidence. It wasn't quite a strut, but it was almost one. He had a lot of thick black hair that he'd combed into a *Grease*-style quiff, and that day he was wearing grey skinny jeans and a burgundy T-shirt that fitted like a glove. He had a cocky, expectant face, but when he caught my eye he broke into a warm smile.

'Hi,' he said to me. 'Are you Olivia?' He propped an elbow on the bar and leaned towards me, still smiling, and I saw that he had perfect white teeth and a dimple in his left cheek. It gave him an adorable, lopsided look, and something fluttered across my stomach.

'Yes,' I said, suddenly aware of my beer-soaked shirt and shiny face.

'I'm Sean,' he said, and I remember feeling nervous then. He looked me right in the eye and didn't once glance away; I found his eye contact almost unsettlingly provocative. Why was he looking at me like that? But then he smiled again and there was a warmth spreading over me, and I smiled back, and we stood there at the bar grinning at each other.

When I finished my shift, we went for a drink down the road, and I knew within minutes that I could live with this Sean. He was the most charming man I'd ever met. He seemed earnest and open, but when I looked into his dark eyes there was something inscrutable about him, something enigmatic, unreadable. He was a puzzle, a riddle, and he excited me, he made me nervous. But then he'd smile that dimpled smile and I'd feel at ease again.

We became very close, very quickly. I learned that he'd recently broken up with his girlfriend, he was 24 years old and currently between jobs. He'd been voted Young Chef of the Year in 2007, and he still had the award in the backseat of his car: it rolled noisily from one end to the other whenever he turned a corner. Although clever, well-mannered and talented, he didn't seem in a hurry to get a new job. He wanted to really enjoy this summer, he told me, he'd been working hard for so long.

I moved in with Sean the next week. His studio apartment was right in town and only a five-minute walk from the bar. Before she went home for summer, Faya drove me to IKEA. I wanted to make the most of this strange living arrangement, I wanted to build myself a home. We bought curtains and cushions and posters for the walls, and I was grateful for her support because Faya made it clear she wasn't keen on Sean: she thought he was shifty. At the time, I thought she was jealous. Sean was genuine, anyone could see that.

Soon Sean started meeting me at the end of every shift. He waited by the bar, always polite, always smiling, and when I finished, we walked home together. Sometimes when we were walking, if I was talking about something serious, he'd stop in his tracks and just look at me, like he wanted to absorb every word I was saying. Only when the conversation lightened would he look away and pick up his stride. I felt like I had his undivided attention, and more than anyone else, I felt he understood me: he got me, he listened, he didn't judge. When I got home from a long shift, he was waiting for me and had made sandwiches and asked how my day was – he was the perfect roommate.

It didn't take long for romance to blossom. With Faya away for summer and Isabel looking after her new baby girl I'd been worried I would feel isolated, but now I had Sean. We both knew it was nothing serious – I'd be going to Brighton in September – but I wanted someone to be close to and we were going to enjoy summer together. We were going to be young and wild and free.

At times I was concerned that Sean was *too* wild: he'd disappear for days at a time, then turn up with his hand bandaged and a story that didn't make sense – he'd fallen behind his cupboard, he'd slammed his hand in a car door, he'd accidentally hit a wall. He had two phones, always carried a big wad of cash on him and would go out 'to see friends' at all times of the night, but I didn't care that his stories were full of holes. It was just a summer romance, after all.

I graduated college with a triple distinction in summer 2010. I told neither of my parents.

I worked hard that summer and saved as much as I could. Double shifts never seemed so bad when Sean was waiting for me at home. Sometimes

I came back to find he had cleaned the whole flat: he made it absolutely spotless, even outside the kitchen where the bins were kept and there was a disgusting maggot infestation. He'd made a cosy den with blankets and cushions, and he lit candles and poured wine. We had lovely, gentle sex, then ordered Domino's pizza, watched films in bed and talked until the sun came up.

I learned a lot about Sean in those first few weeks. The main thing I discovered was that he was a cocaine dealer. It explained a lot, but I was shocked – I'd never been around hard drugs before. It was dangerous, it was what other people did – losers, wasters, not smart, talented people like Sean. At first, I thought he was just a dealer, then I realised how much he took it himself. He'd been doing it all along, even those times we were sitting on the bed, laughing at some silly film – he'd been going to the bathroom every half hour and doing keys of coke. Somehow that made it less of a big deal to me – he'd been doing it all along and I hadn't even known. It couldn't be that scary, could it, if I couldn't even tell? But I still didn't understand how someone like Sean could get so mixed up in this world, and so he explained everything to me.

At 17, he left home to become a chef and that was his introduction to drugs. He told me that lots of chefs take cocaine to stay on their feet all day. After he left his culinary school, he took a job at a large financial company in London, and one day, he found a printer toner cartridge in the kitchen and decided to see if he could sell it. When he got almost a grand for it, he became greedy: he walked through the building and from each floor he stole a cartridge. In his chef whites, who would suspect him? He started selling them ten at a time, and with each ten grand, he'd take himself shopping and buy a new load of coke. But then he grew cocky: he went in on a Sunday and was caught. The company could only prove he'd stolen £10,000 worth of their property, but Sean told me it was more like £100,000. He went to court and was ordered to pay £10,000 in compensation.

Then there was the time he assaulted a police officer – but it wasn't his fault, he'd accidentally knocked him off his motorbike at the traffic lights, he didn't *mean* to – and he owed the officer another £10,000 in compensation. So that was the only reason he turned to drug dealing, to pay back his debts. Couldn't I understand?

'I suppose I can,' I said. 'But you sniff all your profits!'

'I know,' he sighed. 'I shouldn't.'

It didn't take long before Sean was openly doing cocaine in front of me, either when we went out with his friends or when we were at home. But always he was kind to me, always affectionate. I felt safe with him; I trusted him.

And it didn't take long for me to start doing it too. I shocked myself when first I did it. I'd never taken drugs before, except for a puff of weed when I was in Monaco, and I didn't like it and had never done it since. I knew my parents would be aghast if they knew I'd taken cocaine, but unlike smoking, I didn't do it as a silent rebellion. Seeing Sean and his friends use it so much normalised it, and I wanted to fit in, I wanted to be a part of it, whatever it was. Taking it was fun and it did make me feel amazing, but I knew I wouldn't let it take me over. Nothing was going to ruin my future: I was going to university and then I was going to get a job, a good job that paid well, and then I would never have to rely on anyone else again. Nothing would stand in my way.

Sometimes Sean would sit next to me, put his arms around me, rest his head on my shoulder and say, 'Thank you. Thank you for not judging me. Thank you for knowing who I really am. You know I'm not this guy.'

'This guy' was the side of Sean I didn't like. At times he'd get so high he couldn't sleep for days, and he'd sit at the table in his boxers, jigging his knees, exhaling loudly and trying to calm himself. Other times he grew paranoid, convinced I had another man hiding in the house. It was heartbreaking to see but I never said anything, it wasn't my place. He'd been honest with me, and I respected that. Besides, this was just a fling. Since cutting Mother off the weight on my shoulders had lifted; I wasn't prepared to start a moral crusade to stop my summer romance selling drugs.

I didn't tell Sean much about Mother. He knew, of course, that we'd had an argument and she wasn't supporting me financially, but I didn't go into details. I felt like I didn't need to – he knew without me having to say a word.

Mother was still finding new ways to contact me, phoning from withheld numbers and creating new email accounts after I blocked her. I began having strong physical reactions every time she made contact: when I listened to her voicemails or read her emails my heart started racing and my whole body began to boil; blotchy heat rashes spread from my chest to my neck and along my jaw. I started to pick my arm again. But Sean felt like a protective shield: he'd entered my life as she left it, he'd never met her, never been tainted by her. He was all mine.

I told myself that Sean was just for summer, but the more days that passed, the more we became welded together. At night we opened our window to the warm summer breeze, and as the curtains blew, I looked across at the dark shape next to me, his arm flung across my chest, hard and heavy like rope. He slept like a little boy, mouth open, legs curled up, fingers splayed. To me, he was like a cool glass of water when your mouth is dry, or a warm woollen blanket when you've been cold for too long – he was a relief, and I couldn't imagine life without him.

One day, that August, I came home from work to find Sean sitting at the kitchen table, waiting for me. I'd been late for work that day, and in the rush I'd left my phone at home. When I walked into the kitchen, he was holding it in his hand, spinning it on the table and grinning at me.

'You'll never guess who I just spoke to,' he said. 'Your mother.'

I stood there staring at him, my hands tingling, not knowing what to say. What was he doing, picking up my phone? Should I be angry? I felt confused and betrayed. It must have shown on my face because he got up and wrapped his arms around me.

'Don't be cross,' he said. 'I only answered because I know you're hurting.'

'I'm not hurting,' I protested, but he tightened his arms around me.

'I know you are,' he said. 'It's fine, everything's alright. We had a long conversation and I've sorted everything out.'

I pulled away and stared at him. 'What do you mean, you've sorted everything out?' I said slowly.

'Well, I told her that you love her and miss her and you're unhappy not speaking to her. She said she feels exactly the same.' I couldn't speak, I just looked into his face, at those earnest brown eyes staring back at me. 'She was so relieved to hear that you're doing well. She told me how worried she's been about you, she really wants to see you. In fact ...' He tailed off for a moment and looked very pleased with himself. 'When I told her about us, she invited us to come and stay with them next month.'

'Sean,' I began, then stopped. I rubbed my chest; my heart was racing, I felt sick. I sat down at the table and closed my eyes. It felt like all my strength and independence had been suddenly stripped away, and I was naked and exposed. I was a little girl again, quivering in front of Mother and vomiting up strawberries.

'Look, I know you're worried,' Sean said, sitting beside me. 'But it'll be okay. I told her you'd call her tonight. I'm sorry,' he added when I glared at him, 'but I think it's the right thing to do. It'll be okay, I promise. Trust me.'

I did trust Sean, so I called Mother that evening. It went against my better judgement, against everything my body was telling me, but when she answered, Mother was warm and loving, she was understanding and forgiving. She said that Sean sounded lovely, that he'd told her I was hurting; that he understood her pain.

At that point I knew it was game over: she had won. For all those months I hadn't contacted her, hadn't reacted to any of her messages, she'd had no power, but Sean had given her back control. She knew now that she'd got to me. She had hurt me, she had broken me after all.

The conversation with Mother left me in tears. She exclaimed loudly when I told her I'd graduated with a triple distinction. She said how proud of me she was, and the warmth of her praise and affection came flooding back; I knew then that I had missed her, I did still love her. So that was why, when Mother asked if Sean and I would come and visit, I found myself saying, 'Yes, Maman, we'll come.'

* * *

We flew to Nice a few weeks later. My father was on a school trip and would meet us later, so it would be Mother picking us up from the airport. I was terrified to see her, every part of me screaming that this was a bad decision. But Sean didn't agree. He told me that she'd missed me just as much as I'd missed her – more, probably. Anyway, everything was fine now because he'd fixed it.

I saw her immediately, waiting in the arrivals section. She looked older and smaller than I remembered – tired too. Her grey eyes were muted and she'd drawn dark blue liner around them to brighten them. There was a moment, just a few seconds, where I saw her but she hadn't seen me. I watched her peering around to see where we were, standing on tiptoes to look over someone's shoulder. I'd never realised how small she was before. In those few seconds I watched her, she looked vulnerable, and I suddenly felt grateful; she'd taken time out from her day to come and pick us up, she was looking around for us, worried she'd miss us, hoping we were alright. It made me sad to look at her.

Then she saw me and her whole face lit up. She trotted over to us in her floaty blue trousers and white linen tunic and expensive leather sandals, so known to me, so familiar, and she said, 'Oh my little Olive, how I've missed you!' And then her arms were around me and her scent was in my nostrils, white musk and oranges and jasmine, and even though it made me tense up and bad memories came stirring from the depths, she was still my mother, I still loved her. I crumbled in her arms.

Mother drove us to a small village outside Monaco. The restaurant here was one of the best in France, she said, and it was right on the town square so you got a great look at the village. The sun was beginning to set, and we sat outside in dappled light and drank wine and ate slices of cheese. Charming and light and effortless, she was Mother at her best. She got on with Sean like a house on fire – laughing at his jokes, listening intently when he spoke. I thought of all the terrible things she'd said to me over the past few months, but when I looked into her face, I couldn't picture her saying those words.

We didn't mention anything that had happened and I was glad. I wasn't as strong as I thought I was, when she was screaming down the phone to me and I was hanging up on her. Face-to-face, everything changed: I was more scared of her than I thought. Also, I loved her more than I remembered.

When Sean went to the bathroom, it was just Mother and me. I instantly felt uneasy and picked up my menu, pretending I was thinking of ordering more wine. Then I felt her hand on my arm.

'Were you worried to see me, my love?' she asked. I glanced up. She was looking at me fixedly and I stared into her eyes. Close up, they were as grey as ever, and I looked into them, trying to see what was underneath their shiny stillness. What I saw was myself, scared and uncertain, reflecting back at me.

'Yes,' I said finally. 'I was.'

She smiled at me, one of her genuine smiles that made her eyes crease, and took my hand.

'There's no need to be worried. It's all over now, all that nastiness. This is a new start.'

I was so relieved, so grateful to hear her say those words that I could feel sobs rising in my chest. But I gritted my teeth to stop myself from crying and smiled back at Mother. A new start ... well, that sounded nice.

* * *

We had a lovely week with my parents. Looking back now, it stands out as the most enjoyable time I ever spent with Mother – a whole week without conflict or control. I knew what her game was, though: this was her chance to show me how wonderful she was, how much she and my father loved me, how welcoming she'd been to Sean. It felt like a strange version of our old cycle: she'd broken me months ago, back in Chichester, I'd apologised by coming to see her, and by the time I left, we'd be closer than ever. There'd be no doubt that she was the best mother in the world.

But still, it was a special time. Sean and I went from our grotty studio and sagging bed to pristine comfort and long baths and being waited on hand and foot. Mother couldn't do enough for us. We lay on the terrace sunbathing and she brought us pretty plates of antipasti, French cheeses and slices of fresh bread, sweet tomato salads, icy beers for Sean, chilled wine for me. My father chatted happily to Sean about English sport and they cooked together while Mother and I talked about my time at college. We went for late afternoon drives in my little Mini, Sean and me in the front, my parents in the back. They made a big show of strapping themselves in and pretending to be terrified, but afterwards, Mother told me how impressed she was with my driving and I glowed.

She even allowed Sean and me to have some time by ourselves. One day, towards the end of our visit, she put together a picnic, packed an icebox filled with beers, filled up my car with petrol, handed us a map and told us to spend the day exploring Mercantour National Park. We walked around ice-blue lakes, we lay beneath gnarled olive trees, we climbed grey boulders hot from the sun. Before we went home, we had cocktails in a bar overlooking the lake, held hands and watched the last light glimmering on the surface. I felt like I was overflowing with love – for Sean, whom I had grown to love so deeply, and for my parents, whom I also loved, who had made such efforts to welcome him.

Without access to drugs Sean was a different person, and I saw him as a lost boy who'd started a habit that had taken him over. 'You see,' he murmured as we looked out to the lake, 'this is who I really am. The dealing, the coke, that's not me. That's not really me.'

'I know,' I said to him – I thought I did.

* * *

Mother cried when we left. Big fat tears rolled from her enormous grey eyes, and she hugged both Sean and me tightly. She told me to quit my disgraceful pint-pulling job as soon as I got back – I had only a couple of weeks left in Chichester before leaving for university, and she wanted me to enjoy the rest of summer. There'd be no need to get a job while I was at university either, she said – my student finance had all been arranged, tuition paid in full and Father had set up a standing order for living expenses. I'd receive £500 a month, which should be more than enough, but if it wasn't, I shouldn't hesitate to ask for more. Wasn't I lucky, having parents who wanted to help me through university, who didn't want me to be tens of thousands in debt when I graduated? I was lucky – I was, I was.

On the flight home Sean told me he loved me. He told me he loved my parents too, especially my 'Maman', as he'd taken to calling her. Everything was going to be okay now because he loved Maman, and he knew how to deal with her, and he wasn't going to let us disown each other ever again.

'You believe me, don't you, Livvy?' he said in a low voice, his face close to mine.

'Yes,' I said back, squeezing his hand.

Did I believe him? I think I did.

18

TREACHERY

'Pychopaths are incapable of genuinely caring for others, but present themselves as sincere and empathic.'

Everything had changed when we got home. My relationship with Sean turned from a summer fling into the real deal, and he told me that he'd wanted to pull himself together for a long time, and now was his chance. He loved me, he loved my family, he was serious about us He wasn't going to let his drug problem come between us, he was going to get clean.

We made plans for the next year: once I moved into halls in Brighton, Sean would move back home to Birmingham. Away from temptation and friends leading him astray, he'd quit drugs once and for all, get a job, save money, and then he and I would move into a flat for my second year. He took me home to meet his own family, and if I had any remaining reservations about him, they disappeared after that. I adored his mother, Helen, who treated me like an old friend, like an equal. She told me how she had left Sean's father after he cheated on her multiple times; he was controlling and possessive, he emotionally abused her, and she was much better off without him. I loved Sean's stepdad, Stan, who'd been more of a parent to him than his real father had. They were good, decent people and I knew then that this drug nonsense really wasn't him at all – he was above it, like he'd always said.

In September, Sean had an interview in Birmingham. He got the job. It was a sales role – essentially, a glorified door-to-door salesman securing donations for charities. But Sean had a silver tongue, this was what he was best at. His handsome face and easy charm meant that *of course* people opened the door to him, and once he'd given them his spiel, *of course* they reached for their wallets. Whatever he was selling, someone wanted to buy it. Work was his new addiction, and this was one I could get behind.

I moved into halls at Brighton University. Sean drove me to campus and helped me move in. He even stayed for Freshers' Week: we shared my single bed, curled up around each other like shrimps. On the first day, he charmed everyone in halls, and was particularly attentive to the three boys who lived on my floor; he said he wanted to make sure they all knew I was his. By the end of the week, everyone begged him not to go. 'Stay!' they said as I walked Sean to his car. 'No one will know, we don't want you to go!' I smiled to myself, proud that my boyfriend was so charismatic and popular.

After he went back home Sean and I saw each other every weekend. One week, I'd go up to stay with him in Birmingham, the next he'd come down to Brighton. I missed him when he was gone, but I was happy, I loved my course. I learned about photography, web design, film, and I worked hard, even though the first year didn't count towards my final grade.

The other students on my floor were laid-back and friendly and soon we became a tight-knit group. The girls liked to spend time in my room because it was the cosiest: I'd spent a whole day hanging pictures and scarves and arranging fairy lights around my bed. We'd cook dinner in the kitchen and bring it into my room, then we'd get into bed and watch films and talk about our friends and boyfriends, whether we liked our courses and professors, where we saw ourselves in five years' time.

Mother was still on her best behaviour, and we hadn't fought since we'd reunited. She was still a strong presence in my life – she wanted me to call her every other day, and I did – but she seemed to finally understand that I was an adult now. She had to let go.

Sean helped enormously. He seemed to have a sixth sense when it came to Mother; he knew when she was feeling neglected or brewing for a fight, he knew when I needed to phone her. He joked that only he could 'tame the beast', but I didn't like it when he said that. There was scepticism in his voice, like he didn't really believe the 'beast' part. But then he'd only ever seen Mother at her best.

When she heard about his new job Mother asked for Sean's measurements and sent him a bespoke suit and expensive shoes in the post. When winter arrived, she sent him a designer coat – she'd didn't want him getting cold as he went from door to door. It was strange how much she loved him, it unsettled me. Part of me was waiting for her to begin her campaign against him, for her to ruin him, just as she'd done with Lucas and Tim.

During the Christmas holidays she paid for us to go skiing with her and my father in France. This was the first time she ever said anything negative about Sean – just comments about how long he took to get ready in the morning, how long he spent doing his hair. I couldn't argue: Sean was vain. If there was a mirror, he'd be looking into it, pushing back his thick black hair and arching an eyebrow in what he hoped was a droll, sardonic manner.

* * *

It was in halls that I started to see the other side of Sean. I'd seen flashes of another side I didn't like, jealousy and paranoia and aggression, but I always put it down to the coke: it wasn't *really* him. But once I was in Brighton things changed. Sean became convinced I was spending too much time with Tom from my floor. But Tom was just a friend. There was nothing between us at all, but Sean didn't like it. He started being cold to Tom when he visited, then later he became belligerent and aggressive. One night out in the final term of first year, he tried to punch Tom. Thankfully, the other boys got in between them before it kicked off, but things were never the same after that. They'd had enough of Sean's combative, controlling behaviour, they told me. Couldn't I see that he was bad news? No, I said, Sean was a good man. He didn't mean to be like that, this wasn't who he really was. Not *really*. But they didn't agree, and so they wrote me off with him.

I didn't like this new Sean. I didn't understand why he got like this when he wasn't on coke. And he definitely wasn't taking coke when he came to visit, because whenever he was in the shower, I went through all his belongings and checked. When he went to the bathroom, I listened outside for the tell-tale sniff, I watched his eyes and jaw movements as though they fascinated me, but he was clean.

He became secretive, turning his phone over when it flashed up, taking it with him whenever he left the room. One day I asked him if I should be worried. He turned around slowly, looked at me with those big, reproachful brown eyes. How could I ask him such a thing? I knew what his mother had gone through – being cheated on repeatedly by his father, being bullied, controlled – how could I even think Sean would do the same? He had far too much respect for his mother – in fact, for women in general – than to ever do anything like that to me. He would never cheat on me or mistreat me.

And because I trusted him, I believed him.

* * *

I passed my first year of university with straight As, and Mother told me how proud she was. Sean decided he wanted to be in Brighton for the summer, but I was anxious. It was a party town, how would he cope with so many drugs available? It wouldn't be like staying at his parents' house, where he was protected. But it was fine, he insisted, he'd put all that behind him. He was over it – that was the old Sean, new Sean had no time for that. And so he began looking for a new job. He had a friend who worked for a legal recruitment office and he put Sean forward for a role. When I saw Sean's CV, I was startled at how untrue it was.

'You've written that you graduated uni,' I said.

'Yeah.'

'But you didn't.'

'No.'

'Don't you think that's a little risky?' I asked. 'I mean, it's a legal recruitment company, they're going to check up on you. Also, you said you have a year's experience in recruitment, and you don't.'

'Yeah, I know.'

I stared at him. 'Don't you think it's a bit risky, lying like this?'

'Nah,' he said with a shrug. 'Companies never check whether you have a degree or not. And I'll be a great recruiter, it doesn't matter that I don't have experience. Recruitment is about people, and I know how to work people, I know how to manipulate. It won't matter.'

I didn't like what he was saying but I didn't push it. And he was right: it didn't matter. Sean's fraudulent CV got him an interview, and in the interview, he talked his way into the job.

'Told you!' he gloated when he came home. 'I told you!'

'You did,' I conceded. 'Well done.'

It never ceased to amaze me, how Sean could get exactly what he wanted. The word 'no' didn't exist for him. Someone else might be more experienced, someone else might have a more impressive education, but nobody was as smooth-talking as Sean. He lied sombrely, with a crease in his forehead and hurt in his eyes, or he lied flippantly, with a grin and a wink and a raise of his brow. He lied without trepidation, without fear of consequence, without a shred of guilt.

And still I didn't twig.

* * *

Early that summer, I started to get sick. For the first few days it only happened in the morning, and Sean would find me retching over the toilet, gasping and heaving as I vomited. 'It's probably just a bug,' he told me, and I nodded through my tears. It probably was. But then the days went by and I grew sicker and sicker. I couldn't stand up without feeling faint, I was constantly tired; there was a strange throbbing in my belly.

'Could you be pregnant?' Sean asked eventually. I shook my head. At 18, I'd been diagnosed with polycystic ovary syndrome: the doctor had told me that I didn't produce fully formed eggs and I would need IVF if ever I wanted to become pregnant. I wasn't even sure if I wanted children, and part of me felt maybe this diagnosis was the world's way of telling me I shouldn't be a mother. Perhaps I was too broken and damaged; perhaps I would become a parent like my own mother. Even though I knew the chances of getting pregnant were slim to non-existent, I'd still been on the pill, though I'd stopped taking it a few months earlier – it didn't regulate my periods and I didn't want to mess with my ovaries any more than necessary. But after a week of vomiting and exhaustion, Sean came home from work with a pregnancy test for me.

I remember sitting on the edge of the bath, my hands shaking as the blue line appeared. Panic and fear rushed through me, my face felt on fire – but was there part of me that was happy too? I'd been told I would never get pregnant without IVF and here I was, pregnant, naturally, without even trying. I stood up and walked out of the bathroom.

'It's positive,' I said to Sean. My voice sounded flat.

'Positively pregnant or positively *not* pregnant?' he asked.

'Positively pregnant,' I said, and to my surprise his face broke into a smile. He was over the moon. This was our baby, he said, our miracle baby! It would entwine us for life. Marriage didn't mean anything – we could always get a divorce – but having a child would keep us linked for the rest of our lives. And that was what we both wanted, wasn't it?

But it wasn't what I wanted. Hearing Sean say those words made me feel trapped, controlled, and I wasn't ready for a baby. I had two more years of university, I was only 20 – I wasn't ready for any of this.

'Let me tell my mum,' he said. 'She'll be thrilled.'

'No, Sean, please,' I said. 'You can't tell her, I can't do this. We can't do this yet, you know we can't. We're not ready, we're too young. Please listen, please listen to me.'

Eventually he did listen, and we made an appointment at the clinic, where they confirmed my pregnancy and booked in the termination. But Sean didn't stop trying to make me feel guilty. He'd stroke my stomach gently, look down at it wistfully and say, 'Poor baby. Poor, poor baby,' in a hushed, tremulous voice. I felt an almost alien desire to tell Mother. In spite of everything else, I felt this was something she would understand, but Sean said I wasn't allowed to tell her: if he couldn't tell his mother, I couldn't tell mine. Then again, telling people would make it real, and then the baby would be real, and I couldn't let it be: it would hurt too much if it was real.

I had to speak to Mother that night: it was seven o'clock, two days after I'd called her last – those were the rules, as I well knew. I managed to make it through the call without bursting into tears, and Sean sat beside me the whole time to make sure I didn't share our news. Mother moaned about her terrible students, how proud of herself she was that she'd let me study in England, how brilliant her latest sculpture was – really, I just had to see it to appreciate it, words couldn't do it justice – and I nodded as she spoke, knowing she couldn't see me, but needing to do something to motivate me, to give me the strength to get through the call. When she finally asked how I was, I pitched my voice higher, that special voice for Maman, and told her that everything was great, of course. Everything was just fantastic.

My abortion was booked for the next week – the longest week of my life. Sean would wait until he saw me look at him, then he'd sigh and let his eyes trail down to my belly. Tears would pool in the corners of his eyes and he'd shake his head, like the pain was just too much for him to bear. Like I was doing the worst thing possible, a terrible thing, an evil thing, just to spite him. And I *was* doing a terrible thing, wasn't I? I was killing a baby – my baby, *our* baby.

When we arrived at the clinic, Sean was cold and distant as we waited in the little room. I was terrified, aching for some human contact, just the feel of his hand on mine, but he looked determinedly away from my face, staring at the beige walls, at his phone, or else at the invisible swell of my stomach. We waited for hours in that room, and time ticked away. Seven o'clock was approaching, and it was a phone call day for Mother. With trembling hands, I called her, and when she answered, I said, 'Hi Maman!' brightly, but I had a numb feeling in the back of my throat, my voice was quivering, and then before I knew it, I burst into tears.

'Oh, what's wrong, my little Olive?' Mother asked in her warm, soothing voice, and in that moment, I ached for her to wrap her arms around me, for her to sing in my ear like those times she had when I was little.

'I'm pregnant!' I blurted out, and all of a sudden it was real, and I wept harder than ever. Through my tears I saw Sean's body stiffen, his eyes narrow; then he stood up, turned and walked out of the room.

'Pregnant?' Mother repeated, and I could hear the shock in her voice. It all came out then: the clinic, the hospital, how scared I was. But Mother was there for me. She was proud of me, she said, proud that I'd chosen my own future over a baby, proud that I knew I wasn't ready. She calmed me, she made me feel like I could do this. As soon as I recovered, I was to come over and visit her, she said, and she'd look after me and make all the pain go away. But Sean was furious; he couldn't believe I'd told Mother, knowing how desperate he was to tell his own.

Alone, I waited in my seat for the nurse to call me in, and just before she did, Sean rushed back into the room. He kissed me hard on the lips and told me he would be waiting for me when I woke up. Then I was taken into that special room.

And just like that, it was all over.

I woke what seemed like seconds later, and at once everything felt different. The nausea was gone, the strange throbbing in my abdomen had disappeared. My head was mess – but it was over, it was done.

* * *

A few weeks later, university broke up for summer, and we visited my parents again. Mother was still being attentive and loving, rarely criticising me, telling me how proud she was that I'd had the courage to have a termination. She stroked my cheek as she did so; she smiled at me, she patted my hand. *My strong little Olive*, she said. *My grown-up baby girl.*

Sometimes memories flashed into my mind, unannounced and unwelcome, and it was like looking into someone else's life. Mother now wasn't the same Mother who'd hurt me; that was a different time, a different person. I looked at her hands as she sat opposite me, those long, elegant fingers I knew so well, and I remembered all the ways they had hurt me. I saw her hands on my back as she shoved me downstairs, I saw her fingers clasping scissors as she cut off my hair. I saw those hands squirting soap into my pond, those fingers tapping as she typed emails, as she called me bitch, whore, slut. But people could change, after all: she was the proof.

She and my father were so proud of me, they said, that they were going to rent a flat in Brighton for me and Sean to live in for my last two years of university. They didn't want me sharing a shabby student house with six other people, I needed somewhere pretty, quiet; somewhere my professional boyfriend and I could relax. They'd already found a

277

place for us, wasn't that great? A newly decorated duplex in central Brighton that Mother just knew we would love. They would pay the rent and the deposit, and Sean would just pay the bills.

'But Maman, Sean earns good money as a legal recruiter,' I said when he left the room. I was grateful for her offer, but I didn't want her paying my way – I didn't want to give her that control back. 'He gets commission each month, too. He can contribute to rent.'

'No,' Mother said, with a shake of her head. 'I love you both so much that I want to give you a fresh start together in Brighton. I want Sean's wages to go on both of you, not on rent.'

At 20 years old, I would be moving into my very own flat with my boyfriend – it was hard to argue. Mother was caring and sympathetic, she was what I always wanted: a real mother, a mother who loved me. Now I had that, as well as a boyfriend who supported me.

'You're a lucky girl,' Mother said.

I agreed that I was.

Before we went back to England Mother asked us to walk around the house and choose any items of furniture we wanted, she'd then have it shipped over to us.

'This is so kind of you, Maman,' Sean said, and he took my hand and we walked slowly through the house as if it were a showroom. Sean would have taken the lot, but in the end I only asked for a few items: an old chest, some linen bedding, a brown leather chair.

'Here, take this too,' Mother said, coming into the room with one of her paintings. 'You can hang this in your bedroom.' It was a self-portrait. In the painting, Mother was looking down at the viewer, as if she were standing on a stool. She was smiling. Her face was half in shadow and she was strangely formless; the edges of her head blurred into the dark background as if she were part of it. I didn't like the painting at all, but I took it dutifully.

'Thank you,' I said, and she flashed me that glittering smile.

'Now, it's like I'm watching over you.'

* * *

We moved into our new flat and spent time decorating it. We bought window boxes to fill with flowers, we bought matching crockery and oven gloves and scented candles to make our home smell like bergamot and vanilla. Mother said her self-portrait would look good over our bed, but Sean hung it in the toilet.

'She can watch over us in here,' he said with smirk.

Sean was distant and chilly for the next week, but one day I came home from campus to find he'd bought me a special present: a kitten, a perfect Persian kitten with smoky grey fur. I called him Mister. I loved him so much – soft and fluffy like cotton wool, he purred in my lap and followed me around. When I was on the phone to Mother, Mister jumped into my lap and his warm furry presence comforted me. It was unspoken between Sean and me, but we both knew that Mister was our replacement baby, the thing that would fill the raw hole in my heart, the pain I felt so acutely; the pain Sean said he felt too.

Mother was becoming more demanding, but subtly, barely perceptibly. Our phone calls every other day weren't enough now – couldn't I call her every day? It's not like I was busy with a part-time job, was it? She'd spent thousands ensuring I had a lovely place to live and nothing to worry about except work, surely the least I could do was call her every night? She demanded we visit every holiday, every long weekend, and if we were reluctant or wanted to visit Sean's family instead, she made us feel guilty. Didn't we know how much she loved us, how much she wanted to see us? That was why she was paying for our flat – because she loved us so much.

* * *

It took a week for Sean to scope out the drugs in Brighton – New Sean wasn't a match for Old Sean when coke was in sniffing distance, it seemed. I was furious with him but tried hard to let it go; my workload was piling up and I didn't have the energy to fight. Nothing was going to stop me graduating with a good degree, but as my second year progressed, I felt more and more exhausted. Working on weekends was impossible – Sean was all up night doing coke with his new friends. When I tiptoed in at 5am, bleary-eyed and hesitant, to ask if they could please keep it down, Sean rolled his eyes.

'Liv, it's the *weekend*,' he said. 'Get off my back!'

He was so cold, I'd begun to realise. When he was like this, it was as though he was made of stone, like he was my own marble statue: beautiful, but hard, cold-blooded, emotionless.

We began to have arguments, to slam doors and scream at each other. Sean started throwing things in my face: a plate of food, a glass of squash, a mobile phone, a dinner knife. He grabbed my wrists and pinned me down and hissed in my ear that he knew I was fucking around, he knew everything I was doing. I was an unfaithful little bitch, wasn't I? A disgusting cunt, a dirty, cheating whore.

He stalked around the house in a paranoid rage, grinding his teeth and swearing, turning our home upside down as he looked for evidence of my transgressions. He became convinced I had a second, secret phone, from which I called my other lovers, and one night he ordered me to strip so that he could make sure I wasn't hiding it on me. Naked, shivering and humiliated, I stood in front of him as he circled me, and when he was sure I was clean, he looked at me and said, 'For God's sake, put your clothes back on – I don't want to look at *that*!'

I cried myself to sleep while he did lines of coke off the stove, I sobbed into my pillow when he didn't come home. But then in the mornings, he came in from the kitchen or home from his bender, climbed gently into bed with me, put his arms around me and buried his face in my neck, saying, 'I'm sorry, Livvy. I love you so much, I'm so sorry.' And then when I got home from uni that day, he'd bought me flowers and tidied up the house and ran me a bath, and he said he was taking me for dinner, and then after we'd see the latest *Harry Potter* film. We'd have such a lovely night, it'd be so special. It'd be like old times.

I tried to be reasonable about it, I tried to rationalise. Flying into rages and being controlling was how Mother had always been with me – it didn't mean that he didn't love me. Besides, it was just fuelled by drugs. Once Sean sobered up, he walked me to the garden centre, because he knew it was the place I loved most, and he bought me new packs of seeds for my window box and potted plants to place around the house. We stopped for ice creams on the way back and ate them in the park, and he stroked my hand and told me how much he loved me, how no one would ever love me like he did.

I believed him and I loved him, so I forgave him, again and again. Again and again, I lied to Mother over the phone, pitching my voice higher and fixing a smile on my face. I told her all about the lovely weekend Sean and I had just had, leaving out the parts where he spent £500 on coke and pinned me against the wall by my neck.

He was always good with Mother – when he was sober, anyway. Every time I sensed she was itching for a fight or was about to turn on me, Sean knew what to do. He called her up with a cheery 'Hey, Maman!' and told her how much he missed her and how he couldn't wait to see her. Sometimes he took the phone into our bedroom and shut the door while they talked. I didn't like that – he had a way with her, just as he had with me. He could pull me back to him after every paranoid coke-fuelled binge, and he did the same to Mother; every time she teetered on the brink of madness, he hauled her back.

They had a strange relationship, I couldn't quite put my finger on it. Though smitten with each other, at the same time they were competitive, underhand. When we stayed with my parents, Sean and Mother had long talks – sometimes they even went for walks together. My father and I raised our eyebrows at each other and smiled, but I wondered what they were talking about. Later, Mother would tell me how Sean just understood her – her pain, her suffering. He just *got* her. I didn't like hearing her say that. It made me remember when I met Sean, how he'd just got me too.

Mother might have loved Sean but that didn't stop her duplicity. She doted on him to his face, she bought him expensive clothes and shoes, she told him how she couldn't wish for a better future son-in-law. But when he wasn't looking, she pulled the hair away from my ear and whispered nasty things: she said he was vain and obsessed with his appearance, that he was just using them for money. It was the same with Sean: he was adoring to Mother's face, but behind her back, he told me she was trying to come between us, that she was using money to manipulate us. Part of me was glad he saw through Mother's tactics, but another part felt resentful: Sean was bitching about Mother when she'd been so generous to him. It was like they were vying for who had more control over me, and I didn't like that one bit.

* * *

My second year at university was a blur of lectures and essays and deadlines, of fighting with Sean and reuniting with him, of making sure Mother didn't feel neglected. The friends I'd made in halls didn't want to see me anymore because they didn't like Sean; I met up with them individually once or twice but it wasn't the same. I made other friends from my course, but while we studied together, we never went out socially. I stopped going for drinks with my friends, stopped going out almost entirely – it wasn't worth it, all the hassle and grief that came after, all Sean's paranoia and accusations and aggression.

I worked harder than ever, writing essays until the early hours. When Sean went on his benders, I tried to stop worrying and used that time to study instead. I made myself a cup of tea, tidied up my desk and brought Mister into the room and stayed up all night working. Even though things with Mother were better, I was single-minded in my pursuit of success: a good degree didn't just mean a good job, it was an escape.

I finished my second year with a first, and Mother rewarded me with lavish gifts and expensive shopping trips when we visited in summer. I told her I didn't want any presents – all I wanted from her was praise and affection – but she insisted.

'I want to spoil you,' she said, patting my cheek. 'Think of it as a belated 21st birthday present. It breaks my heart not seeing you more, you've grown up so quickly.'

Mother fussed over Sean and me the way she had the previous two summers, but things were different this year. She was beginning to tire of Sean, I could tell instantly. When he wasn't looking, she scanned him with that cool stare of hers, she glowered at his arm around me. She chatted to him in her silken voice, she laughed merrily at all his jokes, but I could see the irritation glinting behind her icy smile. When Sean was cooking with my father or sunbathing on the terrace, she followed me around the house like a shadow, whispering how ungrateful he was, what bad company he was being, how he didn't really care about her. I nodded silently as she spoke – she used to say all those things about me.

That summer, things were different with Sean and me, too. Mother again packed a picnic for us and told us to go for a drive in Mercantour Park, but it wasn't the same as before. We held hands and kissed, but I was detached and reserved. Sean said I was too quiet, I was distant, I didn't want to have sex anymore. I denied it, but it was true and he knew it.

He started becoming more vocal to my parents: he spoke loudly at dinner about how much he loved me, how he was going to propose once I graduated, how he couldn't wait to become a real part of our family. From across the table I smiled at him primly. I still loved Sean but it was exhausting being with him. He was always clean when we stayed with my parents and I was glad of that, even though he did drink my father's wine cellar dry. But I couldn't forget the other Sean – the side I didn't like, the side I was afraid of. When he kissed me, I remembered those times I hadn't wanted sex but he got on top anyway; when he held a friend's baby and cooed, I remembered how he threw me on the floor and choked me.

He'd let his charming mask slip off and shatter, and there was no putting it back on, no matter how hard he tried.

* * *

My third and final year started. Sean was back on drugs, back to his old ways. Our relationship turned toxic, a whirlwind of screaming matches, smashed plates, bruised arms and expensive make-up dinners. Sean had become more and more controlling: he didn't like me going out, he didn't like me seeing friends. Only once did I defy him: I went for end-of-term drinks with friends from my course, even though he'd told me not to. He arrived at the bar ten minutes after me, dark-faced with anger, and physically dragged me away. I tried to forget the shocked, staring eyes of my friends, the way they looked at me with pity. I remembered my invisible curtain, how I used to draw it to shield myself from Mother; now I drew it against Sean too.

Mother was becoming difficult again. I knew she was still scared by what happened two years ago, when she'd almost lost control, but she just couldn't help herself. I was becoming too big for my boots – someone had to bring me down a peg or two. Slowly but surely, I began disappointing her again: I didn't ring when I said I would, I hadn't emailed her enough that week, the tone of my email wasn't warm enough. Every day I had to call her, even though I was drowning in work.

Even without a job I was getting behind. Sean started staying out all night and I stopped being able to sleep. I lay on my back, staring at the ceiling, thinking about where he was, who he was with, what he was doing; or else I lay on my side and faced the empty space where his body should have been.

In the day, when I worked on my dissertation, I was distracted and lethargic. I cuddled Mister and stroked him and cried into his velvet fur.

Whenever I tried speaking to Sean about his addiction he got angry. He'd started to blame his habit on Mother: he needed to get high because she was stressing him out, she was too demanding and controlling, he just needed to forget his problems. What my parents hadn't realised was that by paying our rent, Sean's disposable income had tripled, and he now had more money to spend on all the things he loved – cocaine and alcohol.

I became more and more insular, retreating into the person I was when I was a teen: aloof, remote, unfeeling. At times I wanted to leave Sean, other times I couldn't see a way out. Our lives had become entirely intertwined: we shared a flat, a cat, a car, we loved each other's families. And still, I loved him. When he was Old Sean, the Sean I'd fallen in love with, it was like I couldn't live without him. Before Sean, Mother was unbearable, but with him she was manageable. I would run towards the precipice but Sean would drag me back to him, just as Mother had always done.

* * *

Somehow I managed to graduate from university with a first. I got the highest grade of the year and rang Mother with shaking fingers.

'Well done!' she said. 'I knew you could do it. I'm so glad I supported you financially so you didn't have to get a job. No doubt that was the reason you did so well.'

It felt surreal, university being over. The past few years seemed like a blur; three years had passed in a flash. It had been harder than I thought but I'd done it, I'd fought through the obstacles and escaped unscathed. Or that's what I thought.

My relationship with Sean was at breaking point. He spent more time out than ever before, and he was evasive and aggressive when I asked where he'd been. One day, at the beginning of summer, I was sitting at home with Mister, waiting for Sean to come home. We had no cat food in the house, I'd tried calling him but his phone was off. Mister wound himself around my legs and mewed piteously.

'Okay, I'll go and get you some food,' I said, leaning down to stroke his fluffy head. I went to our local supermarket and bought cat food for Mister and some ready meals for us – I was too tired to cook, but I wanted there to be food in the house when Sean came back. I walked the long way home along the seafront, enjoying the sun on my face and trying to feel positive. It was the beginning of summer, I'd just graduated, I was 22, young and free. I remember taking deep breaths of sea air, hoping that somehow it would cleanse me, freshen me, blow away the darkness that seemed to follow me.

And that's when I saw him: Sean.

Sean, but it couldn't be Sean because he was with another woman, a blonde woman. He had his arm over her shoulder, he was holding her, he was kissing her. It couldn't be Sean, except it was. I stood there staring at him, at him and this voluptuous, red-lipsticked stranger, and my stomach throbbed. Blood was pulsing in my ears, roaring like the sea. I wanted to turn and flee; to run, to get away from him as fast as I could, but my feet were glued to the floor, my legs were like lead. I stared at him as wave after wave of horror rolled over me: it couldn't be, it just couldn't be.

But it was, it was.

He didn't come home until midnight. I was waiting up for him. I'd planned what I was going to say but when he walked in, I couldn't think what it was. I wanted to say something cutting, to make him feel some of the pain and incredulity that I was feeling now, but my mouth stayed shut, my arms tightly folded.

'What's up with you?' he said as he kicked off his shoes and sank down onto the sofa.

'I saw you,' I managed to choke out.

'Saw me where?' he said casually, without a hint of concern on his face.

'Who is she?' I asked.

'Who's who?' he shot back.

We stared at each other.

'Sean, stop it,' I said eventually. 'I saw you. Tonight. With her. Kissing her.' I tried to keep my voice level, but it was shaking.

'Ah,' is what he said.

'How long has this been going on? And don't lie to me.'

'A while.' Then he looked at me accusingly: 'You weren't giving me any attention.'

'How long?'

'I dunno,' he said. 'Three months, four months.'

I couldn't believe what I was hearing. Four months behind my back and I hadn't even realised. Shame rose in me like bile. I wanted to scream and shout, to cry and throw things. Instead I said, 'I want you out! You can stay tonight, but tomorrow you need to go.'

'Okay,' he said with a shrug, like my words meant nothing to him, like *I* meant nothing to him. The next morning, I went for a long walk along the seafront; I had told Sean when I came back he needed to be gone. I walked for miles, thinking and crying silently to myself, wondering whether to call Mother. I so desperately wanted to be babied, to have someone tell me they loved me and it wasn't my fault and everything would be alright. I knew I was young, but I didn't feel it anymore: I felt overripe, past my best, like shrivelled fruit fermenting in a jar. No one would love me like Sean did. Why had he done this?

When I came home, hours later, Sean had gone, and so had all his things. He'd taken everything we'd bought together: the furniture, the framed posters, the kitchen gadgets. All that remained was my own belongings and the few items we'd taken from my parents' home: the chest, the bedding, the old leather chair. *The painting of Mother, watching over me with a smile*. I flung myself onto the bed where Mister was curled up, sleepy and oblivious, and I cried like my heart had broken.

It was my fault, I knew that. I should have known better, I should have realised sooner. I opened myself up to his coldness, I allowed him to possess me, I let his words melt sweetly over me. I tried to warm his marble stillness, but it was too hard, too cold, and now I was battered and bruised from the effort.

19

DOMINION

'To the psychopath, strangers are disposable;
family members are possessions.'

When I called Mother the next day to tell her what happened, I could hear the excitement in her voice. She said all the right things – 'Oh darling, how terrible,' and 'It's his loss, I'll tell you that now' – but I knew what she was thinking. Sean had gone: this was her time to take back control. 'I'm getting on the next flight,' she told me grandly. 'Maman will make it all better.' When I asked if my father could come too, she said no, this was a women-only time.

When she arrived the first thing she did was have the locks changed; then she took me to dinner. For the duration of the meal she told me how she'd always disliked Sean. The boy was a sponge, a sneak, she said. He was a user, a parasite. She'd always known he was a liar.

'Why didn't you tell me?' I asked her. I felt so stupid. My friends in halls had been right all along – Sean was bad news – and apparently everyone had seen it but me.

'I didn't want to hurt you,' she said, looking surprised. 'I couldn't bear to hurt you.'

'Well, it's for the best,' I said. 'He wasn't good for me anymore. I feel drained. Like he's taken everything from me, he's drained me right out. I feel like a ghost.'

'Is that right?' Mother said, sipping her wine.

'Yes, like half a person.'

'I see,' she said, watching me carefully. 'I see.'

The next day, she took me shopping to replace all the things Sean had taken. 'Never fear, Maman is here,' she said whenever she bought a new item for the house. It was like she wanted me to make a mental note of every single thing she did, everything she bought. How loving she was, to fly from France to console her heartbroken daughter; how generous to buy new things for the flat. No one could ever say she wasn't the best mother in the world. I thanked her profusely, but I begged her not to buy anything. I told her that now I'd graduated, I was going to get a job, I wanted to be fully independent.

But Mother just laughed and said, 'You're not earning yet, my love.'

* * *

When Mother left, I phoned up to put the house and the bills in my name. That's when I realised the mess Sean had left me in. He'd somehow managed not to pay the water bill since we moved in, and I was £1,500 in arrears. I was also saddled with an £800 gas and electricity bill, a £200 estate agent's fee and a £700 phone contract bill taken out in my name. When I went to the bank to get a credit card, I was told I couldn't have one. Why? Because of my terrible credit rating. Sean had taken out a £2,000 loan in my name and had racked up a £2,500 debt on a credit card, also in my name. When I deleted his profiles and accounts from my laptop I found a Craigslist advert he'd set up, looking for a 'Mature older woman for fun sex, no strings'. I wept with fury and humiliation. My parents had given Sean everything: a lovely flat (rent-free), new furniture and clothes, expensive holidays and shoes. All he had to do was pay the bills and love me. Instead, he'd cheated on me and controlled me, lied to me and stolen from me. At 22, I had a negative credit rating – I was destitute.

Mother didn't seem shocked when I told her. 'What a mess,' she said. 'We'll pay off the bills, of course.' I felt like my hands were tied: I didn't want her help, I couldn't bear the idea of being indebted to her, but if the bills weren't paid, I would have to move out. I knew I could get a crummy flatshare with six other people but I so desperately wanted to stay in my little flat with Mister. It was home, even though it was bare and I was alone. I couldn't stand any more upheaval, any more moves: all I wanted was to get a job and start earning.

'I'll pay you back,' I told her. 'Every penny you give me from now on, I promise I'll pay it all back.'

'Don't be silly,' she said briskly. 'I like helping you.'

'But I don't want to be helped anymore,' I said. 'I'm 22, I want to pay my own way. You've done enough for me, now it's my turn. As soon as I get a job, I'll start paying you back. I'll set up a standing order.' I needed her to hear what I was saying, to acknowledge that this was just a loan, to get me out of the mess Sean had left me in.

But she just laughed, squeezed my shoulder and said, 'You're a funny little thing.'

* * *

That August, I got a job, my first proper job. I was now an SEO assistant working at a digital marketing agency. I loved my job and I was good at it, and every time I sat down at my desk in the morning, I felt a flash of triumph, despite my misery: I was a grown-up, I was professional. I'd done it! Despite her protests, I started paying Mother back in large instalments. After paying rent and bills and Mother, I had barely anything to live on, but I didn't care: I was moving forward, independent. Soon, I would owe nothing.

Despite how he treated me, I knew I still loved Sean. In the nights I worried about him, stroking Mister and trying not to feel sorry for myself. But then one day in September I came home from work and he was waiting on the front step. Thinner than I remembered, his face was puffy and dough-like. He looked tired, dishevelled, and his big dark eyes were dull.

'I'm sorry,' he said as I approached the door. 'I'm so sorry.'

'You need to go,' I said, fumbling for my key and avoiding his eye. I couldn't bear to look at him, at his rumpled clothes and hopeless, staring eyes.

'Olivia, please,' he said, standing up. 'I'm so sorry. I'm sorry for everything. I fucked up. What I did was unforgivable, I'll never forgive myself, I hate myself.'

'Good!' I said icily, and his face crumpled. I had to make myself say the words – it hurt my heart to see him.

'I'm so sorry,' he repeated, looking at the floor and shaking his head. 'But you have to believe me …' He looked up again and his face was desperate. 'All the things I did … it wasn't me, it wasn't really me, it was the coke. It makes me into someone I'm not and I hate it. I don't want to do it anymore, I want to get clean. I want to be with you, I love you.'

'Too late,' I said.

I tried to get the key in the lock, but he moved in front of me.

'Please,' he said, and now tears were rolling from his wounded brown eyes. 'Olivia, I have no one else, I have nowhere to go. I can't stay with my friends because then I'll never get clean, you know that. Please, just let me come in for a little bit, let me explain.'

I knew I shouldn't, but I let him upstairs: we would talk, he could have a cup of tea and a bite to eat and a shower, and that would be it. Then he needed to go. He agreed readily, but of course he never left. He told me how sorry he was, how much he'd missed me; that he'd lost his job the day before: he'd fallen asleep on the toilet after one of his benders, and when staff opened the door to check he was okay, there were lines of coke on top of the cistern. He'd realised – far too late, he knew – that cocaine was ruining his life. It had already cost him his job and the woman he loved, and he wasn't going to let it continue. It had turned him into someone he wasn't, paranoid and possessive – but he wasn't like that really, not *really*, and I knew that, I knew who he really was. I knew the real Sean.

'Sean,' I said once he'd finally stopped speaking. 'How can you expect me to trust you? You cheated me in as many ways as a person can be cheated.'

'I know,' he said miserably, dropping his head. 'But it's different now, I promise it's different.'

'Why is it different?'

'Because I've asked for help,' he said, and he raised his head and looked at me steadily.

'How?'

'I've spoken to Narcotics Anonymous and set up meetings,' he said.

'Good.'

Then he tilted his head back and blinked at me.

'And I've spoken to your mother.'

For a moment I couldn't understand what he'd said. I stared at him, hostile and unbelieving. He smiled at me.

'I told her everything this morning. About the coke, how it took me over.'

'Why?' I blurted out. 'Why tell her? You know how much she hates drugs!'

'I needed to,' he replied. 'I needed her to know the real reason I did these terrible things. Why I mistreated you, why I got us into so much debt, why I panicked and ran. Maman knows me, just like you do. She knows who I really am. And that's why she's being so supportive. She wants us back together.'

I shook my head. I couldn't understand what he was saying. He was lying – surely, he was lying, surely, Mother wouldn't want me back with Sean after everything he'd done – but when I called her, she said it was true.

Of course she forgave Sean – he'd confessed, hadn't he? He was trying to get help. Who was I to judge him? He'd made mistakes and he'd owned up to them, and that took balls. He wanted to make things right now, and I needed to let him.

'Maman, he cheated on me for *months*,' I whispered, as Sean stroked Mister on the sofa and pretended not to hear.

'So?' she shot back. 'He was troubled, he had issues. He was an addict. Besides, you weren't giving him enough attention, you were hardly ever putting out.'

'Maman!' I said. 'He took out loans in my name! He stole from me.' I knew it sounded petty to list all the bad things Sean had done, but these weren't petty things, were they?

'I think you'll find that he stole from *me*,' she sniped. 'And I've forgiven him. Now it's your turn.'

I sat down heavily. I knew she loved the fact that Sean had confided in her, that they'd had a long talk behind my back, discussing our relationship and sex life. If I knew Mother, she would see it as some kind of victory that Sean had been honest with her when he'd lied to so many others. it would have brought them closer together.

'Sean and I spoke for two hours today,' she continued, and now I could hear the triumph in her voice. 'He told me everything, Olivia. *Everything*. It's time to be the bigger person. You need to forgive him and help him. He needs your support if he's to get clean.'

I looked across the room at Sean. He was sitting silently on the sofa, stroking Mister and gazing at the floor. I loved him, I'd missed him. I'd missed his buffer from Mother, and I'd missed the good times, when he was Old Sean, when we would laugh for hours over nothing and cook for each other and go for walks, holding hands. But I wasn't sure if Old Sean existed anymore – maybe he was just a figment of my imagination. Sean was capable of things I never imagined: not just cheating on me but lying to me, creeping behind my back for months. Applying for loans and credit cards in my name, never paying bills, incurring thousands of pounds of debt and hiding it all from me. I didn't know who that Sean was. Had Old Sean even existed, or did I just want to believe he did? Perhaps he was the same as Mother, and that's why they had such a special connection: with her, you saw only what she wanted you to see; if you saw anything else it was because you yourself wanted to see it.

'So, I'm happy to pay off all the debts and bills Sean wrote up,' she continued. 'But only on the condition that you take him back, that you're a team again.'

I rubbed my forehead. I was finding it hard to process what Mother was saying. Was this bribery, was it blackmail? 'I'll call you tomorrow, Maman,' I managed to say, and hung up. Sean came over and sat beside me, Mister in his arms.

'I know you don't trust me,' he began. 'I wouldn't trust me either. But please, just give me a chance. I'm going to do it this time, Olivia, I really am. I'm going to go to my meetings and get a new job and get clean, and make it all up to you. Please let me, please.'

'I need to think about this,' I said. 'You can stay on the sofa for now.'

I didn't let Sean back in our bedroom for a month – it felt like the only bit of control I had left. I'd been set on moving on without him, moving forwards by myself, but now I couldn't see a way out. He'd wormed his way back in and got Mother onside, and now I was trapped.

'No one will love you like I do,' he said.

'No one will love you like Sean does,' Mother said.

I nodded and tried to believe it.

* * *

Things were good for the first few months. Sean got a new recruiter job and attended his addiction meetings diligently. If he went out with his new work friends, he would have one drink and come home. He was attentive and affectionate, cooking dinner for me every night, running baths and tidying the flat and telling me how much he loved me, how grateful he was that I'd believed in him. The thing was, I didn't believe in him. I was proud he'd been clean for months now and seemed serious about it, but I didn't trust him anymore. I couldn't forget his total lack of shame when confronted about the other woman.

'Ah,' he'd said, before blaming it on me.

I couldn't get his face out of my mind: how cold he'd looked, how emotionless. This man who'd been at my side for more than three years, who said he loved me, hadn't felt the slightest bit of guilt at what he'd done, no matter how much he professed the opposite now.

I managed to track down the girl I'd seen him with. I sent her a polite message on Facebook, telling her that I wanted to have a chat with her, woman to woman. She agreed. We talked for half an hour, and I learned that she was called Jess, and as far as she was concerned Sean had been her boyfriend for six months. She'd had no idea I existed until he broke things off with her the previous month, telling her he'd got back together with his ex-girlfriend. I learned that Jess and Sean had gone for romantic weekends away when he'd told me he was going home; that she'd stayed over at my house ('Sean's house', as she called it) when I was visiting my parents. The last time Sean and I went to Monaco, Jess had lived in our house and looked after Mister. Sean, she said, was a pathological liar. He'd lied about everything to her, lied so smoothly and so professionally, and she'd devoured every word. 'You know there were other girls too, don't you, Olivia?' she said before we hung up. 'Oh yes, there were others, and lots of them.'

I thanked Jess for her honesty, telling her I didn't need to know about the other women. I didn't tell Sean I'd spoken to her. Confused and overwhelmed, I didn't trust anyone. The only person I trusted was myself, and I decided that for now I was going to keep my cards close to my chest. When I thought of Jess and Sean together, of her lying in my bed with my cat, of him taking her away for intimate weekends while I sat at home, oblivious, I felt fury like I'd never felt before, but I also felt broken, like I'd been flattened, annihilated by his betrayal. So I hardened my heart – I wouldn't think about it.

The one area of my life that was going well was work. I'd become close to one of the writers at work, Sofia, and in the day, I could forget about Mother and Sean as we talked and laughed at our desks. Because Sean was on his best behaviour, I started to go out again, not worrying about whether he'd get jealous or possessive. I could see his face when I came back from an evening out, the way his mouth was twitching, how desperate he was to ask questions and prod and probe, but he knew he couldn't. Not yet, anyway.

Sofia and I started going out for drinks, and one night I opened up to her about Sean. I hadn't told anyone apart from Mother – I was too ashamed, too humiliated. I remember as I told her all the things Sean had done that her eyes grew bigger and bigger: the cheating, the lying, the way he'd controlled me. I told her about the loans and credit cards in my name, about the things he had done before – the dealing and stealing and the criminal convictions. I told her how I knew, no matter what he said, that he didn't feel any shame for what he'd done; that if she met Sean, she'd love him.

'I'm not being funny, Olivia,' Sofia said. 'But he sounds like a psychopath.'

'Really?' I said lightly, although something jabbed in my gut. 'If you think that, you should hear more about my mother!' I said this with a laugh, like it was a joke. Sofia had met Mother that summer when she'd visited the office, and she'd liked her, as everyone did when they first met her. But I wasn't ready to tell the truth about Mother yet. Besides, a psychopath? Psychopaths were murderers, rapists and serial killers. They weren't people like Sean, who were just deceitful and vulnerable and messed up.

But I began to be more open about Sean with my friends. I spoke to Faya and Isabel, whom I'd barely seen in the past year. I didn't tell them everything, only about the cheating, but that was enough.

'I don't understand why you're still with him,' Faya said.

'I'm starting to give up on you,' Isabel told me.

'But he's sorry,' I told them. 'He's sorry and he wants to change. And no one will ever love me like Sean loves me.'

* * *

It all went wrong just before Christmas 2013. We were staying with my parents for the holidays, and Sean and I would be flying to France after work on the Friday. I had to work in London that day, so the plan was that he would bring our suitcases to the airport after work and we'd meet there. That Thursday night, he went for Christmas drinks with his work.

'Try to be home by midnight,' I told him. 'You still haven't packed and we need to be fresh for tomorrow.'

'I'll be home by 11,' he said with a smile. But that night he didn't come home. I waited up until two, trying to phone him, but his phone was off. When I woke up in the morning, he still wasn't home: his phone was still off. I knew what had happened; someone at work would have had cocaine. I knew Sean would have had a drink and found it impossible to say no. He would have had a line, then he would have got the dealer's contact details from his friend and bought more himself. I called him throughout the day and finally, when I was on the train to the airport, he picked up. There was no sorry, no explanation – he'd just needed to get fucked, and I didn't have the energy to argue.

'I've already packed your suitcase for you,' I told him. 'You just need to pick it up – and my case – and get the train to the airport.'

'I don't think I'm going to come,' he said.

I was silent on the other end of the line. I could hear him breathing. When I hung up, he didn't ring back. On the train I burst into tears, which was strange as I didn't feel upset. I felt tense, taut; like I was being pulled in too many directions, like I was stretched out too thinly, or rolled out flat like dough. I was going to break at any moment.

I cried again when I arrived at the airport, when I went through security with only my handbag. I cried on the flight, turning my head away from the other passengers and looking out the window so they wouldn't see my tears. I cried when we landed, when I saw my parents waiting for me in arrivals, when I flung myself into Mother's outstretched arms. I told them what had happened on the drive home. My father was furious, I'd never seen him like that before.

'You need to end this, Olivia,' he told me. 'Enough is enough.'

'I know!' I sobbed. 'I know!'

Mother was oddly quiet.

The next day, over breakfast, I asked my father if he would come home with me in the New Year to help me kick Sean out – I didn't think he was going to go quietly this time.

'Of course,' he said, 'of course I'll come.'

'Let's not be hasty,' Mother said. 'Let's not talk about anyone moving out. This was just a setback – Sean fell off the wagon, that's all. It happens.'

Father and I stared at her.

'Jose, she can't get back with him after this,' my father said. He looked baffled.

'It's no big deal,' Mother said. 'He slipped up just the once, he's sorry. I've already spoken to him.'

'When?' I asked, startled.

'This morning,' Mother said, 'and last night too.' She smiled that smile I hated. 'I've fixed everything. Sean's devastated at what happened, but he's going to move past it. It's almost the New Year, everything will be different once you've put all this behind you.'

'Maman,' I started. I couldn't believe what I was hearing. 'You know this isn't just about the coke, don't you? It's everything else, it's *him*. You don't know what he's done.'

'What's he done?' my father asked, looking worried. So I told them everything. I told them how controlling Sean was, how terrifying he could be; I told them about the verbal abuse, the physical abuse, all those times I locked myself in the bathroom because I was afraid of his rages, all those times he'd kicked the door down and dragged me out. I told them about Jess, what she'd said about the other girls, how she said Sean was a pathological liar, how he'd looked me in the eye when he knew my heart was breaking and he hadn't felt a thing. Mother sighed and rolled her eyes like I was being a drama queen.

'Everyone has faults,' she said. 'What's there to gain by listing his?'

I could tell my father was angry, and later, I heard them arguing downstairs. My father wanted me to break up with Sean, he wanted him out of my life once and for all. Mother said it wasn't an option. But this time my father held as firm as he could, and that infuriated Mother. She screamed at him that this was all his parents' fault – that because Granny and Grandad had always tried to split them up, my father didn't know what love was. He didn't know that they needed to fight for Sean the way *he*, my weak, spineless father, should have fought for Mother, all those years ago. But this time he wouldn't make the same mistake, she'd be sure of that.

I knew then that by uniting us in September, Mother had got what she wanted: finally, she was a part of us, the third wheel in our relationship. She was our fairy fucking godmother, picking up the pieces of our broken relationship and gluing us back together again, even though none of our pieces fitted together anymore. We would be indebted to her forever. There was another reason too, but I couldn't quite see it then.

Mother spent much of that holiday in secret communication with Sean. She whispered to him on the phone, coming into the living room where I was watching TV with my father to mouth 'It's Sean!' and then stepping back out again. They wrote to each other incessantly, and she delighted in showing me their long email thread. When I asked to see what she'd written, she covered up the screen with a smile and said, 'No, it's private,' or 'Nosy, it doesn't concern you!' By the time I went home after New Year it was agreed that I would take Sean back. Mother would come and visit in mid-January to check up on us, and Sean was sober again and ready to get back on track. My father was silent and grim-faced, but Mother said I wasn't to think about the bad things that had happened, I was to think of the good times, and how no one would love me like Sean did.

I returned home to a spotless house and a perky, apologetic Sean. I let him wrap his arms around me, I let him kiss my neck, I let him climb on top. I closed my eyes and drew my curtain across him. I knew what I had to do, but I was frozen, impotent: I wanted to act, but I was afraid to.

I went back to work and told Sofia what had happened over the holidays. 'This is it now, right?' she asked. 'You won't consider taking him back after this, surely?'

'I've already taken him back,' I said, and she stared at me. 'It's not as simple as you think,' I added defensively. 'My mother wants us back together.'

'Your *mother*?' she said. 'Your *mother*?'

'Yes,' I said, looking away from her and back to my screen. I could feel her eyes on me.

'I need to tell you something,' Sofia said. 'I'm still your friend, and I'm here for you. But you need to know that I'm seriously losing respect for you.'

'Okay,' I said, like the words didn't sting. When I spoke to Isabel later, she said the same thing – she too was losing respect for me. Her words also hurt, but they were true; I'd lost respect for myself too. I wavered between blind fury and an awful, noiseless grief, but I still didn't know what I was grieving for. My relationship with Sean? My trust in Mother? My non-existent self-respect? I called Sean's mother, Helen and wept down the phone to her.

'Olivia,' Helen said to me in a low voice. 'Sean's my son and I love him. But I also love you. If I were your mother ...' She paused and I held

my breath. 'I'd tell you to run a mile and never look back. Sean's not …
he's not good for you. You'll be better off without him, I know that. Better
and happier and safer without him.'

I scrolled through my social media account and I looked at the
pictures of Sean and me: cuddled up with Mister on the sofa, sitting in
the sun with Mother in Monaco, laughing with friends in Brighton. It
was all a lie, I realised, just as false as the photos of happy families that
hung on our walls back home. I looked at Sean's account and it was the
same, but worse. That photo of me and Sean looking pretty in a fancy
restaurant? That was one of our make-up meals after he threw plates at
me while I cowered in the corner. That photo of Sean at work drinks in
a designer suit, the one he'd captioned 'Success'? His entire outfit was
bought by Mother, and hours later, he'd fallen asleep by our toilet in a
puddle of his own vomit. I was tired of it all. I was tired of living a lie, tired
of avoiding the truth.

A few days before Mother's visit, I came home to find Sean sitting in
the kitchen in his boxers, a ring of dried-up coke in each nostril and long,
fat lines on the table. He hadn't lasted two weeks this time. I looked at
him. 'Sofia says you're a psychopath,' I said. I don't know what made me
say it; I'd tried not to even think about it since she first articulated it. Sean
glanced up at me, his eyes dull, his face bored.

'Course I fucking am!' he said. 'Jesus, how could you not have known?'

It wasn't a question. I heard what he'd just said and I knew I should
be feeling things, but still I felt numb. I went into my bedroom, closed
the door, opened my laptop and googled 'psychopath'. Then I read
about the hallmarks of a psychopath, the warning signs you're caught
up with one: pathological lying, superficial charm, need for stimulation,
grandiose sense of self, cunning and manipulative, lack of remorse,
shallow emotional response, callousness, poor behavioural controls,
early behaviour problems, sexual promiscuity, impulsivity, failure to
accept responsibility, juvenile delinquency, criminal tendencies.

As I read the symptoms, these terrible traits I recognised so well, something strange happened to my body. A feeling of coldness ran over me: something raw, something glacial, flooding through my blood like ice; but at the same time there was heat, wave after wave of it, rolling up through my chest and over my face until I felt like I was burning alive. I remember lying back on my bed and shaking, putting the palms of my hands on my cheeks, and it hurt, it actually hurt, this combination of fire and ice, this pain, my shame, my blindness for not knowing, for not seeing. I'd been foolish, sightless, peering through the darkness without ever wanting to truly see. But now I saw.

'Psychopath. *Psychopath* ...' I whispered the word to myself and it hissed around my room, snake-like, stealthy. It made me think of forked tongues and glittering eyes, but also of Mother's long fingers, her shiny white teeth, the way she tossed her head back as she laughed. The way she clapped her hands and weaved her body, the way her mouth quivered when she told her lies, the way her eyes slid slyly over to me afterwards – jubilant, defiant, remorseless.

The psychopath I'd just read about was Mother. It was also Sean, but she was the stronger one, shrewd and resolved and calculated. Sean hurt me because he was selfish and weak and greedy: he wanted to screw other girls, so he cheated; he wanted coke, so he lied; he wanted money, so he stole. Mother hurt me because she simply wanted to – that was the difference. She was always in control, unlike Sean, who was weak; weak enough to allow cocaine to shatter his mask, to ruin all his hard work pretending to be someone he wasn't. They saw themselves in each other, but she was the one who held the power.

I lay on my bed until I stopped shaking. I took deep, slow breaths until my heart stopped pounding, then I stood up, smoothed back my hair, and went back into the kitchen. Sean was sitting where I'd left him.

'I want you to leave,' I said, and my voice sounded like it was coming from someone else. 'When I come home tomorrow, I want you gone. Is that understood?' I could see him thinking, wondering whether he had the energy to fight, to persuade, to cajole, to drag me back as he always had – as Mother always had. He sighed, then shrugged, and I knew there was no fight left in him.

'Okay,' he said.

'I don't want you speaking to my mother. Do you understand? Not a thing.'

He nodded. 'Okay.'

And he was as good as his word. Finally, we were on the same page. When I came home from work, he was gone. This time he'd only taken his own possessions. I sat down on the sofa and I cried, but this time from relief: one down, one to go. But I had to keep up the pretence.

* * *

The day before Mother arrived, I phoned her.

'Sean's gone,' I said. 'It's over.'

She was aghast, furious I'd made this decision without her, furious at me for being so selfish.

'We'll discuss this tomorrow,' she said.

'Okay,' I said, and I made my voice thin and wobbly, the way she liked it to be.

She and my father arrived the next evening. They told me to come to their hotel for drinks and a chat. When I got to the hotel bar, they were already there, and I watched them for a moment as though they were strangers to me. My father, in his woolly cardigan, bespectacled and rosy-cheeked, holding his ale and glancing around the room; Mother beside him, in a scarlet tunic with lips to match, sitting in her chair, straight-backed and proud. I could feel her strength; I could almost see it, radiating around her like an aura. But I was strong too.

I slid into the seat opposite them and waited for Mother to start. What she had to say was this: I had been selfish beyond belief to treat my poor Maman and Sean in this way. I had given absolutely no regard to my Maman's heartache and pain, to the fact that she also loved Sean, that she saw him as a son. Maman had supported me every step of my life, she'd loved me unconditionally. No one would love me like Maman and Sean, and he and I were a team. I was to stay with him and support him and love him, and then everything would be fine. Maman would continue to support us, as she had always done, and it would be wonderful, we'd all be closer than ever. But first, I had to apologise.

She looked at me expectantly, waiting for me to break, to cry, to tell her how sorry I was and how she was the best mother in the world. Then she would forgive me, and she'd forgive Sean also, and I'd be so grateful to her, to my generous, forgiving Maman, who always looked after me, always had my best interests at heart.

But I was seeing clearly now: Mother wanted me back with Sean because that's how she could control me. I'd told her everything he had done, how he was breaking me, draining me, turning me into half a person, a ghost, something weak and insubstantial and meaningless. And that was what she wanted, that was how she saw me. I belonged to her, I was an extension of herself, so I could exist only on her terms – I couldn't be my own person, I couldn't have conviction or confidence, otherwise she wouldn't be able to control me. My whole life she'd used me – to paint herself a certain way, to get what she wanted, to feel powerful and validated. She was toxic, just like Sean, but she was worse than him, so much worse, because she was my mother. They'd circled me like vultures, gaslighting me, preying on my insecurities, twisting things until I couldn't see what was real anymore. But now I could see.

I stood up. 'No, I'm not doing any of that,' I said. 'I'm not apologising to you, you're a psychopath.' My father's head jerked up; Mother said nothing, but her eyes glittered. Usually, I would have been afraid, but I wasn't anymore – I didn't care, I could do this, I was strong. 'Don't call me again. Don't email me, don't text me. I never want to hear from you again. Got that? Ever again!'

Then, without saying goodbye, I turned on my heel and marched out. I walked back home and locked the door and drew the curtains and blared Cher songs as loud as I could. I didn't want to hear the banging at the door, the shouting through the letterbox, the tapping at the windows. I was impervious to it now, I was bored of it.

I called Sofia, I called Faya, I called Isabel, and I told them everything. I would need their support moving forward, because if there was one thing I knew, it was that Mother wouldn't go quietly.

PSYCHOPATHY SYMPTOM #15

Lack of remorse

Psychopaths are incapable of feeling true remorse. They have no regard for the effects their actions may have on other people, no matter how damaging these might be. Because they feel no guilt, psychopaths can easily shrug off responsibility for causing other people pain, either rationalising their behaviour, blaming other people, or denying it altogether.

20
MALICE

'Psychopaths are incapable of feeling true remorse.'

When Mother realised I was serious about cutting her off, she first reached out to Sean. She wrote emails saying how devastated she was to have lost him, how her heart ached that she hadn't been able to say goodbye. She told him that he was more of a son to her than I'd ever been a daughter, and was he sure a reconciliation was out of the question? Sean replied politely but forwarded the emails to me, asking if I could make her stop. I'd been receiving emails too, of course, which I'd ignored, but I sent just the one, asking her to stop contacting Sean and me, because neither of us wanted to hear from her. This was her reply:

Dear Olivia,

By not replying to my messages all you're doing is showing me how much you're hurting – you sad, spiteful, unloved daughter of mine. How dare you tell me not to contact Sean anymore. I have FAR MORE love, respect and honest feelings for him than for you, and I always will do. If that's rubbing salt into your open and weeping wounds, then tough titties, is all I can say.

You are a far bigger criminal than he is, at least he has his drugs as an excuse, unlike you, a spoilt, pathetic child who throws tantrums when things don't go your way. You are an evil, double-crossing, unscrupulous slut, and you don't even have the side effects of coke to hide behind!

Love Maman

I deleted the email, as I deleted all the others, and blocked her email address again. It didn't always work; she set up alternate accounts to harass me, and my blacklist grew longer and longer. From one of her new accounts Mother emailed Granny, cc-ing me into the exchange. The email was over 2,000 words, and in it, she threw out all my 'dirty little secrets': Did Granny know how much I'd been lying to her? Did she know I'd been up to my eyes in a cocaine-fuelled underworld? Did she know I'd had an *abortion*? Yes, I'd aborted my own baby – and oh, it would have been Granny's first great-grandchild – oh, the pain, oh, the agony! Mother was only telling Granny because she wanted to build bridges with her – because they'd both loved me, because they'd both been betrayed by me.

When I read that email I shivered with anger. The idea of Mother using my pain to 'build bridges' with Granny – the one woman she despised more than me – was unbearable. I knew exactly what she was doing: she knew that Granny loved me, *really* loved me, and she wanted to create a wedge between us. By telling her what I was 'really like' she thought she'd gain an ally and weaken my support system – but Granny saw straight through it. She wasn't upset by anything Mother said, only that I hadn't confided in her myself. Poor Granny, I'd wanted to protect her from all this, from my self-inflicted turmoil. I'd wanted to keep her separate from Sean's tawdry world.

Mother's email backfired. Any doubts I might have had, any prickling of uncertainty that I was doing the wrong thing, were eradicated with that email. Using my pain and the things I'd gone through to make fake peace with a woman she hated was going too far; the very fact that she couldn't see what she was doing was wrong only fuelled my desire to cut her off for good. I changed my email address, I changed my number. I even changed my locks again, just in case Mother had secretly stashed her own key when she'd changed them after Sean left. My nightmare returned, that terrible dream of Mother watching me drown, and I'd wake up trembling and sweating, convinced I could hear a key turning in the lock, certain I could hear her quick, light footsteps creeping over to my bed.

After I told Granny everything, she returned the favour. She told me everything too: all the things she'd kept from me before because she knew I loved Mother, she knew the truth would have hurt. She told me about my early childhood, those times I couldn't remember or had blocked out. How my grandfather always knew there was something wrong with Mother, how my father refused to see it. There was a strange relief in knowing that it wasn't me that made her this way; Mother had always been disturbed, no matter how well she hid it.

But she wasn't concerned with hiding it now. As it slowly began to dawn on her that this time there would be no clawing me back, no controlling and manipulating, she started to be more open in her abuse. When her emails to my old account bounced back, she began emailing my work account. Every day when I turned on my computer there was a new message from her, and I read it while sipping my coffee, trying to feel as little as I could. This was just part of my strange new morning routine, I wouldn't let it bother me. But I wasn't Mother, I wasn't cold and unfeeling. Her emails, designed to hurt, did so:

Olivia,

You are a sick pervert, a pathetic, lonely, snivelling little pig, and I have nothing to say to you again. The idea that I ever was your mother fills me with shame and disgust, so thank you for failing so spectacularly as my child. After seeing you in January, the baby I gave birth to, the little girl I sang to, I felt no love or affiliation to you whatsoever. To me, you are dead. Now I have buried you, and it's as if your existence was all a bad dream.

Josephine

Her emails had a powerful physical effect on me. My face and neck flushed red, my heart raced, and before I knew what I was doing, I was rolling my sleeves up and picking at my arm. But the difference this time was that my anguish didn't have to be a secret anymore. Over the years I'd tried different coping mechanisms – invisible curtains that shielded me, closing myself off so I wouldn't feel my own pain – but my new mechanism was better. I was open, for the first time in my life; I was honest about what had happened. There was no hiding now, no more shame. Whenever a new email arrived at work, I read it aloud to Sofia and we laughed at her callous absurdity.

* * *

One day I arrived at work to find an envelope on my desk. Inside were photos of Mother setting fire to cards I'd made for her, burning pictures of me and presents I'd bought. There was a letter attached that she'd addressed to her 'schizophrenic daughter': it said: 'Just destroyed every trace of you from our home. It's as if you never existed.' I held the letter in my hand, reading the words from the woman who'd carried and given birth to me, this woman who hated me. I knew her handwriting so well, the confident, looping script; I knew her neatness, the way she addressed the letter and wrote the date and underlined it. I knew the way she would have licked the stamp, sticking it down with a flourish, thumping her fist onto it for good measure. What else did I know? I knew she wanted to obliterate me.

When she began threatening to show up at my work I started having panic attacks. After the second one I was so distressed, I was taken to see the HR team and I told them everything. Under their guidance, I wrote Mother a Cease and Desist Letter, a legal document stating that she was not to contact me in person, via phone, email or any social media channels, and if she did, I would take legal action. It didn't have the intended effect. Next morning, another email was waiting for me.

> URGENT: A disgusting cockroach has been harassing me for the past two decades – do you know how to deal with this type of pest? Maybe if I sent my own laughable Cease and Desist Letter the cockroach might die … or perhaps I should just kill it myself? Hit it with a swatter, then crush it into sludge with my shoe? Do cockroaches understand Cease and Desist Letters?

> Olivia,
> Your attempts at appearing grown-up by sending us legal letters are comical. Well, guess what? I've got my own lawyer, and together we're going to end you once and for all, you sad setback from another life. You think you've got one up because you paid back the money for Sean's debts? What a farce! When a parent gives their child money it is ALWAYS a loan, and now I'm not your mother anymore, I want my money back. I'm about to sue your sorry ass for all the money I've ever spent on you. Watch this space …
> Josephine

Her bluster scared me, but it didn't take much research to realise that her threats of legal action were hollow. In her search to wield control, she hopped from one tactic to another. If she couldn't have financial command over me and she couldn't take legal action, then how could she hurt me? By going after my job. And so she began emailing Sofia and other people at my work, any email addresses she could find. She dug up old photos of me in Monaco, silly photos she'd taken of me and Lucas giggling and kissing as we raised glasses of wine – wine she'd insisted on pouring us – and sent them around the office.

> Olivia,
>
> I feel a lot better now I've told your work and your dear friend Sofia the truth about you: that you're a sick and manipulative little girl, a disgusting, vulnerable and ashamed wreck – and an easy, drunk whore, as these pictures prove. Enjoy being controlled by Sofia – she's got her claws well and truly into you, just how you like it. Good luck with your pathetic new 'life', hiding out in your cheap flat like a paedophile, with nobody to love but your sad and ugly cat!
>
> Josephine

She emailed the CEO at my work to tell him that Sofia and I were harassing her during work hours, that we were sending her abusive and hurtful emails, that we should be reprimanded and dealt with. Thankfully, by this point Mother's tactics were common knowledge in the office and her email went unanswered. Every day, someone came up to me with a new story: Mother sent them an email warning against my compulsive lying, Mother set up a Twitter account and was replying to every company Tweet. I only found out in 2018 that she'd also been phoning the senior management, telling them that I was heavily using drugs.

She seemed to enjoy the legal angle best, and sent email after email documenting the pretend progress of her court case. She emailed from my father's account as if she were him, but I knew Father, I knew he would never write these words. I blocked him too.

I couldn't change my work email address and she knew it. Though I continued to block her, she set up new accounts every week. She said I owed her £60,000 for the money she'd spent on my education – but she'd waive it if I apologised, paid £1,000 towards the debt, wrote her a letter explaining why I'd acted so disgracefully, and returned a silk scarf my father bought me the previous summer. If I did those four things, she'd forgive me. But now I could see her behaviour for what it was: desperate power plays, nothing more.

* * *

And so I learned to ignore her emails, though when she threatened to pay me a visit, I was still scared. I developed a visceral fear of seeing her; just thinking of her turning up at my work and encroaching on the life I'd built made my heart pound. I was so afraid she would one day come barging into my office, sleeves rolled up and eyes gleaming, that I spoke to the doorman of our building and begged him not to let her in if ever she showed up. He remembered Mother from when she visited my work the previous summer – everyone always remembered her – and he promised he wouldn't let her in.

Every time there was a knock at the door at home I started sweating. I knew I would never feel safe there, I knew I had to move. I got a promotion and a raise and so I celebrated by moving to a new flat. Finally, I felt safe. But Mother wasn't finished yet.

* * *

One day, several months later, Sofia asked me how I felt about her writing an article on Mother – specifically, what it was like to grow up with a psychopath for a mother. Initially, I was confused: I'd read Sofia's crime-focused articles, why would she want to write a piece about Mother? But the more I thought about it, the more I felt like it was something I wanted to do. Being open about what had happened and refusing to be ashamed had been my unexpected salvation, my shield against Mother's attempts to sabotage me. Perhaps it would be cathartic, getting it all out on paper: acknowledging what I'd gone through and how it had damaged me; not glossing over my turmoil, not allowing her to tarnish me. I told Sofia I wanted to do the piece. She called it 'My Mother, The Psychopath' and a few years later, it would be read by an editor at Penguin Random House.

We were careful; we changed all the names – I was 'Katie', Mother was 'Joan' – and altered any details that meant we could be identified. Unlike Mother herself, I didn't want to ruin her or destroy her life, I just wanted her out of mine. When the article was published in April 2016, my friends and colleagues were shocked: even though they'd witnessed some of Mother's behaviour, no one but those I was closest to knew the full extent of it. At work people read the article with round, incredulous eyes, and they told me how upset it made them, how sorry they felt for me. I didn't want anyone's pity, but these reactions helped to validate me: I wasn't making a fuss over nothing, I wasn't weak or a drama queen, I wasn't a silly, spoilt brat. A psychologist I knew through a friend contacted me after reading it. She said she thought the psychopath diagnosis was correct, that I was right to sever ties and that I must never let her back in.

* * *

A year went by and Mother began to go quiet. Not silent – that would have been expecting too much – but quiet. She still emailed now and then, flitting between angry, aggressive messages and more subtle attempts to manipulate: she sent photos of my father, knowing it would hurt me to see him; she sent photos of their cat and her new litter of kittens, with a note attached saying 'Love Maman', as if we'd never fallen out at all. But she couldn't hurt me the way she wanted to anymore.

I was happier than I'd ever been, and Granny said you could tell just by looking at me. I looked lighter, like a weight had been lifted. I had a new boyfriend from work – James, who couldn't have been more different to Sean if he'd tried. I loved him deeply, everything about him: his gentle eyes, his infectious laugh, his patient, compassionate support.

It was James who taught me the meaning of unconditional love. He loved me for me: selflessly, genuinely, without expecting anything in return. He gave me a security and comfort I'd never experienced before, and I cherished the fact he'd never met Mother, never been used by her to get to me. Her mouth had never even uttered his name. He was pure, pristine, unsullied by her smut.

But one day at work, James came back from lunch to find a note on his desk: someone called Joan had called, asking to speak to him because she was worried about Katie.

'Joan?' James said, reading the note with a frown. 'I don't think I know any Joans. And who's Katie?' He glanced at me. 'Do you know any Joans?'

'No,' I said, shaking my head. 'Maybe they got the wrong person.'

'Probably,' he agreed, and he folded up the note and walked over to his desk. It was as he walked away that I remembered the names from the article the year before. I remember staring at James's back as he walked away from me and feeling suddenly terrified. All the old feelings came flooding back, those feelings I'd tried so hard to forget, and suddenly, waves of heat were rolling up my face again; my heart was drubbing in my chest, my stomach twisting and churning. As I sank into my chair, I took deep breaths, clasping my desk with both hands. I felt like I was clinging to the edge of safety: if I let go, I would fall; I would topple into darkness.

There was something about Mother using the names from the article that I found so insidious, so acutely unsettling. It was more than just her way of letting me know she'd read the piece, it was her playing along as if she were a part of it. Then there was the fact she'd asked to speak to James – how did she know about him? My social media accounts were locked down and I'd deleted anyone who Mother was vaguely friendly with from school. I had to use Twitter for work but my account was strictly professional and there had been no mention of James whatsoever. I couldn't bear the idea of Mother reaching out to him, of her honeyed tones seeping out the receiver into his ear, defiling his goodness with her noxious words. *What was she planning to say to him if she got through?* It made me shudder to think.

I had no idea how she'd found the article either – neither Sofia nor I had shared it on Twitter, knowing Mother regularly checked our accounts. It was testament to how well we'd hidden it that she took a year to discover its existence, but once she'd seen that title, 'My Mother, The Psychopath', she would have known. I remembered how she'd said nothing when I called her that, how she'd been silent but her eyes had glittered. Perhaps some psychopaths didn't know what they were, but I knew she did, just as Sean did.

But now I was on high alert. Something was coming, I knew it. I didn't have to wait long to find out what it was.

A few days later, I was making coffee in the kitchen at work. I was chatting away about my new kitten and how he liked to use our sofa as a toilet when my friend Nick popped his head round the door.

'There's someone waiting at reception for you, Olivia,' he said.

'Oh, who?' I said, distracted.

'She said "Josephine aka Joan"?' he replied, shrugging a shoulder. 'I dunno, she said you'll know what it means.'

I stared at him as prickles of horror began to creep over me. I remember backing up against the wall because I needed the support, I needed something to lean on; to feel my world was not collapsing.

'Oh my God, it's my mother!' I whispered, and suddenly people started springing into action. James led me to the cosy seats under the stairwell and I cowered in his arms, shivering uncontrollably, terrified I would look up to find my mother grinning triumphantly down at me. The doorman recognised Mother and refused to let her up. After a while, when she realised I wasn't coming down, she wrote me a note. Clipped to it were her travel receipts – a plane boarding pass from Nice, a train ticket from London, and a brief description of her journey. This is what the note said:

> I've come <u>ALL</u> this way to tell you that I'm <u>so dreadfully sorry</u> for being <u>THE ABSOLUTE WORST</u> mother in the world. Can you find it in your little heart to forgive me?

I wasn't like Mother. I knew I was strong now, I knew I was tough, but also I was soft. Cutting her off had hurt me deeply. I knew that it was the right thing to do, but that knowledge couldn't take away the feelings of sadness that slinked over me. This was my mother, my own flesh and blood, who had taken a taxi and then a flight and then a train and then another train and then another taxi to come and see me; my mother, who'd held my hand as we watched a baby butterfly beat its wings. My mother, who in spite of everything, I still loved.

But I knew Mother. I could hear her saying those words she'd written, and they weren't contrite, remorseful words, they were dripping in sarcasm and hatred. I could sense the urgency in the note, that old desire of hers to 'have it all out', to scream and to shame me, to have me break and sob at her feet. But I wasn't going to fall into her traps anymore.

My work were wonderful – they took one look at me and told me to go home, James too. We were escorted to the back entrance and into a waiting taxi, and I clung to James until we got home. Mother didn't know where we lived but I double-locked our door all the same, then I climbed into bed and wrapped myself in the duvet while James brought me cups of tea and kissed my forehead and told me everything was going to be alright.

My friends kept me up to date with Mother's antics that day. She returned to reception three more times and apparently, she was very agreeable, asking politely where I was, if reception knew where I lived. Did they know if I was in today? Did they know if I was still at number

47? She just wanted to see her daughter, that's all, and she'd come all this way. Eventually, she was asked to leave, and this was when Mother let that mask of hers slip. She agreed to go quite pleasantly, but then just as she was walking through the automatic doors, she turned and shouted, 'That Olivia ... that Olivia is a *fucking bitch*!'

And there it was: her true colours, her real face. She hid it with a mastery that floored me, but when that camouflage had no more purpose, she shrugged it off, shameless. She had been exposed, but still she was brazen, crueller, nastier and more vengeful than before.

EPILOGUE

That was two years ago. My mother has made no attempts to see me since – at least, not that I know of – and I'm happier now than I ever thought I could be. James and I have been together for four years; we're saving to buy our own house and looking forward to the future. I used to worry about what kind of parent I might be. What if the part of me that shares my mother's DNA kicks in? What if I start to recreate our old cycle with my own child? But I know now that if I ever do have children, I will be a good mother, because I'm not like her: my mother is a psychopath, and I am not, and that's all there is to it.

It took me a long time to see the truth, but now I know the only thing I could have done was to run and never look back. This is the advice I will always give to anyone in the same position: if someone is hurting you and manipulating you and causing you fear, get rid of them. Know that it's not your fault, and never let someone without conscience convince you that you're not of value. Don't listen to protestations of change, because psychopaths are incapable of it. Do not pity, you cannot redeem the unredeemable.

I know I made the right decision, but I would be lying if I said it came without sorrow. Because this was my mother. Our relationship was complex and toxic, painful and potent, shaped by the intricate labyrinth of her disturbed psyche. I'm not ashamed to say I still have feelings of love for her. That doesn't mean I'm weak, it means I'm strong. I choose to move forward without bitterness, to cast aside the anguish and the agony, because unlike my mother, I can feel empathy and remorse: I choose to bestow them on her.

I love and miss my father very much, but his passive inaction, his idle meekness, is harder for me to understand than my mother's torment. When I speak of my father I always use the past tense. It feels like he died years ago, only stories and memories remain. By continuing to remain at my mother's side, he destroyed his relationships with his three brothers and mother. Granny tells me how proud of me she is, that she's never seen me so happy, that she loves my kind, 'sensible' James. But while she and I are close, the idea that she will never see her son again is unendurable, and my heart breaks for her. But I choose to forgive my father too. I refuse to have my life tainted by bitterness.

My mother has faded from my life, but she hasn't gone entirely. In 2017 I got a new job, and it took less than a week for her to track me down. She sent me an email: the subject matter was 'I FOUND YOU', the message inside was blank. Her presence may have ebbed away but she is still here, faintly, like the black wisps of smoke after you blow out a match.

I have often wondered what she is capable of, and there are times when I get scared. She's been quiet for too long. It's irrational, I know, but when something prickles at the back of my neck, I still feel those watchful eyes on me. I can almost see her, lurking in the gloom of night, gleaming eyes, glittering teeth, crouched upon the edge of sight.

ACKNOWLEDGEMENTS

OLIVIA

I would like to thank my boyfriend – 'the sensible one' – for his unconditional love, support, humour and strength. I'll see you down the aisle one day, mate! Thank you also to my Granny, for her continual support and care, for telling me the truth when I asked for it, and for always putting me first.

Thank you Cousin El, Sharpie and Duffy for your friendship and memories as I delved back into my past, and thanks to our editor and everyone at Penguin Random House for giving me the opportunity to tell my story. Thank you to EB, my first director – not only for helping start my career, but also for denying my mother the chance to destroy it! Special feline thanks to Benedict, and also to my sweet Mister – gone but never forgotten.

Thank you to my best friend, S. M. Nelson, for bringing my story to life so eloquently. Matching tattoo? Thank you also for believing we could write a book that may help other young people in similar situations to find their strength . . . even if the only 'book' you'd written before was Harry Potter fan fiction!

And finally, thank you to my mother, for making me the woman I am today – even if she didn't intend to.

S.M. NELSON

Thank you to 'Olivia' for allowing me to tell your incredible story – not once, but twice. Thanks for your bravery, honesty and trust in me throughout this process. Now we really are linked for life – with or without a tattoo!

Thank you to our editor for seeing the potential in my article, and thanks to everyone at Ebury and Penguin Random House who believed in this book. Thank you Law, SAJ and NJC for your edits and advice, and thanks to all my friends and family for their love and patience this year. Special thanks to KD and DM for their unending hospitality while I wrote – and of course, thank you for all the rosé! I couldn't have done this without it.

And thank you TLD, for everything.

HELPLINES

The National Association for People Abused in Childhood (NAPAC)

The NAPAC supports adult survivors of any form of childhood abuse, and provides a support line and local support services.

Tel: 0808 801 0331

www.napac.org.uk

Emergence

Emergence is a user-led organisation committed to supporting carers, family and friends of those who identify with the diagnosis of personality disorder.

www.emergenceplus.org.uk

The Consortium for Therapeutic Communities (TCTC)

TCTC is a charity for those involved in the delivery of relationship-based support and treatment, and provides a directory of therapeutic communities in the UK.

www.therapeuticcommunities.org